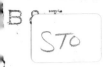

DETECTION OF
DEVELOPMENTAL

DETECTION OF DEVELOPMENTAL PROBLEMS IN CHILDREN
Birth to Adolescence
Second Edition

Edited by
Marilyn J. Krajicek, R.N., Ed.D.
Alice I. Tearney Tomlinson, R.N., M.S.
Rocky Mountain Child Development Center
School of Medicine
University of Colorado Health Sciences Center

University Park Press
Baltimore

UNIVERSITY PARK PRESS
International Publishers in Medicine and Human Services
300 North Charles Street
Baltimore, Maryland 21201

Copyright © 1983 by University Park Press

Typeset by Oberlin Printing Company
Manufactured in the United States of America by The Maple Press Company

Library of Congress Cataloging in Publication Data
Main entry under title:

Detection of developmental problems in children.

Includes index.
1. Children—Medical examinations.   2. Child development—Testing.
I. Krajicek, Marilyn J.   II. Tomlinson, Alice I. Tearney.   [DNLM: 1. Child development disorders—Diagnosis—Nursing texts.   WY 149 D479]
RJ50.D47   1981   618.92'0075   82-21900
ISBN 0-8391-1789-2

Contents

Contributors

Lawrence Bernstein, M.D., Assistant Clinical Professor, Department of Pediatrics and Neurology, School of Medicine, University of Colorado Health Sciences Center, 4200 E. Ninth Avenue, Denver, Colorado 80262; Private Practice in Child Neurology, 950 East Harvard Avenue, Denver, Colorado 80210

Robert H. Bradley, Ph.D., Professor of Educational Foundation, and Director, Center for Child Development and Education, University of Arkansas at Little Rock, Little Rock, Arkansas 72204

Kathleen Bryant, M.A., Assistant Professor, Department of Physical Medicine and Rehabilitation, Department of Otolaryngology, School of Medicine, University of Colorado Health Sciences Center, 4200 East Ninth Avenue, Denver, Colorado 80262

Elna Cain, R.N., M.S., Child Health Nursing Consultant, Colorado Department of Health, 4210 East 11th Street, Denver, Colorado 80220

Paul S. Casamassimo, D.D.S., M.S., Associate Professor and Chairman, Department of Growth and Development, University of Colorado School of Dentistry; and Chief of Dentistry, Rocky Mountain Child Development Center, School of Medicine, University of Colorado Health Sciences Center, 4200 East Ninth Avenue, Denver, Colorado 80262

Marion Downs, M.A., Professor of Otolaryngology (Audiology), University of Colorado Health Sciences Center, 4200 East Ninth Avenue, Denver Colorado 80262

Beverly A. Entwistle, R.D.H., M.P.H., Assistant Professor and Research Associate, University of Colorado School of Dentistry; Chief of Dental Hygiene, Rocky Mountain Child Development Center, School of Medicine, University of Colorado Health Sciences Center, 4200 East Ninth Avenue, Denver, Colorado 80262

Patricia Komich, O.T.R., Chief, Occupational Therapy, Rocky Mountain Child Development Center, School of Medicine, University of Colorado Health Sciences Center, 4200 East Ninth Avenue, Denver, Colorado 80262

Marilyn J. Krajicek, R.N., Ed.D., Associate Professor, School of Nursing; Assistant Professor of Pediatrics; Director of Nursing, Rocky Mountain Child Development Center, School of Medicine, University of Colorado Health Sciences Center, 4200 East Ninth Avenue, Denver, Colorado 80262

Annette Lansford, M.D., Practitioner of Developmental Pediatrics, and Director, Child Disability Clinic, Carle Clinic, 602 West University Avenue, Urbana, Illinois 61801

Rita Lillo, R.N., M.S., Clinical Specialist in Childhood Diabetes, Barbara Davis Children's Diabetes Center, University of Colorado Health Sciences Center, 4200 East Ninth Avenue, Denver, Colorado 80262

Philomena Lomena, Ed.D., Assistant Professor, Department of Economics, University of Northern Colorado, Greeley, Colorado 80639

Linda Lord, R.P.T., M.P.H., Physical Therapist, Special Education Preschools, Jefferson County Schools, 809 Quail Street, Lakewood, Colorado 80215

Marie-Louise Lubs, Ph.D., Associate Professor of Pediatrics, Genetics Division, Mailman Center for Child Development, University of Miami Medical School, Miami, Florida 33124

Harold P. Martin, M.D., Associate Professor of Pediatrics and Psychiatry, School of Medicine, University of Colorado Health Sciences Center, 4200 East Ninth Avenue, Denver, Colorado 80262

Paula Henkin Roberts, R.N., M.S., Nursing Consultant, 9669 North Sorrel Road, Castle Rock, Colorado 80104

James Sprague, M.D., Assistant Professor of Ophthalmology, School of Medicine, University of Colorado Health Sciences Center, 4200 East Ninth Avenue, Denver, Colorado 80262; and Chief, Division of Ophthalmology, Denver General Hospital, Denver, Colorado

Alice I. Tearney Tomlinson, R.N., M.S., Nursing Consultant, Rocky Mountain Child Development Center, School of Medicine, University of Colorado Health Sciences Center, 4200 East Ninth Avenue, Denver, Colorado 80262

Nancy Weaver, M.S., Educational Consultant, 7123 South Newport Way, Englewood, Colorado

Preface

There continues to be an increasing need for and emphasis on the importance of the early identification of children with potential developmental delays. These children and their families may have problems that may necessitate a multidisciplinary approach to assist in formulating an appropriate plan for intervention.

The second edition of this book has been expanded to include the assessment needs of children from birth to adolescence. Additional content relating to sensorimotor integration difficulties, neurological assessment, dental problems and a teaching approach to working with children with chronic conditions has been included, and previous chapters have been updated.

With the trend of expanding nursing to provide comprehensive services to children and families, the nurse is in a strategic position to make evaluative decisions regarding outcomes. Utilizing the nursing process includes identification, assessment, evaluation, and intervention. Disposition may also include referral to a variety of specialists. If a case is complex, referral may be to a team of specialists for an in-depth evaluation and treatment plan. The information in this book can be a valuable resource to practitioners in other disciplines.

Marilyn J. Krajicek
Alice I. Tearney Tomlinson

EMBRYONIC DEVELOPMENT

AGE days	LENGTH mm.	STAGE Streeter	GROSS APPEARANCE	C.N.S.	EYE	EAR	FACE
4		III	Blastocyst				
8	.1	IV	embryo, trophoblast, endometrium				
12	.2	V	ectoderm, amnionic sac, endoderm, yolk sac				
18	1	VIII	ant. head fold, body stalk, heart	Enlargement of anterior neural plate			
22	2	X early somites	foregut, allantois	Partial fusion neural folds	Optic evagination	Otic placode	Mandible Hyoid arches
26	4	XII 21-29 somites		Closure neural tube Rhombencephalon, mesen., prosen. Ganglia V VII VIII X	Optic cup	Otic invagination	Fusion, mand. arches
32	7	XIV		Cerebellar plate Cervical and mesencephalic flexures	Lens invagination	Otic vesicle	Olfactory placodes
38	11	XVI		Dorsal pontine flexure Basal lamina Cerebral evagination Neural hypophysis	Lens detached Pigmented retina	Endolymphic sac Ext. auditory meatus Tubotympanic recess	Nasal swellings
43	17	XVIII		Olfactory evagination Cerebral hemisphere	Lens fibers Migration of retinal cells / Hyaloid vessels		Choana, Prim. palate
47	23	XX		Optic nerve to brain	Corneal body Mesoderm No lumen in optic stalk		
51	28	XXII			Eyelids	Spiral cochlear duct Tragus	

EMBRYONIC DEVELOPMENT CHART

The embryonic ages for Streeter's stages XII – XXIII have been altered in accordance with the human data from Iffy, L. et al: Acta Anat. 66 : 178, 1967

EXTREMITIES	HEART	GUT, ABDOMEN	LUNG	UROGENITAL	OTHER
					Early blastocyst with inner cell mass and cavitation (58 cells) lying free within the uterine cavity.
					Implantation Trophoblast invasion Embryonic disc with endoblast and ectoblast
		Yolk sac			Early amnion sac Extraembryonic mesoblast, angioblast Chorionic gonadotropin
	Merging mesoblast anterior to pre-chordal plate	Stomatodeum Cloaca		Allantois	Primitive streak Hensen's node Notochord Prechordal plate Blood cells in yolk sac
	Single heart tube Propulsion	Foregut		Mesonephric ridge	Yolk sac larger than amnion sac
Arm bud	Ventric. outpouching Gelatinous reticulum	Rupture stomatodeum Evagination of thyroid, liver, and dorsal pancreas.	Lung bud	Mesonephric duct enters cloaca	Migration of myotomes from somites
Leg bud	Auric. outpouching Septum primum	Pharyngeal pouches yield parathyroids, lat. thyroid, thymus Stomach broadens	Bronchi	Ureteral evag. Urorect. sept. Germ cells Gonadal ridge Coelom, Epithelium	Rathke's pouch
Hand plate, Mesench. condens. Innervation	Fusion mid. A-V canal Muscular vent. sept.	Intestinal loop into yolk stalk Cecum Gallbladder Hepatic ducts Spleen	Main lobes	Paramesonephric duct Gonad ingrowth of coelomic epith.	Adrenal cortex (from coelomic epithelium) invaded by sympathetic cells = medulla Jugular lymph sacs
Finger rays, Elbow	Aorta Pulmonary artery Valves Membrane ventricular septum	Duodenal lumen obliterated Cecum rotates right Appendix	Tracheal cartil.	Fusion urorect. sept. Open urogen. memb, anus Epith. cords in testicle	Early muscle
Clearing, central cartil.	Septum secundum			S-shaped vesicles in in nephron blastema connect with collecting tubules from calyces	Superficial vascular plexus low on cranium
Shell, Tubular bone				A few large glomeruli Short secretory tubules Tunica albuginea Testicle	Superficial vascular plexus at vertex

EMBRYONIC DEVELOPMENT CHART

FETAL DEVELOPMENT

AGE weeks	LENGTH cm. C-R	LENGTH cm. Tot.	WT. gm.	GROSS APPEARANCE	CNS	EYE, EAR	FACE, MOUTH	CARDIO-VASCULAR	LUNG
7	2.8				Cerebral hemisphere; Infundibulum, Rathke's	Lens nearing final shape	Palatal swellings; Dental lamina, Epithel.	Pulmonary vein into left atrium	
8	3.7				Primitive cereb. cortex; Olfactory lobes; Dura and pia mater	Eyelid; Ear canals	Nares plugged; Rathke's pouch detach.; Sublingual gland	A-V bundle; Sinus venosus absorbed into right auricle	Pleuroperitoneal canals close; Bronchioles
10	6.0				Spinal cord histology; Cerebellum	Iris; Ciliary body; Eyelids fuse; Lacrimal glands; Spiral gland different	Lips, Nasal cartilage; Palate		Laryngeal cavity reopened
12	8.8				Cord-cervical & lumbar enlarged, Cauda equina	Retina layered; Eye axis forward; Scala tympani	Tonsillar crypts; Cheeks; Dental papilla	Accessory coats, blood vessels	Elastic fibers
16	14				Corpora quadrigemina; Cerebellum prominent; Myelination begins	Scala vestibuli; Cochlear duct	Palate complete; Enamel and dentine	Cardiac muscle condensed	Segmentation of bronchi complete
20						Inner ear ossified	Ossification of nose		Decrease in mesenchyme; Capillaries penetrate linings of tubules
24		32	800		Typical layers in cerebral cortex; Cauda equina at first sacral level		Nares reopen; Calcification of tooth primordia		Change from cuboidal to flattened epithelium; Alveoli
28		38.5	1100		Cerebral fissures and convolutions	Eyelids reppen; Retinal layers complete; Perceive light			Vascular components adequate for respiration
32		43.5	1600	Accumulation of fat		Auricular cartilage	Taste sense		Number of alveoli still incomplete
36		47.5	2600						
38		50	3200		Cauda equina, at L-3; Myelination within brain	Lacrimal duct canalized	Rudimentary frontal maxillary sinuses	Closure of: foramen ovale; ductus arteriosus; umbilical vessels; ductus venosus	
First postnatal year +					Continuing organization of axonal networks; Cerebrocortical function, motor coordination; Myelination continues until 2-3 years	Iris pigmented, 5 months; Mastoid air cells; Coordinate vision, 3-5 months; Maximal vision by 5 years	Salivary gland ducts become canalized; Teeth begin to erupt 5-7 months; Relatively rapid growth of mandible and nose	Relative hypertrophy left ventricle	Continue adding new alveoli

FETAL DEVELOPMENT CHART

GUT	UROGENITAL	SKELETAL MUSCLE	SKELETON	SKIN	BLOOD, THYMUS LYMPH	ENDOCRINE
Pancreas, dorsal and ventral fusion	Renal vesicles	Differentiation toward final shape	Cartilaginous models of bones Chondrocranium Tail regression	Mammary gland		Parathyroid associated with thyroid Sympathetic neuroblasts invade adrenal
Liver relatively large Intestinal villi	Müllerian ducts fusing Ovary distinguishable	Muscles well represented Movement	Ossification center Sternum	Basal layer	Bone marrow Thymus halves unite Lymphoblasts around the lymph sacs	Thyroid follicles
Gut withdrawal from cord Pancreatic alveoli Anal canal	Renal excretion Bladder sac Müllerian tube into urogenital sinus Vaginal sacs Prostate	Perineal muscles	Joints	Hair follicles Melanocytes	Enucleated R.B.C.'s Thymus yields reticulum and corpuscles Thoracic duct Lymph nodes; axillary iliac	Adrenalin Noradrenalin
Gut muscle layers Pancreatic islets Bile	Seminal vesicle Regression, genital ducts		Tail degenerated Notochord degenerated	Corium, 3 layers Scalp, body hair Sebaceous glands Nails beginning	Blood principally from bone marrow Thymus-medullary and lymphoid	Testicle-Leydig cells Thyroid-colloid in follicle Anterior pituitary acidophilic granules Ovary-prim. follicles
Omentum fusing with transverse colon Mesoduodenum, asc. & desc. colon attach to body wall. Meconium. Gastric, intest. glands	Typical kidney Mesonephros involuting Uterus and vagina	In-utero movement can be detected	Distinct bones	Dermal ridges hands Sweat glands Keratinization		Anterior pituitary-basophilic granules
	No further collecting tubules			Vernix caseosa Nail plates Mammary budding	Blood formation decreasing in liver	
						Testes-decrease in Leydig cells
						Testes descend
	Urine osmolarity continues to be relatively low			Eccrine sweat Lanugo hair prominent Nails to fingertips		
			Only a few secondary epiphyseal centers ossified in knee		Hemoglobin 17-18 gm Leukocytosis	
			Ossification of 2nd epiph. centers-hamate, capitate, proximal humerus, femur New ossif. 2nd epiph. centers till 10-12 yrs. Ossif. of epiphyses till 16-18 yrs.	New hair, gradual loss of lanugo hair	Transient (6 wk) erythroid hypoplasia Hemoglobin 11-12 gm 7S gamma globulin produced by 6 wks. Lymph nodes develop cortex, medulla	Transient estrinization Adrenal-regression of fetal zone Gonadotropin with feminization of ♀ 9-12 yr. (onset); masc. of ♂ 10-14 yr. (onset)

FETAL DEVELOPMENT CHART

Acknowledgments

Support in part for the development of this guide was made possible by the following grants: Maternal-Child Health Grant Project 926, Bureau of Community Health Services, U.S. Department of Health and Human Services; Colorado State (MCH) Mental Retardation Grant (on contract for 1981–82, C-291028); and Regional Office of Administration on Developmental Disabilities, U.S. Department of Health and Human Services (grant #59-P-4012918-10).

Special appreciation is extended to Susan Thornton, Opal Every, Kathleen Krepps, Jay Lawson, Ellie Kazuk, and Bill Frankenburg.

DETECTION OF DEVELOPMENTAL PROBLEMS IN CHILDREN

I. Nursing Assessments
Screening for
Developmental
Problems

A. A Home Visit Assessment
of a Child and Family
with a Potential
Developmental Problem

Marilyn J. Krajicek, R. N., Ed. D.
Alice I. Tearney Tomlinson, R. N., M. S.

THE PUBLIC HEALTH OR SCHOOL NURSE is often contacted to assess a child and his or her family in the home environment when the child has been identified as having a potential developmental problem. There is a distinct advantage in observing individuals in the environment that is the most natural and usual to them. By being a part of a child's and family's home life, if only temporarily, the nurse is provided an opportunity to more fully and rapidly understand their concerns or problems from their own frame of reference. Sometimes concerns and anxieties are discussed fully at a home visit, while at other times, the home visit serves as a starting point to encourage family members to communicate their problems.

When it is determined that a home visit is necessary, an appointment must be made and confirmed with the family. The following outline is included as a guide that may help nurses and other health care professionals to observe and evaluate the lifestyles of children and families in their own environment.

It is essential that the appointment be scheduled so that the identified patient, as well as the siblings, if possible, can be present. If there are extended family members living permanently in the home, it is advisable that they also attend. In two-parent homes, presence of both parents may depend on their working schedules. If both parents cannot be present, the parent who spends the greater amount of waking hours with the child should plan to be there.

I.   DESCRIPTION OF ENVIRONMENT
    A.   Type of community and neighborhood (homogenous, mixed, industrial, residential, apartment complex); area of the city; apparent socioeconomic level; upkeep of the area. These items are often indicators of the family's stature in the neighborhood.
    B.   Home: A short description of the residence, including adequacy of living facilities, safety, as well as furnishings for daily living activities. Include description of play facilities; types of toys (developmental in nature); provision for reading and music for children and adults (other than television), i.e., record player, radio, musical toys, etc.
        1.   Is there a storage area for the child's belongings?
        2.   Is the child required to care for his or her own room and toys in a manner appropriate for his or her own development?
    C.   Sleeping arrangements: Are they appropriate? Is there indication of infantilization? Does the child sleep with the parents in the parents' room, or does he or she have a separate room and bed?
II.   BEHAVIOR IN HOME
    Observation of the child's behavior at home provides the most reliable information for comparison with his or her behavior outside the

home, such as in the clinic, at school, or in other public places. Home behaviors may range from quiet, pleasant, cooperative, and placid, to anxious, depressed, manipulative, overactive, oppositional, and angry. Making note of these behaviors and the situations in which they occur is helpful in assessing the home environment.

For the school age child who demonstrates behavior problems, the nurse should refer to the Conners Rating Scale (Hyperkinesis Index, 1975).

III.   INTERACTION

    A.   Observations of interactions are crucial during the visit and include: sibling/sibling, sibling/parent or others, and child/objects in the environment. What is the general tenor of the environment? (e.g., annoying, tense, restrictive—other than necessary for safety measures; positive or negative feelings conveyed, praise given, discipline used; intervention and planning rather than crisis approach).

    B.   Include a short paragraph on each family member present, with physical description, and note all interactions during the visit. Ask young children to show you where they sleep, what they play with, and their favorite toy. For older children, elicit their concerns for themselves and other family members. If possible, spend some time with each family member.

IV.   DAILY ROUTINE

    A.   Daily routine can be ascertained through an open-ended question, encompassing the family routine from awakening until retirement at night.

        1.   Are routines accomplished in a spontaneous or a restricted manner?

        2.   Obtain the routine of each family member, including his or her regular activities away from home as well.

    B.   Screening tools may be used in the family environment, depending on the need and purpose of the visit (see Chapter I, Part B on screening for choice of appropriate tools). The home visit also offers an excellent opportunity to screen other unidentified siblings as well.

V.   SUPPORT SYSTEM FOR FAMILY

    A.   Peers outside the family

    B.   Local physical facilities for recreation and outside interests

    C.   Relatives, friends, church groups and other organizations

Table 1 lists categories of a typical history form that may be useful in pinpointing problems in a child's family environment, pre- and postnatal history, and so on. Many developmental centers use such forms and can provide a copy on request.

Table 1.   Major categories explored by typical history form

Background information
i.e., parents' occupations and ethnic backgrounds
Past pregnancy history
i.e., past miscarriages, premature births, deformities
Pregnancy
i.e., medicines taken, X-ray exposure, alcohol consumed
Family history
i.e., relatives with abnormalities or chronic illnesses
Birth history of identified child
i.e., ages when child pulled to stand, finished toilet training
Nutrition history
i.e., amount of food groups eaten, snacking, mealtime behavior problems
Health history
i.e., childhood diseases, immunizations, accidents, allergies
Health care list
i.e., places the child has received care, physicians' names
School involvement
i.e., preschool, special education, tutoring

Table 2 includes information that can be used to develop a pedigree if the nurse believes a child's delays may be transmitted genetically. Included with the table is a sample pedigree.

REFERENCE

The Hyperkinesis Index. 1975. Abbott Laboratories, Chicago.

SUGGESTED READINGS

Conners, C. K. 1969. A teacher rating scale for use in drug studies with children. Am. J. Psychiatry 126:884–888.

Conners, C. K. 1970. Symptom patterns in hyperkinetic, neurotic, and normal children. Child Dev. 41:667–682.

Conners, C. K. 1973. Rating scales for use in drug studies with children. Psychopharmacol. Bull. (Special Issue). 24–29.

Table 2.   Drawing and interpreting pedigrees

1. The upper edges of the symbols, for each generation, should be even. A line connects the upper edges of the symbols that represent a sibship. With respect to the couple seeking counseling, her side of the family is usually drawn out on one page and his on another.
2. The mating line is between two symbols; male partner is on the left, female on the right.

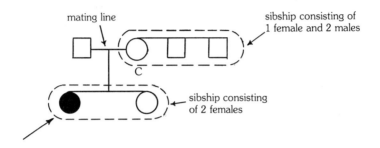

3. The consultant (marked by C) is the individual who *seeks* counseling. The proband (marked by an arrow) is the most immediate family member who is affected. If a couple is seeking counseling, the woman is considered to be the consultant whether or not she is affected, unless the disorder affects the husband or *his* blood relatives. An affected child is usually the proband.
4. Birthdates are indicated for the proband and each immediate family member as well as for all affected individuals. Approximate ages are noted for all other individuals or when exact birthdates are not known.
5. Maiden names are written in parentheses after first names. They are included for each affected female, carrier, or at-risk married female.
6. Married names are given for each married female who is affected, is a carrier, or is at-risk for being either a carrier or affected.
7. Sets of sibs, stillborns, and abortions are arranged in chronological order from oldest to youngest. Distant relatives may be grouped and the number of individuals noted—3, N.
8. Causes of death and/or health problems are listed for all family members below or above their respective symbols.
9. A key to indicate the symbols for the conditions in question is noted on the pedigree page. For example: ■ diabetes

⬛ cleft lip

⬛ diabetes and cleft lip

Table 2 and the pedigree information on the following two pages reprinted with permission from Genetics for the Professional. Genetics Unit, University of Colorado Health Sciences Center, 1980.

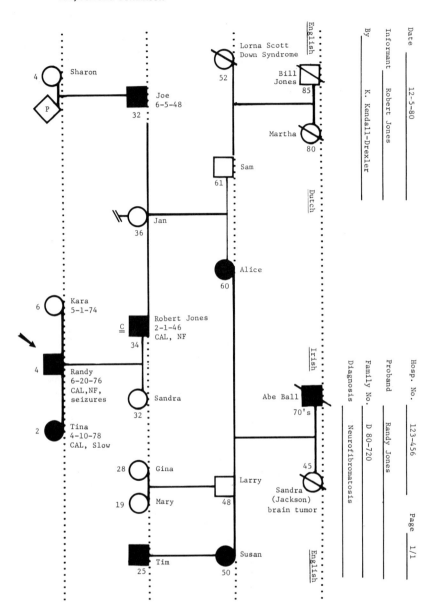

Date ___12-5-80___

By ___K. Kendall-Drexler___   Informant ___Robert Jones___

Hosp. No. ___123-456___   Page ___1/1___

Proband ___Randy Jones___

Family No. ___D 80-720___

Diagnosis ___Neurofibromatosis___

Sample Pedigree

Pedigree Symbols

☐	male	☐	proband or propositus or index case
○	female	○ 25	25-year-old female
☐	male consultant	⟨p⟩	pregnancy
③	3 females	⬜	deceased male
n	more than 1 male	[☐]	adopted male
◇	sex undesignated	⊘ stillbirth	stillbirth, female
■	affected with trait	◉	abortion, female (indicate month of occurrence and type, SAB or TAB)
■•	affected with trait and examined	◪	abortion, male
○•	not affected with trait and examined	◈	abortion, sex unknown
◑	carrier of trait	☐—⊤—○	no issue
⊙	carrier of X-linked trait		

☐—○ or ☐—○   mating

I ☐—○—☐ II   multiple mating

☐═○   consanguineous mating

⟨monozygous twins⟩   monozygous twins

⟨dizygous twins⟩   dizygous twins

⟨twins of unknown zygosity ?⟩   twins of unknown zygosity

I. Nursing Assessments
Screening for Developmental Problems

B. Utilization of Screening Tools

Paula Henkin Roberts, R.N., M.S.

MANY NEW AND EXCITING CHANGES in the fields of child development, assessment, screening, and nursing itself have occurred in recent years. Indeed, so much has been written about the importance of early identification and intervention, casefinding, and monitoring of individuals' current levels of function—all in the name of *prevention*—that confusion of terms often results. Before discussing the use of specific screening tools, which is the main purpose of this chapter part, it is important to review terminology regarding screening.

DEFINITION OF TERMS

Screening tests "sort out apparently well persons who probably do not have a disease from those who probably do have the disease. A screening test is not intended to be diagnostic. Persons with positive or suspicious findings must be referred to their physicians for diagnosis and necessary treatment" (Wilson and Lungner, 1968).

There are four types of screening that may be employed: *mass screening*, *selective* or *prescriptive screening*, *multiple screening*, and *multiphasic screening*. Following are some examples of these types of screening:

1.   An entire population may be screened by *mass screening* techniques, e.g., newborn screening for phenylketonuria.
2.   A given group of people at higher risk for a condition than the general population may be screened by *selective* or *prescriptive screening*, e.g., Jewish people for Tay-Sachs disease.
3.   Ruling out two potential problem areas at one time may be accomplished by *multiple screening*, e.g., hearing and vision screening used in the schools.
4.   Extending the number of screening measures used on a given individual from the 2 or 3 measures used in multiple screening to a battery of as many as 10 may be achieved by *multiphasic screening*, e.g., a well-child visit.

Other characteristics of screening, should also be cited here. As outlined by Frankenburg et al. (1973), they include *surveillance*, *sensitivity*, *specificity*, and *standardization*:

1) Screening measures may be used to periodically follow an individual or group, monitoring their present state of well-being, e.g., periodic urinalysis; this screening factor is called *surveillance*.
2) Screening tools should have some degree of *sensitivity* (accuracy in correctly differentiating an individual with a disease from the general population).
3) Screening tools should also have some degree of *specificity* (accuracy in correctly differentiating individuals who do not have the disease from those who do).

4) Some screening tools are *standardized*, meaning as compared with a standard (i.e., development).

With the advent of so many tools for screening, it is necessary to distinguish between categories of tests now available for documenting developmental problems in children. Melinda B. Kemper and William K. Frankenburg, in *Perspectives on Measurement: A Collection of Readings for Educators of Young Handicapped Children* (Kemper and Frankenburg, 1979), have discussed the differences between screening, diagnosis, and assessment tools:

1. *Screening* is the first step in identifying individuals who possibly have a developmental problem from those who do not. Screening tests are designed to be applied to large numbers of children; thus, they are usually short, objective, easy to administer and score, and can be given by trained volunteers or paraprofessionals. They are often standardized and examined for their reliability (consistency in measurements) and validity (the test measures what it is purported to measure). When abnormal findings result, referral for diagnostic evaluation is necessary.

2. *Diagnosis* involves a thorough analysis of a problem, often identified by screening, in order to determine the nature and/or cause. Thus, tests used to make a diagnosis are time-consuming, require skilled administration and interpretation by professionals, and are consequently more expensive than screening measures. The complexity of diagnostic tests results from the questions they must answer.

3. *Assessments*, on the other hand, are a means of estimating the current skills and abilities of a child who has already been identified as abnormal by screening and who has an established diagnosis. Assessment tools and practices measure current skills and abilities in a variety of areas. These tools, therefore, usually appear as checklists and are most often given by an individual working closely on an ongoing basis with the child. The tools are easy to administer and generally provide a means of planning an intervention program for the child initially, then later measuring the resulting progress. Thus, assessments often provide for the establishment of goals and objectives to be attained in programming for a handicapped child. However, caution should always be exercised with assessment tools, since many of them have not been standardized nor been examined with regard to their reliability or validity.

Table 1 differentiates into the categories of screening, diagnosis, or assessment a range of tests that are actively employed by nurses, physicians, teachers, therapists, and others working with children in order to *prevent* the occurrence of undetected developmental problems and/or

Table 1.   Screening, diagnostic, and assessment tools for detection of developmental problems in children

Name	Age range	Year published	Administration time	Type			Standardized	Reliability	Validity
				S*	D*	A*			
Neonatal Behavioral Assessment Scale (Brazelton)	1st few days of life	1973	30 min.			X			
Denver Developmental Screening Test (DDST) and revised form (DDST-R)	0–6 yrs.	1968	15–20 min.	X			X	X	X
Receptive-Expressive Emergent Language Scale (REEL)	0–3 yrs.	1971	Approx. 15 min.	X			X	X	
Behavioral Developmental Profile (Marshalltown)	0–6 yrs.	1975			X				
Callier-Azusa Scales	0–adult	1975				X		X	
Developmental Profile (Alpern-Boll)	0–12 yrs.	1972	30–40 min.			X	X	X	X
Learning Accomplishment Profile (LAP)	0–6 yrs.	1975				X	X Limited (in progress)		(in progress)
Slosson Intelligence Test (SIT)	0–adult	1964	10–30 min.	X			X >4 yrs.		X >4 yrs.

*S = Screening; D = Diagnosis, A = Assessment

Author/Address	Comments
Brazelton, T.B., Spastics International Medical Publications, in association with W. Heinemann Medical Books, J.B. Lippincott Co., London, Philadelphia	Evaluates control over interfering motor activity; response to animate and inanimate stimulation. Stimulation assessment of neurological adequacy and estimates of attentional excitement.
LADOCA Project & Publishing Foundation, Inc., E. 51st Ave. & Lincoln St., Denver, CO 80216	Screens gross motor, fine motor-adaptive, language, and personal skills.
Bzoch, K.R. and League, R., University Park Press, 300 North Charles St., Baltimore, MD 21201	Evaluates language. Structured parent interview.
Dept. of Special Education, Marshall-Poweshiek Joint-County System, 1 Westwood Dr., Marshalltown, IA 50158; or The Marshalltown Project, 507 E. Anson, Marshalltown, IA 50158	Assesses gross motor, fine motor, conceptual, language, social, and self-help skills. (For handicapped and culturally deprived children.)
Stillman, K. (Ed.), South Central Regional Center for Services to Deaf Blind Children, 2930 Turtle Creek Plaza, Suite 207, Dallas, TX; or University of Texas at Dallas, Callier Center for Communication Disorders, 1966 Inwood Rd., Dallas, TX 75235	Assesses gross motor, fine motor, language, social, and self-help skills. (For low-functioning deaf blind and multihandicapped individuals.)
Alpern, G.D., and Boll, T.J., Psychological Development Publications, 7150 Lakeside Dr., Indianapolis, IN 46278	Assesses gross motor, fine motor, language, conceptual, social, and self-help skills. Interview.
Griffen, P.M., and Sanford, A.R., Kaplan School Supply Corp., 600 Jonestown Rd., Winston-Salem, NC 27103	Assesses gross motor, fine motor, conceptual, language, social, and self-help skills. Provides criterion-referenced record of current skills.
Slosson, R.L., Western Psychological Services Publishers and Distributors, 12031 Wilshire Blvd., Los Angeles, CA 90025	Observation of individual performance. (Similar to Stanford-Binet Intelligence Scale.)

Table 1. *Continued*

Name	Age range	Year pub-lished	Admin-istration time	Type S*	Type D*	Type A*	Stan-dardized	Relia-bility	Valid-ity
Home Observation for Measurement of the Environment (HOME)	0–3 yrs., 3–6 yrs.	1976 1978				X	X	X	X
Vineland Social Maturity Scale	0– adult	1936 1941 1965	10–15 min.	X			X	X	X
Neonatal Perception Inventories	New-borns					X			
Verbal Language Development Scale (MECHAM)	0–15 yrs.	1971	Varies up to 30 min.			X			
Memphis Comprehensive Developmental Scale	0–5 yrs.	1974				X			
Hearing Development and Communication Questionnaire (HEAR)	0–2 yrs.	1979	20 min.	X				X	X
Portage Guide to Early Education	0–6 yrs.	1976				X			
Boyd Developmental Progress Scale	0–8 yrs.	1974		X				X	X
SEEC Developmental Wheel	0–5 yrs.	1976				X			

*S = Screening; D = Diagnosis, A = Assessment

Author/Address	Comments
Caldwell, B.M., and Bradley, R.M., Center for Child Development and Education, University of Arkansas, 33rd and University, Little Rock, AR 72204	Interview and observation.
Doll, E.A., American Guidance Service, Inc., Publishers Bldg., Circle Pines, MN 55014	Structured parent interview. Good with exceptional children. Describes child's habitual or customary behavior.
Broussard, E.R., and Hartner, M.S., 1971, In: Hellmuth, J. (ed.), Exceptional Infant: Studies in Abnormalities, Vol. 2, pp. 432–449. Brunner/Mazel, New York; and E.R. Broussard, 201 Lytton Ave., Pittsburgh, PA 15213	Checklist.
Mecham, M.J., American Guidance Service, Inc., Publishers Bldg., Circle Pines, MN 55014	Interview to assess speech and language skills.
Quick, A.P., Little, T.L., and Campbell, A.A., Fearon Publishers, 6 Davies Dr., Belmont, CA 94002	Assesses gross motor, fine motor, conceptual, language, social, and self-help skills of developmentally delayed preschool children.
Downs, M.P., BAM World Markets, Inc., P.O. Box 10701, University Park Station, Denver, CO 80210	Screens hearing of infants.
Bruma, S., Shearer, M., Frohman, A., and Hilliard, J., Cooperative Educational Service Agency, P.O. Box 564, Portage, WI 53901; or Portage Project, 412 E. Slifer St., Portage, WI 53901	Assesses gross motor, fine motor, conceptual, language, social and self-help skills.
Boyd, R.D., Inland Counties Regional Center, Inc., P.O. Box 6127, San Bernardino, CA 92408	Measures three areas of function: motor skills, communication skills, and self-sufficiency skills.
Swanson, L.E., and Staff, Early Childhood Education, 804 W. Bode Rd., Schaumburg, IL 60194	Assesses gross-fine motor, conceptual, language, social, and self-help skills. (May be used for educational planning program evaluation.)

Table 1. *Continued*

Name	Age range	Year published	Administration time	S*	D*	A*	Standardized	Reliability	Validity
SEED Developmental Profile	0–4 yrs.	1975				X			
Vision Up	0–6 yrs.					X			
Griffiths Mental Developmental Scale for Testing Babies	0–2 yrs.	1954	20–40 min.			X	X Sample small		
Gesell Developmental Schedules	4 wks.– 6 yrs.	1925 1938 1940	20–40 min.	X					
Developmental Screening Inventory (DSI)	1–18 mos.	1966	20–30 min.	X					
Kahn Intelligence Test	1 mo. and older	1964		X					
A Developmental Approach to Case-finding	1–36 mos.	1969 1980		X					
Bayley Scales of Infant Development: Motor Scale and Mental Scale Infant Behavior Record	2–30 mos.	1969	45–60 min.			X	X	X	X
Prescreening Developmental Questionnaire (PDQ)	3 mos.– 6 yrs.	1975	5 min.	Pre- X					X
Cattell Infant Intelligence Scale	3–30 mos.	1930 1940	20–40 min.			X	Small number	X	

*S = Screening; D = Diagnosis, A = Assessment

Author/Address	Comments
Herst, J., Wolfe, S., Jorgensen, G., and Pallan, S., Sewall Rehabilitation Center, SEED Program, 1360 Vine St., Denver, CO 80206	Assesses gross motor, fine motor, conceptual, language, social, and self-help skills. Intended for use with severely handicapped children to obtain "functional" assessment.
Croft, N.B., and Robinson, L.W., Educational Products and Training Foundation, 6025 Chestnut Dr., Boise, ID 83704	Assesses gross motor, fine motor, conceptual, language, social, and self-help skills.
Griffiths, R. 1954., The Abilities of Babies, McGraw Hill Book Co., New York.	Only standardized infant assessment on British children. Available only to testers trained by Griffiths.
Passamanick, B., Psychological Corporation, 757 Third Ave., New York, NY 10017	Nice clinical tool for therapists. Needs updating.
Knobloch, H., Dept. of Pediatrics, Albany Medical College, Albany, NY 12208	Screens gross motor, fine motor, adaptive, language, and personal social skills. Shortened version of Gesell Developmental Schedules.
Box 1441, Missoula, MT 59801	Appropriate for verbally or culturally handicapped children. Special adaptation for blind and deaf children.
Haynes, U.H., U.S. Dept. of Health and Human Services, HEW Publication HSA 795-210-1980, Superintendent of Documents, U.S. Government Printing Office, Washington, DC 20402	Focuses on vulnerable child. Evolution of basic neurological patterns and maturation of CNS.
Bayley, N., The Psychological Corp., 1372 Peachtree St., NE, Atlanta, GA 30309	Evaluates gross and fine motor skills and attentional, fine motor, problem-solving, language, and other areas of early cognitive development. Evaluates interpersonal, affective, motivational, and interest levels of sensory experience.
Frankenburg, W.K. et al., LADOCA Project & Publishing Foundation, Inc., E. 51st Ave. and Lincoln St., Denver, CO 80216	Parent-answered questionnaire. Designed as prescreen for Denver Developmental Screening Test (DDST).
Cattell, P., The Psychological Corp. 1372 Peachtree St., NE, Atlanta, GA 30309	Better for exceptional children. Items derived from other tests. Measures intelligence.

Table 1. *Continued*

Name	Age range	Year published	Administration time	Type			Standardized	Reliability	Validity
				S*	D*	A*			
Sequenced Inventory of Communication Development (SICD)	4 mos.–4 yrs.	1975				X	Limited sample	X	X
Preschool Attainment Record	6 mos.–7 yrs.	1967	15-20 min.		X		X		
Stycar Vision Tests	6 mos.–7 yrs.	1960		X					
Stycar Hearing Tests	6 mos.–7 yrs.	1960		X					
Denver Eye Screening Test (DEST)	6 mos. & over	1972	5–10 min.	X			X	X	X
Quick Screening Scale of Mental Development	1–9 yrs.	1963	30–45 min.	X					
Minnesota Preschool Test	1½–6 yrs.	1938 1940		X			X	X	
Developmental Test of Visual-Motor Integration (Beery) (VMI)	2–15 yrs.	1967			X		X	X	X
Valett Developmental Survey of Basic Learning Abilities	2–7 yrs.	1966				X			
Quick Test	2 yrs.–adult	1958 1962	5–10 min.	X			X	X	X

*S = Screening; D = Diagnosis, A = Assessment

Author/Address	Comments
Hedrick, H.L., Prather, E.M., and Tobin, A.R., University of Washington Press, Seattle, WA 98195	Variety of subtests measuring receptive and expressive language development
Doll, E.A., American Guidance Service, Inc., Publishers Bldg., Circle Pines, MN 55014	Interview assessing gross motor, fine motor, conceptual, language, social, and self-help skills
Sheridan, M.S., Institute of Psychological Research, 3/4 Quest, Rue Fleury St., West, Montreal 357, Prov. Quebec, Canada	Observation of individual performance. Screens vision.
Sheridan, M.S. (same as Stycar Vision Tests)	Observation of individual performance. Screens hearing.
Barker, J. et al., LADOCA Project & Publishing Foundation, Inc., E. 51st Ave. & Lincoln St., Denver, CO 80216	Individually administered vision screen.
Banham, K.M., The Psychological Affiliates, Chicago Plaza, Brockport, IL 62910	Questionable usefulness because of poor standardization.
Goodenough, F. et al., American Guidance Service, Inc., Pubishers Bldg., Circle Pines, MN 55014	Items have poor appeal to young children. Assesses development of mental ability.
Beery, K.E. and Bucktenica, N.A., Follett Publishing Co., Customer Service Center, Box 5705, Chicago, IL 60680; or Follett Publishing Co., 1010 W. Washington Blvd., Chicago, IL 60607	Often used as screening test for pre-writing skills. Fairly complete test of visual-motor integration functioning in young children.
Valett, R.E., Consulting Psychologists Press, 577 College Ave., Palo Alto, CA 94306	Assesses gross motor, fine motor, conceptual, and language skills. Intended for use with developmentally delayed, mildly retarded children. Covers additional areas of visual, tactile, and auditory discrimination. Aid in planning individual learning programs.
Ammons, R.B., and Ammons, C.H., Psychological Test Specialists, Box 1441, Missoula, MT 59801	Quick screen of verbal-perceptual intelligence.

Table 1. *Continued*

Name	Age range	Year published	Administration time	Type S*	Type D*	Type A*	Standardized	Reliability	Validity
Stanford-Binet Intelligence Scale (Form L-M)	2 yrs.– adult	1972	30–90 min.		X		X	X	X
Carolina Developmental Profile	2–5 yrs.	1976				X			
Full Range Picture Vocabulary Test	2 yrs. & up	1948 1950 1952	10–15 min.	X				X	
Arthur Adaptation of Leiter International Performance Scale	2–9 yrs.	1950	30–60 min.		X		X	X	X
Illinois Test of Psycholinguistic Abilities (ITPA)	2–10 yrs.	1960 1968			X				
Developmental Sentence Analysis	2–7 yrs.	1974			X		X	X	
Goldman-Fristoe Test of Articulation	2 yrs.– adult	1967 1972			X			X	
Peabody Picture Vocabulary Test (PPVT), Revised	2½–18 yrs.	1959 1965 1981	12–15 min.	X	X			X	X 7 yrs. of age
Developmental Indications for Assessment of Learning (DIAL)	2½–5½ yrs.	1975	20–30 min.	X			X	X	X
McCarthy Scales of Children's Abilities (MSCA)	2½–8½ yrs.	1972	45–50 min.		X		X	X	X

*S = Screening; D = Diagnosis, A = Assessment

Author/Address	Comments
Terman, L.M., Merrill, M.A., and Thorndike, R.L., Test Dept., Box 1970, Iowa City, IA 27514; or Houghton-Mifflin Co., 666 Miami Circle, NE, Atlanta, GA 30324	Primarily verbal items, with some performance items for preschool years. Strongly predictive of academic achievement.
Lillie, D.L., and Harbin, G.L., 803 Churchill, Chapel Hill, NC 27514; or Kaplan School Supply, 600 Jonestown Rd., Winston-Salem, NC 27103	Assesses gross motor, fine motor, conceptual, language, and social skills. Intended for use with mildly handicapped children.
Ammons, B.B., and Ammons, H.S., Psychological Test Specialists Box 1441, Missoula, MT 59801	Quick initial verbal screening device. Little correlation with the Stanford-Binet Intelligence Scale.
Arthur Grace, Stoelting Co., 1350 South Kostner Ave., Chicago, IL 60624	Useful with children who have auditory deficits, speech and language problems or motor handicaps. Evaluates nonverbal skills.
Kirk, S.A., McCarthy, J.J., and Kirk, W.D., University of Illinois Press, University of Illinois, Urbana, IL 61801	Not generally considered an adequate measure of language development when used alone, but often used as part of a test battery.
Lee, L.L., and Koenigsknecht, R.D., Northwestern University Press, 1735 Benson Ave., Evanston, IL 60201	Evaluates recorded language samples for expressive syntax and morphology. Sometimes used as part of language test battery.
Goldman, R., and Fristoe, M., American Guidance Service, Inc., Publishers Bldg., Circle Pines, MN 55014	May be more interesting for young children than Photo Articulation Test. Assesses articulation of consonant sounds.
Dunn, L.M., American Guidance Service, Inc., Publishers Bldg., Circle Pines, MN 55014	Screens/evaluates receptive vocabulary. Useful with children with expressive deficits. Should be used only in connection with other tests.
Makdell, C., and Goldenberg, I. DIAL Inc., Box 911, Highland Park, IL 60035	Screens gross motor, fine motor, concepts, and communication skills to identify children with potential learning problems.
McCarthy, I., The Psychological Corp., Psychological Measurement Division, 757 Third Ave., N.Y., NY 10017; or Psychological Corp., 304 E. 45th St., N.Y., NY 10017	Considered one of the least "culturally biased" tests. Most useful with children who have mild learning disabilities. Determines general intellectual levels.

Table 1. *Continued*

Name	Age range	Year pub-lished	Admin-istration time	Type S*	D*	A*	Stan-dardized	Relia-bility	Valid-ity
Peabody Individual Achievement Test (PIAT)	2½–18 yrs.	1970	30–40 min.			X			
California Pre-school Social Competency Scale (CPSCS)	2½–5½ yrs.	1969		X			X		
Comprehensive Identification Process (CIP)	2½–5½ yrs.	1975	30–40 min.	X			X		
Developmental Articulation Test (HEJNA)	3–8 yrs.		10 min.		X				
Marianne Frostig Develop-mental Test of Visual Perception	3–8 yrs.	1964 1966			X		X	X	X
The Extended Merrill-Palmer Scale	3–5 yrs.	1978					X		
Denver Audio-Metric Screen-Test (DAST)	3 yrs. & older	1972	5–10 min.	X			X	X	X
Test of Auditory Comprehension of Language (TACL)	3–7 yrs.	1973			X		X	X	X
Photo Articula-tion Test	3–12 yrs.	1969			X		X	X	X
Goldman-Fris-toe-Woodcock Auditory Skills Test Battery	3 yrs.– adult	1976			X		X	X	X

*S = Screening; D = Diagnosis, A = Assessment

Author/Address	Comments
Dunn, L.M., and Markwardt, F.C., American Guidance Service, Inc., Publishers Bldg., Circle Pines, MN 55014	Interview to measure school readiness and academic achievement.
Levine, S., Elzey, F.F., and Lewis, M., Consulting Psychologists Press, Inc., 577 College Ave., Palo Alto, CA 94306	Observation of individual performance; general development screen. Measures adequacy of interpersonal behavior and degree of social responsibility.
Zehrbach, R.R., Scholastic Testing Service, 480 Meyer Rd., Bensenville, IL 60106	Observation of individual performance; general development screen.
Hejna, R.F., Speech Materials, Box 1713, Ann Arbor, MI 48106	Assesses consonant sounds on developmental scale.
Frostig, M., and Maslow, P., Consulting Psychologists Press, 577 College Ave., Palo Alto, CA 94306	Evaluates eye-hand coordination and school readiness. Measures five operationally defined perceptual skills.
Stutsman, R., Stoelting Co., 1350 South Kostner Ave., Chicago, IL 60624	Based on structure of intellect model. Test too new for practical usefulness to be established.
Drumwright, A. et al., LADOCA Project & Publishing Foundation, Inc., E. 51st Ave. and Lincoln St., Denver, CO 80216	Individually administered hearing screen.
Carrow, E., Learning Concepts, Inc., 2501 N. Lamar, Austin, TX 78705	Evaluates receptive syntax and morphology. Useful as part of test battery.
Pendergast, K., Dickey, S., Selmar, J., and Soder, A., The Interstate Printers & Publishers, Inc., Danville, IL 61832	Diagnostic articulation test.
Goldman, R., Fristoe, M. and Woodcock, R., American Guidance Service, Inc., Publishers Bldg., Circle Pines, MN 55014	Auditory discrimination, selective attention, memory, and sound-symbol subtests used to identify specific deficiencies in auditory functioning.

Table 1. *Continued*

Name	Age range	Year pub- lished	Admin- istration time	Type S*	Type D*	Type A*	Stan- dardized	Relia- bility	Valid- ity
The Houston Test for Language Development (Houston)	3–6 yrs. (Also 6 mos.– 3 yrs.)	1963 1958	30 min.		X		X	X	X
Language Facility Test	3–15 yrs.			X					
Screening Test for Auditory Comprehension of Language	3–7 yrs.			X				X	
Cooperative Preschool Inventory	3–6 yrs.	1970		X					
Riley Pre- school Develop- mental Screen- ing Inventory	3–5 yrs.			X					
Columbia Mental Maturity Scale	3 6/12– 9 11/12			X					
Parent Readi- ness Evaluation of Preschoolers (PREP)	3 9/12– 5 8/12			X					
Ayres Battery	4–7–10 yrs.	1964 1969			X		X	X	X
Animal Crack- ers, A Test of Motivation to Achieve	Pre- school, kinder- garten, 1st grade			X					
Bender Visual Motor Gestalt Test	4 yrs.– adult	1938 1974			X		X	X	X

*S = Screening; D = Diagnosis, A = Assessment

Author/Address	Comments
Crabtree, M., Houston Test Co., P.O. Box 35152, Houston, TX 77035	Establishing basis for objective evaluation of language functioning in children.
Carrow, E., Learning Concepts, Inc., 2501 N. Lamar, Austin, TX 78705	Observation of individual performance to screen speech and language.
Carrow, E., Learning Concepts, Inc., 2501 N. Lamar, Austin, TX 78705	Observation of individual performance to screen speech and language.
Caldwell, B.M., Educational Testing Service, 1947 Center St., Berkeley, CA 94704	Observation of individual performance to screen school readiness and academic achievement.
Riley, C.M.D., Western Psychological Services, 12031 Wilshire Blvd., Los Angeles, CA 90025	Observation of individual performance to screen school readiness and academic achievement.
Burgemeister, B.B., Brum, L.H., and Lorge, I., Harcourt Brace Jovanovich, Inc.; Health Care Publications Division, 737 3rd Ave., New York 15017	Observation of individual performance; general development screen.
Ahr, A.E., Priority Innovations, Inc., P.O. Box 792, Skokie, IL 60076	Observation of individual performance to screen school readiness and academic achievement.
Ayres, A.J., Western Psychological Services, 12031 Wilshire Blvd., Los Angeles, CA 90025	Various subtests provide potential breakdown of problems underlying functional deficits in fine motor area. Used with children who have or are suspected to have visual-perceptual or visual-motor problems.
Adkins, D.C., and Ballif, B.L., CTB/McGraw-Hill, Del Monte Research Park, Monterey, CA 93940	Observation of individual performance to screen general development.
Bender, L., American Orthopsychiatric Association, Sales Office, 49 Sheridan Ave., Albany, NY 12210	Developmental levels can be scored with reliability, but neuropsychological and emotional indicators are less reliable.

Table 1. *Continued*

Name	Age range	Year pub-lished	Admin-istration time	Type S*	Type D*	Type A*	Stan-dardized	Relia-bility	Valid-ity
Test of Basic Experience (TOBE)	Pre-school, kinder-garten, 1st grade	1975	125 min.	X					X
Wechsler Pre-school & Pri-mary Scale of Intelligence (WPPSI)	4–6½ yrs.	1967			X	X	X	X	X
School Readi-ness Survey (SRS)	4–6 yrs.	1967		X				X	
Ready or Not? Handbook for School Readi-ness Checklist	4–6 yrs.				X				
Screening Test of Academic Readiness (STAR)	4 6/12–6 5/12			X					
McCarthy Screening Test (MST)	4–6½ yrs.	1978	20 min.	X			X	X	X
Primary Academic Sentiment Scale (PASS)	4 4/12–7 3/12			X					
Sprigle School Readiness Screening Test (SSRST)	4 6/12–6 9/12			X					
ABC Inventory	4 9/12–5 11/12	1965	9 min.	X				X	

*S = Screening; D = Diagnosis, A = Assessment

Author/Address	Comments
Moss, M.H., CTB/McGraw-Hill, Del Monte Research Park, Monterey, CA 92940	Observation of individual performance to screen school readiness and academic achievement.
Psychological Corporation, 304 E. 45th St., New York, NY 10017	Provides separate verbal and performance scores.
Jordan, F.L., and Massey, J., Consulting Psychologists Press, 577 College Ave., Palo Alto, CA 94306	Observation of individual performance to screen school readiness and academic achievement. (Parent-administered.)
Auston, J.J., and Lafferty, J.C., Research Concepts, Division of Test Maker, Inc., 1368 Airport Rd., Muskegon, MI 49444	Checklist to assess school readiness and academic achievement.
Ahr, A.E., Priority Innovations, Inc., P.O. Box 792, Skokie, IL 60076	Observation of individual performance to screen school readiness and academic achievement.
The Psychological Corporation, Psychological Measurement Division, 757 Third Ave., New York, NY 10017	Norms based on McCarthy Scales of Children's Abilities. Screens R-L orientation, verbal memory, Draw-A-Design, numerical memory, conceptual grouping, and leg coordination; designed to identify children likely to encounter difficulty in coping with school work.
Thompson, G.R., Priority Innovations, Inc., P.O. Box 792, Skokie, IL 60076	Observation of individual performance to screen school readiness and academic achievement.
Sprigle, H.A., and Lanier, J., Psychological Clinic & Research Center, San Marco Blvd., Jacksonville, FL 32207	Interview to screen school readiness and academic achievement.
Adair, N., and Blesch, G., Educational Studies & Development of Test Maker, Inc., 1357 Forrest Park Rd., Muskegon, MI 49441; or Research Concepts, 1368 E. Airport Rd., Muskegon, MI 49441	Identifies children who may not likely fail in kindergarten and who are not likely to be ready for 1st grade.

Table 1. *Continued*

Name	Age range	Year published	Administration time	Type S*	D*	A*	Standardized	Reliability	Validity
Preschool Readiness Experimental Screening Scale (PRESS)	5 yrs. pre-kindergarten			X					
Primary Self Concept Inventory	Kindergarten– 6th grade			X				X	X
Kindergarten Auditory Screening Test	Kindergarten, 1st grade			X					
Screen	Kindergarten, 1st grade			X					
Wide Range Achievement Test (WRAT)	5 yrs.– adult	1965	20–30 min.	X					
Search	5–7 yrs.	1977	20 min.	X					
Meeting Street School Screening Test (MSSST)	5–7½ yrs.	1969	20 min.	X			X	X	X
First Grade Screening Test	End of kindergarten– early 1st grade			X					
Auditory Discrimination Test (Wepman)	5 yrs.– adult	1973	5 min.	X					
Predictive Screening Test of Articulation	1st grade			X					

*S = Screening; D = Diagnosis, A = Assessment

Author/Address	Comments
Rogers, W.B., Jr., and Rogers, R.A., 1972. Clinical Pediatrics 2(10): 253–256.	Observation of individual performance to screen school readiness and academic achievement.
Muller, D.G., and Leonetti, R., Learning Concepts, 2501 W. Lamar, Austin, TX 78705	May be administered to individual children or to small groups to screen school readiness and academic achievement.
Katz, J., Follett Publishing Co., Customer Service Center, Box 5705, Chicago, IL 60680	Observation of individual performance to screen hearing.
Senf, G.M., and Comrey, A.L., Computer Psychometric Affiliates, Inc., Chicago, IL 60607	Observation of individual performance to screen school readiness and academic achievement.
Jastak, J.F., Bijou, S.W., and Jastak, S.R., The Psychological Corporation, 1372 Peachtree St., NE., Atlanta, GA 30309	Measures achievement in reading, spelling, and arithmetic.
Silver, A.A., and Hagin, R.H., Walker Educational Book Corp., 720 Fifth Ave., New York, NY 10019	Detects learning difficulties and helps prevent later school failure.
Hainsworth, P.K., and Siqueland, M.L., Crippled Children & Adults of Rhode Island, Inc., Meeting Street School, 333 Grotto Ave., Providence, RI 02906; or Meeting Street School, 667 Waterman Ave., E. Providence, RI 02914	Early identification of children with learning disabilities.
Pate, J.E., and Webb, W.W., American Guidance Service, Inc., Circle Pines, MN 55014	Observation of individual performance to screen school readiness and academic achievement.
Wepman, J., Western Psychological Services, Publishers & Distributors, 12301 Wilshire Blvd., Los Angeles, CA 90025	Measures development of auditory discrimination.
VanRiper, C., and Erickson, R.L., Continuing Education Office, Western Michigan University, Kalamazoo, MI 49001	Observation of individual performance to screen articulation.

Table 1. *Continued*

Name	Age range	Year published	Administration time	S*	D*	A*	Standardized	Reliability	Validity
Individual Learning Disabilities Classroom Screening Instrument (ILDCSI)	Grades 1–3	1970		X					
Piers-Harris Children's Self Concept Scale ("The Way I Feel About Myself")	Grades 3–12	1969	15–20 min.			X	X	X	X
AAMD Adaptive Behavior Scale	Based on adaptive level functioning in residential setting or community	1969 1974 1975			X				
AAMD Adaptive Behavior Scale Public School Version	Adaptive behavior	1969 1974			X				
Preschool Language Scale–Revised Edition	1–7 yrs.	1979	20–30 min.	X			X	X	X
The Milani Comparetti Motor Development Screening Test	0–2 yrs.	1977	4–8 min. depending on experience	X					
The HOME Screening Questionnaire	0–6 yrs.	1981	15–20 min.	X			X	Less reliable under 1 year	

*S = Screening; D = Diagnosis, A = Assessment

Author/Address	Comments
Meier, J.H., Cazier, V.O., and Giles, M.T., Learning Pathways, Inc., Box 1407, Evergreen, CO 80439	Designed to aid classroom teachers in systematic identification of children who have difficulty learning academic material.
Piers, E.V., Counselor Recordings & Tests, Box 6184 Acklen Station, Nashville, TN 37212	Self report instrument on development of children's self attitudes and correlates of these attitudes.
Nihira, K., Foster, R., Shellhaas, M. and Leland, H., American Association on Mental Deficiency, 5201 Connecticut Ave. NW, Washington, DC 20015	Objective descriptions and evaluations of adaptive behavior. Behavior rating scale for mentally retarded, emotionally maladjusted, and developmentally disabled individuals.
Lambert, N., Windmiller, N., Cole, L., and Figueroa, R., University of California, Berkeley, Dept. of Education, Berkeley, CA 94720	Assists in appropriate school placement. Used to plan intervention strategies and remediation activities.
Zimmerman, I.L., Steiner, V.G., and Pond, R.E., Charles E. Merrill Publishing Co., A Bell & Howell Co., Columbus, OH 43216	Evaluates auditory comprehension and verbal ability as well as articulation. Has Spanish bilingual scale.
Trembath, J., Meyer Children's Rehabilitation Institute, University of Nebraska Medical Center, Omaha, NE 68131	A simple, rapid neurodevelopmental examination which can be easily incorporated into routine health care management.
Frankenburg, W.K., Coons, C.E., and Gay, E.C., LADOCA Project & Publishing Foundation, Inc., E. 51st Ave. at Lincoln St., Denver, CO 80216	Not recommended for use in middle- to upper-SES population. Designed to sample aspects of social, emotional, and cognitive support available to a young child in his or her home. (Parent questionnaire)

monitor intervention programs. (Note: Neither the author nor the editors personally endorse all the tests listed in the table; the purpose has been to provide a representative sampling of available tools.)

TYPES OF SCREENING TESTS

How, then, should a nurse concerned about *prevention* of handicapping conditions proceed in determining the presence or absence of developmental problems?

The type of screening test used is important. The *criteria* that should

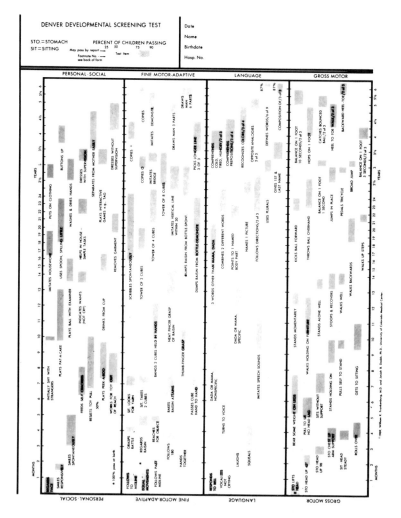

Figure 1. Denver Developmental Screening Test (DDST), 1969.

be used *in selecting a screening tool* are the following (Frankenburg, 1973):

1. Is the screening tool *acceptable* to the patient, the family, and the nurse?
2. Is the tool *reliable* (are screening results consistent each time the tool is used)?
3. Is the tool *valid* (does it measure what it is supposed to measure)?
4. Is the total *cost reasonable?*

The Denver Developmental Screening Test

One standardized screening tool for "assessing" development in preschool children that deserves special mention is the Denver Developmental Screening Test (DDST) (Figure 1) and revised form (DDST-R) (Figure 2). The DDST was carefully standardized on over 1,000 normal preschool

1. Try to get child to smile by smiling, talking or waving to him. Do not touch him.
2. When child is playing with toy, pull it away from him. Pass if he resists.
3. Child does not have to be able to tie shoes or button in the back.
4. Move yarn slowly in an arc from one side to the other, about 6" above child's face.
   Pass if eyes follow 90° to midline. (Past midline; 180°)
5. Pass if child grasps rattle when it is touched to the backs or tips of fingers.
6. Pass if child continues to look where yarn disappeared or tries to see where it went. Yarn should be dropped quickly from sight from tester's hand without arm movement.
7. Pass if child picks up raisin with any part of thumb and a finger.
8. Pass if child picks up raisin with the ends of thumb and index finger using an over hand approach.

9. Pass any enclosed form.
   Fail continuous round motions.
10. Which line is longer? (Not bigger.) Turn paper upside down and repeat. (3/3 or 5/6)
11. Pass any crossing lines.
12. Have child copy first. If failed, demonstrate

When giving items 9, 11 and 12, do not name the forms. Do not demonstrate 9 and 11.

13. When scoring, each pair (2 arms, 2 legs, etc.) counts as one part.
14. Point to picture and have child name it. (No credit is given for sounds only.)

15. Tell child to: Give block to Mommie; put block on table; put block on floor. Pass 2 of 3.
    (Do not help child by pointing, moving head or eyes.)
16. Ask child: What do you do when you are cold? ..hungry? ..tired? Pass 2 of 3.
17. Tell child to: Put block on table; under table; in front of chair, behind chair.
    Pass 3 of 4. (Do not help child by pointing, moving head or eyes.)
18. Ask child: If fire is hot, ice is ?; Mother is a woman, Dad is a ?; a horse is big, a mouse is ?. Pass 2 of 3.
19. Ask child: What is a ball? ..lake? ..desk? ..house? ..banana? ..curtain? ..ceiling? ..hedge? ..pavement? Pass if defined in terms of use, shape, what it is made of or general category (such as banana is fruit, not just yellow). Pass 6 of 9.
20. Ask child: What is a spoon made of? ..a shoe made of? ..a door made of? (No other objects may be substituted.) Pass 3 of 3.
21. When placed on stomach, child lifts chest off table with support of forearms and/or hands.
22. When child is on back, grasp his hands and pull him to sitting. Pass if head does not hang back.
23. Child may use wall or rail only, not person. May not crawl.
24. Child must throw ball overhand 3 feet to within arm's reach of tester.
25. Child must perform standing broad jump over width of test sheet. (8-1/2 inches)
26. Tell child to walk forward, ⊂◯⊃⊂◯⊃ heel within 1 inch of toe.
    Tester may demonstrate. Child must walk 4 consecutive steps, 2 out of 3 trials.
27. Bounce ball to child who should stand 3 feet away from tester. Child must catch ball with hands, not arms, 2 out of 3 trials.
28. Tell child to walk backward, ⊂◯⊃⊂◯⊃ toe within 1 inch of heel.
    Tester may demonstrate. Child must walk 4 consecutive steps, 2 out of 3 trials.

DATE AND BEHAVIORAL OBSERVATIONS (how child feels at time of test, relation to tester, attention span, verbal behavior, self-confidence, etc,):

Figure 1.   Key to DDST.

children in the Denver metropolitan area. This factor alone increases user confidence in the stability of this tool, for it was thus possible to develop normative data on when mastery of certain developmental tasks occurs on a large number of children from varying socioeconomic backgrounds. The DDST is concise and easy to administer. It establishes a range of normality for accomplishing developmental milestones, encouraging a broader look

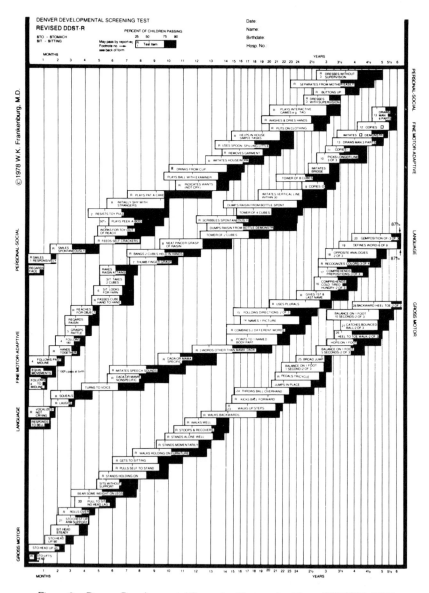

Figure 2.   Denver Developmental Screening Test, revised form (DDST-R), 1978.

at the preschool child in the areas of *personal-social* skills (relating to people and independence), *fine motor-adaptive* skills (hand-eye coordination, problem solving, and perception), *language* skills (hearing, use and interpretation of the spoken word), and *gross motor* skills (posturing, locomotion, and coordination) (Frankenburg, Dodds, and Fandal, 1973).

The DDST does well what it is designed to do; that is, it aids the nurse in screening preschool development. It does not measure the developmental level of a child, nor tell the level at which the child functions. (To do this a *diagnostic* developmental exam must be administered.) The DDST tells the screener how the child compares with the standardization population; in other words, is his or her development age appropriate (*normal*)? Or is it *questionable* or *abnormal*, or perhaps even *untestable*? If, upon a second screening, the child continues to fall into either the *questionable, abnormal,* or *untestable* categories, then follow-up is indicated. The DDST affords the nurse an opportunity to screen the development of a child; it is essential, therefore, that the nurse carefully administer each test item according to procedures outlined in the test manual (Frankenburg et., 1973).

Other standardized Denver screening tests to check vision, articulation, and hearing are also described in Table 1. Such screening tools are examples of *first-stage* screening procedures (Roberts, 1977). In the last several years much work and effort have gone into development of *second-* and *third-stage* screening procedures with the Denver tool, which should be of interest and assistance to the nurse.

Prescreening Development Questionnaire

The Prescreening Developmental Questionnaire (PDQ) based on the DDST is a multiple-stage tool designed to assist those professionals who have limited time and staff assistance to screen the development of preschool children more frequently and regularly (Figures 2 and 3). Through the PDQ, which uses parents as screeners, larger populations of children may be screened and developmental surveillance of children accomplished more quickly and cost-effectively.

Questions on the PDQ were developed from items on the DDST. The entire parent questionnaire contains 96 questions on current child behavior, arranged in chronological order based on the age at which 90% of the DDST standardization population passed the test items. After the age of the child to be screened is determined, 10 age-appropriate questions are selected to be answered by the parent or caregiver. Based upon the parent's answers, the questionnaire is then scored to determine the existence or nonexistence of developmental problems—*first stage* screening.

Experience in using the PDQ and DDST indicates that for those populations with limited formal parental education (less than high school education) testing is more effective if a short form of the DDST, rather than the PDQ, is administered as a *first stage* screening. (Then if any questions arise

4-year

DENVER PRESCREENING DEVELOPMENTAL QUESTIONNAIRE

Please read each question carefully before you answer. Circle the best answer for each question.
YOUR CHILD IS NOT EXPECTED TO BE ABLE TO DO EVERYTHING THE QUESTIONS ASK.

Child's Name: _Ronald Jones_

Date: _5/28/76_

Birthdate: _5/20/72_

YES   —CHILD CAN DO NOW or HAS DONE IN THE PAST
NO   —CHILD CANNOT DO NOW, HAS NOT DONE IN THE PAST
            or YOU ARE NOT SURE THAT YOUR CHILD CAN DO IT.
R   —CHILD REFUSES TO TRY
NO-OPP—CHILD HAS NOT HAD THE CHANCE TO TRY

4-year check—Answer 71 through 80

71. Can your child pedal a tricycle at least ten feet? If your child has never had a chance to ride a tricycle his size, circle NO-OPP. (YES) NO R NO-OPP

72. After eating, does your child wash and dry his hands well enough so you don't have to do them over? Circle NO-OPP if you do not allow him to wash and dry his hands by himself. (YES) NO R NO-OPP

4-year, 3 month check—
Answer 73 through 82

73. Does your child put an "s" at the end of his words when he is talking about more than one thing such as blocks, shoes, or toys? (YES) NO R NO-OPP

74. Without letting your child hold onto anything, have him balance on one foot for as long as he can. Encourage him by showing him how, if necessary. GIVE HIM THREE CHANCES. Estimate seconds by counting slowly. Did your child balance 2 seconds or more? (YES) NO R NO-OPP

Figure 3.   Sample questions for 4-year-old age group on the Denver Prescreening Developmental Questionnaire.

75. Without letting your child take a running jump, ask him to jump length-wise over this paper. Did he do this without landing on the paper?   YES   NO   R   NO-OPP

76. Have your child draw this figure in the space below. DO NOT SAY "CIRCLE." *Do not help or correct your child.* Say to your child, "Draw a picture just like this one," and point to the picture on the right.   YES   NO   R   NO-OPP

Look at these examples when scoring your child's drawing.

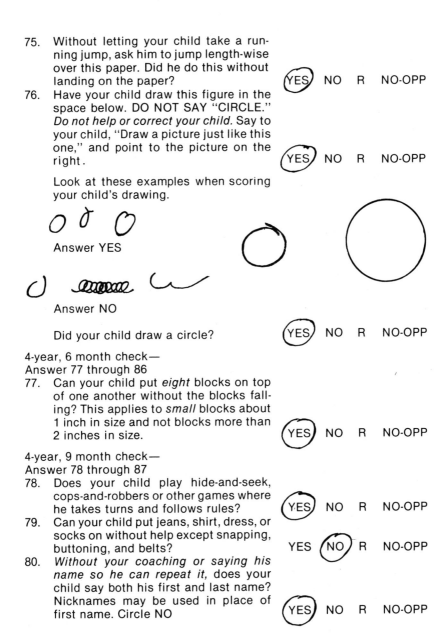

Answer YES

Answer NO

Did your child draw a circle?   YES   NO   R   NO-OPP

4-year, 6 month check—
Answer 77 through 86

77. Can your child put *eight* blocks on top of one another without the blocks falling? This applies to *small* blocks about 1 inch in size and not blocks more than 2 inches in size.   YES   NO   R   NO-OPP

4-year, 9 month check—
Answer 78 through 87

78. Does your child play hide-and-seek, cops-and-robbers or other games where he takes turns and follows rules?   YES   NO   R   NO-OPP

79. Can your child put jeans, shirt, dress, or socks on without help except snapping, buttoning, and belts?   YES   NO   R   NO-OPP

80. *Without your coaching or saying his name so he can repeat it,* does your child say both his first and last name? Nicknames may be used in place of first name. Circle NO   YES   NO   R   NO-OPP

about the child's development, a full DDST—*second stage* screening—should be given.) For those populations with formal parental education (high school or more) the PDQ can be administered as a first stage screening. (If any questions then result, the full DDST can be completed as a second stage screening.)

What is a short DDST and how is it employed? Once the age of the child to be screened is determined and the age line accurately drawn, then the examiner administers three test items immediately to the *left* of (not touching or intersecting in any way) the age line in each of the four sectors of the DDST. If all items are passed, no further screening is required at this stage. If, however, *any* test item is failed or the child refuses to do one or more items, then rescreening with a full DDST should immediately occur (Fandal, Kemper, and Frankenburg, 1979).

NURSE AS COMMUNITY LIAISON

Use of prescreening, screening, and assessment tools helps the nurse accomplish the goal of *prevention* of handicapping conditions in children. Not only are developmental problems thus likely to be identified earlier, providing an opportunity to document objectively the child's progress over time, but the nurse is given the chance to assist, support, and encourage the family in dealing with their handicapped child. Screening analyses enable the nurse to point out the strengths as well as the weaknesses of the child under consideration. In addition, the nurse can assume the role of liaison between the child, his or her family, medical and educational resources, and the local community. Following are suggestions of ways a nurse can be an effective community liaison for a child and family with developmental problems (Erickson, 1978):

a) It is initially important to have the parents *actively involved* in the care and decision making regarding the child.
b) Include the parents and child as *team members* in the screening, referral, evaluation, diagnosis, and intervention processes.
c) When assessing a child for developmental problems be *objective* in approach and in intervention measures instituted and consider future management plans that may be developed and implemented with the child.
d) Make certain the plans are realistic and acceptable to the child and his or her family.
e) Be *knowledgeable* about local, state, regional, and national resources.
f) Encourage parents to keep *ongoing records* of the child's medical and developmental history.
g) *Point out abilities* and disabilities of the child.
h) Assist parents in *working with professionals*. The success of intervention programs depends on good communication, cooperation, and follow through.

i) *Listen* carefully to what parents and children say and encourage other professionals involved with the family to do the same.

j) Be aware of the *limitations* and *deficiencies of remediation programs* operating in the community and help the family to minimize deficiencies as much as possible.

k) Whenever possible, encourage the family to join and be active in *parent groups* that share mutual concerns.

Several recently developed resources for nurses involved in assessing child growth and development merit attention here. One, the Nursing Child Assessment Satellite Training Project (NCAT), developed by Kathryn Barnard, Ph.D. of the School of Nursing at the University of Washington, is designed to teach nurses about "newly developed child health assessment strategies." NCAT includes the following scales: the teaching scale, birth to 3 years; and the feeding scale, birth to 1. In addition, it focuses on the child's home environment to determine how it stimulates and supports child development, using the *Home Observation for Measurement of the Environment* adapted for the NCAT series by Caldwell and Bradley (1976). Another excellent resource is: *Screening Growth and Development of Preschool Children: A Guide for Test Selection* (Stangler, Huber, and Routh, 1980), which examines screening measures for development, hearing, growth, speech, language, and vision.

SCHOOL-AGE CHILDREN

Increasing numbers of school-age children are being identified as having school problems including reading, spelling, writing, or arithmetic difficulties; attention problems; impulse control disturbances; and emotional lability. Such youngsters demand more time, attention, and educational resources than their chronological age classroom peers. In addition, the move to integrate all children with handicapping conditions into the public school system (in compliance with PL 94-142) poses challenges for teachers, school psychologists, and school nurses. For these reasons, it is important to screen *school-age* children for vision, hearing, speech and language, perception, adaptive, and self-help skills. The sooner these areas are identified and if necessary treated, the greater the chances that the child will experience school success rather than failure. The intervention program and the individual child's progress can be monitored on an ongoing basis by use of assessment tools.

CONCLUSION

In conclusion, detection of developmental problems in preschool and school-age children continues to be a vital area of activity for nurses. The use of both new and old screening tools contributes to early identification of problems, to intervention, and to the promotion of health and wellness.

REFERENCES

Barnard, K. E. et al. 1978. Nursing Child Assessment Satellite Training Series. University of Washington, Seattle.

Caldwell, B. M., and Bradley, R. H. 1976. Home Observation for Measurement of the Environment; Birth to Three and Three to Six. Little Rock, Ark.

Erickson, M.P. 1978. Developmental screening. In: J. B. Curry and K. K. Peppe (eds.), Nursing Approaches to Care, pp. 159–181. C. V. Mosby Co., St. Louis.

Fandal, A., Kemper, M. B. and Frankenburg, W. K. 1979. Needed: Routine developmental screening for all children. In: Pediatric Basics, No. 24. Medical Marketing Services Department, Gerber Products Co., Fremont, Mich.

Frankenburg, W. K. 1973. Pediatric screening. In: I. Schulman (ed.), Advances in Pediatrics, Vol. 20, p. 150. Yearbook Medical Publishers, Inc., Chicago.

Frankenburg, W. K., Dodds, J. B. and Fandal, A. W. 1973. Denver Developmental Screening Test Manual/Workbook for Nursing and Paramedical Personnel. University of Colorado Medical Center, Denver.

Kemper, M. B., and Frankenburg, W. K. 1979. Screening, diagnosis, and assessment. In: T. Black (ed.), Perspectives on Measurement: A Collection of Readings for Educators of Young Handicapped Children, No. 1. Technical Assistance Development System (TADS), division of the Frank Porter Graham Child Development Center, University of North Carolina at Chapel Hill.

Roberts, P. 1977. Nursing assessments. Screening for developmental problems. D. Use of screening tools. In: M. J. Krajicek and A. I. Tearney (eds.), Detection of Developmental Problems in Children. A Reference Guide for Community Nurses and Other Health Care Professionals, 1st Ed., pp. 31–46. University Park Press, Baltimore.

Stangler, S. R., Huber, C. J., and Routh, D. K. 1980. Screening Growth and Development of Preschool Children: A Guide for Test Selection. McGraw-Hill Book Co., New York.

Wilson, J. M. G., and Lungner, C. 1968. Principles and practice of screening for disease. World Health Organization Public Health Pap. 34:1.

SUGGESTED READINGS

Cross, L., and Goin, K. W. (eds.). 1977. Identifying Handicapped Children: A Guide to Casefinding, Screening, Diagnosis, Assessment, and Evaluation. Walker and Co., New York.

Erickson, M. L. 1976. Assessment and Management of Developmental Changes in Children. C. V. Mosby Co., St. Louis.

Frankenburg, W. K., and Camp, W. K. 1975. Pediatric Screening Tests. Charles C Thomas, Springfield, Ill.

Frankenburg, W. K., Camp, B. W., DeMersseman, J. A., and Voorhees, S. F. 1971. The reliability and stability of the Denver Developmental Screening Test. Child Dev. 42:1315–1325.

Frankenburg, W. K., Camp, B. W., and Vannatta, P. A. 1971. Validity of the Denver Developmental Screening Test. Child Dev. 42:475.

Frankenburg, W. K., and Cohrs, M. E. 1973. Acceptance of home screening: How to reach the unreached. Clin. Res. 21(2):299.

Frankenburg, W. K., and Dick, N. P. 1973. Development of preschool aged children: Racial-ethnic and social class comparison. Clin. Res. 21(2):318.

Frankenburg, W. K., and Goldstein, A. D. 1971. Procedure for Selecting Screening Technicians. University of Colorado Press, Denver.

Johnston, R., and Magrab, P. (eds.). 1976. Developmental Disabilities: Evaluation, Treatment, and Education. University Park Press, Baltimore.

I. Nursing Assessments
Screening for Developmental Problems

C. Physical Examination of the Child

Elna Cain, R. N., M. S.

COMMUNITY NURSES AND PRACTITIONERS with skills in assessment and intervention who provide wellchild care in clinics, homes, and other community settings are often the first to identify health risks, health problems, developmental delays, and potential handicaps in young children. Infants and toddlers need frequent assessments not only because they are growing rapidly but because numerous congenital defects may not be identifiable immediately after birth. Parents of infants and toddlers need much support and education to help them prevent health problems and minimize problems when they first appear.

A number of abnormalities found in older children are developmental—occurring as a result of growth. Other problems result from poor health practices. As a child grows, the nurse can use a physical examination as an opportunity to teach the child and his or her parents about preventive health care. This chapter contains an outline for such an examination.

All nurses have at some time done physical examinations of patients. It has long been common practice for nurses to examine affected body parts. Now emphasis has shifted so that nurses often do systematic, complete examinations.

The way to learn to do a physical examination is to practice. All nurses have a store of information and experience to draw upon. The techniques and tools of performing a physical examination involve many of the skills with which nurses are familiar, even though nurses may not always have had the opportunity to practice them regularly.

TECHNIQUES

The techniques of physical examination are: *inspection*—looking at, observing; *palpation*—feeling lightly or firmly, probing, and pressing; *percussion*—tapping, striking directly or indirectly (indirectly includes striking finger held on body with percussion hammer or finger of other hand); *auscultation*—listening, usually with a stethoscope.

TOOLS

The nurse's most basic and important tools for a physical examination are the hands, eyes, ears, and other senses. These tools are all that is necessary for gathering a breadth of valuable information. A number of other tools are useful to add when resources are available and as the nurse's skills are refined. These items and the equipment desirable are listed at the end of each part of the physical examination outline in this chapter.

USE OF THE PHYSICAL EXAMINATION OUTLINE

The outline below is designed for the beginning examiner (or as a refresher for the experienced one). It includes listings of normal findings in children;

findings within the range of normal (which can be a wide and sometimes confusing range); and some "not present" specifics; that is, things to check as not present that are aimed at ensuring absence of deformity, syndromes, and relatively obscure disease conditions. Although the body areas are listed in the order in which they are most often recorded, examination does not have to proceed in the exact order of the outline. Thoroughness, thoughtfulness, and a systematic examination are the most important considerations. Confidence, based on sophistication in decision making, depth of knowledge, and evolution of skills, increases with study, practice, and periodic verification of the nurse's findings.

If some of the examining tools are not available, if some techniques seem too complicated, or aspects to check too numerous, items can be completed when the time is right. Simply looking at (inspecting) and feeling (palpating) an entire child yields a wealth of useful and valid data to combine with historical data for decision making (see Figure 1).

APPROACHES AND SUGGESTED EXAMINATION SEQUENCES

To gain maximum cooperation from an infant or child, it is best to start by establishing a pleasant relationship with the parent, then seek to establish a relationship with the child by talking, using a toy, or doing a screening procedure such as the Denver Developmental Screening Test. Save upsetting procedures for last. Before beginning the examination, wash your hands in warm water. Establish a routine for infants and for older children that is followed consistently. Include all body areas in the routine. Allow for some flexibility to fit the responses of each child.

It is usually easiest to examine an infant of up to about 6 to 9 months of age on a padded table. Older infants and children of up to 3 or 3 ½ years of age are usually best examined while sitting on the parent's lap. Older children can sit alone on a chair or table. All need to lie down for examinations of the abdomen and genitalia (and infants must be supine to check for congenital dislocated hip).

The following are suggested routines or sequences of examination for infants and older children. (The child must be undressed, but it is not necessary to do it all at once. Have the parent or child do the undressing.)

Infants

Examine top-to-bottom front, then top-to-bottom back. Have undressed except for diaper. Place baby face up on table → head (except eyes, nose, mouth, throat, ears) → face → head and neck nodes → neck → clavicles → arms (including axillary nodes) → hands → chest (including listening to heart and anterior lungs) → abdomen → legs → feet. → Remove diaper. Inguinal area → genitalia → anus. For dislocated hip → leave diaper on table. Turn baby on his or her stomach, matching diaper area to diaper. →

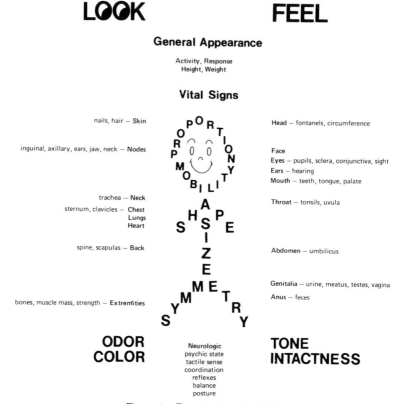

Figure 1.   Examination of a child.

back of head → neck → spine → back of chest (including listening) → *buttocks → back of legs.* → Turn face up. Replace diaper. → *neurological tests* (not already included) → *eyes → nose → mouth → throat → ears.*

Toddlers, Preschoolers, School-Age Children

Examine top, front, and back, then bottom, front, and back. Have undressed from waist up. → *head → face* (except eyes, nose, mouth, throat, ears) → *head* and *neck nodes → neck → clavicles → arms → hands → chest* (including listening front and back). → Replace shirt, blouse, or dress. Have clothes from waist down removed except underpants. → *legs → feet.* → Have child lie down on table. → *abdomen.* Pull underpants down. → *genitalia → anus.* Replace underpants. → Have child walk for observation of gait, touch toes, and do standing *neurological tests → eyes → nose → mouth → throat → ears.* A drape or sheet may be substituted for the child's own clothing.

PHYSICAL EXAMINATION OUTLINE

I.   Measurements
    A.   Temperature
    B.   Pulse
    C.   Respirations
    D.   Blood pressure
    E.   Height or length
    F.   Weight
    G.   Head circumference
Record height, weight, and head circumference percentile for age on graph or standardized forms.
Instrumentation: thermometer, blood pressure apparatus with child-size cuffs, scales, tape measure, measuring board.

II.   General Appearance
    A.   Alert
    B.   Active
    C.   Well nourished
    D.   Healthy appearing
    E.   Strong voice quality (or cry)
    F.   No striking physical features
    G.   Warm, close mother-child relationship
    H.   Readily responsive to examiner
Describe activity and appearance of child as observed during contact and examination.
Technique: *inspection.*

III. Skin
    A.   Warm
    B.   Color consistent with racial background
    C.   No cyanosis or jaundice
    D.   Hematocrit (or hemoglobin) within normal limits
        (Anemia cannot be determined by skin color.)
    E.   Good turgor (Skin is elastic and returns readily to normal position after pinching.)
    F.   No lesions, bruises, abrasions, or rashes
    G.   No birthmarks
Skin is examined on each part of the body as other examinations are made of that part. Hair and nails are part of the skin.
Techniques: *inspection, palpation,* including use of hematocrit centrifuge, or hemoglobinometer.

IV.   Lymph Nodes
Nonred, nontender, and cool nodes to 3 mm diameter may be normal; to 1 cm in cervical and inguinal areas, usually normal. (Specific sites to check are included throughout outline.)
Techniques: *inspection, palpation.*

V.   Head
    A.   Symmetrical (May be asymmetrical in early weeks of life.)
    B.   Fontanels closed (Posterior closed by 2 months, anterior by 18 months. If open, fontanels should not be bulging or sunken when infant is sitting.)
    C.   No suture ridges felt (Ridges may be felt to 6 months.)
    D.   Hair evenly distributed without bald or worn spots or unusually low forehead or neck hairline
    E.   Hair: color, texture, sheen
    F.   Scalp clear of lesions, scaling, or foreign bodies
    G.   Occipital lymph nodes not enlarged

Techniques: *inspection, palpation* primarily. May add *percussion* and *auscultation.*

VI.   Face
    A.   Generally
        1.   Well proportioned
        2.   Symmetrical at rest and in movement
        3.   Features similar to those of parents

Technique: *inspection.*

    B.   Eyes
        1.   Color of irises
        2.   Pupils equal in size, round in shape
        3.   Pupils constrict and dilate in response to light (bright and dim)
        4.   Pupils clear
        5.   Light reflection falls on same area of both pupils
        6.   Eyes move together (Muscle imbalance may be normal for 6 months, but follow closely. Refer if imbalance persists, as early care is critical.)
        7.   Eye covered when other eye fixed on object does not move when cover removed (cover test)
        8.   Follows object side-to-side, up and down, and obliquely (By 4 months most babies can follow 180° side-to-side.)
        9.   Eyes converge when object brought close to nose
      10.   Red reflex observed (Light shown through pupil at close range reflects red glow similar to the yellow reflection from a cat's eyes.)
      11.   Eyes not sunken
      12.   No circles under eyes
      13.   Sclerae and conjunctivae clear
      14.   Lids level
      15.   No epicanthic folds (Inner lid folds normal in children of Mongolian race.)

16. Eyes not unusually widely or closely set
17. Vision 20/(20, 30, 70, etc.)

Technique: *inspection* including use of light and vision screening equipment. Use of ophthalmoscope may be learned from references and/or a person with skill in its use.

C. Ears
    1. External ears well shaped and symmetrical
    2. Symmetrically placed and set so that part of each ear falls above an imaginary line drawn from outer corner of eye to occiput
    3. Ear canals open
    4. Tympanic membranes pearly gray with light reflex, umbo, long process, and short process of malleus visible
    5. Hearing screening passed (Audiometer screening for older children; bell, whisper, or other screening techniques, together with history and language development, may be used for younger children.)
    6. Lymph nodes behind ears not enlarged

Techniques: *inspection,* including use of otoscope and hearing screening equipment: *palpation.*

D. Nose
    1. Patent bilaterally
    2. No nasal drainage or crusting
    3. Septum midline
    4. Mucosa pink and firm
    5. Bridge of nose not unusually flat or broad
    6. No pain or tenderness on pressure over sinuses

Techniques: *inspection*, including use of light; *palpation.*

E. Mouth
    1. Mucous membrane, tongue, and gums pink, moist, and without lesions or redness
    2. Tongue proportionate to mouth, symmetrical at rest and in movement, extends to gum margins
    3. Palate intact and not unusually high or narrow
    4. Teeth (number of) have no dental caries and are clean (Estimate of average number of teeth is obtained by subtracting 6 from age in months up to 20 primary teeth. Refer if no teeth by 12 months of age.)
    5. No malocclusion, overlapping, or unusual spacing of teeth noted
    6. No drooling noted (after 2 years)
    7. Lymph nodes under jaw not enlarged

Techniques: *inspection*, including use of light; *palpation.* For dental assessment, see Chapter 9.

    F.   Throat
        1.   Pink and moist with no redness, pus, or drainage noted
        2.   Tonsils not obstructing airway, not touching in midline, no pus or crypts
        3.   Uvula midline and single
        4.   No consistent mouth breathing
        5.   Gag reflex present

Technique: *inspection*, using light and tongue blade.

VII.   Neck
    A.   Mobile, symmetrical
    B.   No pain evident when neck flexed chin to chest
    C.   Not webbed or unusually short (Babies have short necks.)
    D.   Trachea midline
    E.   Thyroid not palpable
    F.   Sternocleidomastoid muscles symmetrical with no swelling or masses
    G.   Anterior and posterior neck lymph nodes not enlarged

Techniques: *inspection, palpation.*

VIII.   Chest
    A.   Generally
        1.   Symmetrical and not unusually shaped at rest and with movement
        2.   Clavicles at same level and smooth
        3.   Sternum not sunken or protruding
        4.   No beading on ribs
        5.   Breasts flat with nipples symmetrical (There should be no breast engorgement or development from 1 month of age to puberty.)
        6.   Axillary lymph nodes not enlarged

Techniques: *inspection, palpation.*

    B.   Lungs
        1.   Respirations regular at rate of (number) per minute (Some irregularity is normal.)
        2.   Chest expands equally with breathing
        3.   Breath sounds clear and equal on both sides anteriorly and posteriorly
        4.   No rales (fine crackles on inspiration), friction rub (coarse or grating sound), or wheezes (musical sounds on inspiration or expiration) heard

Techniques: *inspection, palpation, auscultation,* including use of stethoscope.

    C.   Heart
        1.   Pulse rate (number) per minute, regular and full

2. Heart sounds clear with regular rhythm; rate slightly faster on inspiration than expiration (There are two parts of the normal heart sound, commonly called lubb-dubb or S_1 S_2. Either may normally be heard as a "split" sound in children, especially "dubb" or S_2. Extra sounds, blowing or whispering sounds, or unusual rhythm indicate need for referral, although in many cases the unusual sounds may be normal and not indicate heart pathology.)

Techniques: *inspection, palpation, auscultation,* including use of stethoscope.

Items covered are adequate for beginning examination of the chest. Increased skill and additional points to check can be gained by study of references and/or the assistance of a preceptor. Percussion, a useful method in chest examination, may be added in the same manner.

IX. Abdomen
A. Symmetrical, protruding (Children's abdomens may normally protrude until puberty.)
B. Firm muscle tone
C. Umbilicus not protruding, no umbilical hernia
D. Bowel sounds present every 20 seconds (Heard as metallic short tinkling, they are normally heard every 10 to 30 seconds. Should listen to bowel sounds before deep palpation.)
E. Abdomen nontender on light or deep palpation or when pressure quickly withdrawn
F. Liver palpable 1 cm below costal margin (Not always palpable. Best felt on inspiration. May be normally palpable up to 2 cm below right lower rib throughout childhood.)
G. Spleen not palpable (Rarely palpable up to 2 cm below left lower rib. Should be soft and nontender.)
H. No masses felt on superficial or deep palpation
I. Inguinal lymph nodes not enlarged
J. Femoral pulses felt equally bilaterally

Techniques: *inspection, palpation, auscultation,* including use of stethoscope.

As with the chest, increased skill and additional points to check may be gained by study and/or use of a preceptor. Percussion may be added in the same manner.

X. Genitalia
A. Urinary stream strong and wide
B. Urine clear yellow
C. Urine negative on dip stick screening

D.   Male
   1.   Testes in scrotum. (Examine gently, placing pressure in inguinal area on side being palpated with other hand. Left testicle is normally lower than right. Testes are not consistently found in scrotum but presence of both at some time should be determined.)
   2.   Meatus at tip of penis and not inflamed
   3.   No inguinal hernia or hydrocele noted
   4.   No loose or constricting foreskin (if circumcised)
   5.   Foreskin not contricting (if not circumcised)(Foreskin usually becomes easily retractable by 4 years. Do not forceably retract foreskin.)
E.   Female
   1.   Meatus and vaginal opening visible
   2.   No discharge from vagina (until near puberty)
   3.   Clitoris small
   4.   Labia symmetrical, not adherent or enlarged
Techniques: *inspection, palpation,* with use of urine dipstick. Note pre-teen and teen signs of adolescent sexual maturation—i.e., growth of genitals, hair density and distribution, breast development.

XI.   Anus
A.   No irritation, fissures, or tags
B.   Stool soft and formed (if observed)
Techniques: *inspection, palpation*; rectal examination may be added with the assistance of a preceptor or study of references.

XII.   Extremities
A.   Mobile with full range of joint movements possible actively and passively
B.   Of equal length, strength, muscle mass, mobility, and temperature
C.   Muscle tone firm
D.   Long bones straight
E.   Feet mobile (Feet turning in, out, down, or up usually within normal limits until child has been walking 1 to 2 years if they can be passively overcorrected.)
F.   Legs straight. (Bowed legs usually normal to 2½ years, flat feet to 3½ years, knock-knees from 2 to 3½ years. There is much normal variation.)
G.   Walks easily and fluidly with good balance (Broad-based gait normal to 3 years.)
H.   Inguinal, gluteal, and thigh folds symmetrical (Asymmetry may be normal, but it is an alert to examine infants and toddlers carefully for signs of dislocated hip.)

I. Legs abduct equally when knees and hips are flexed in frog position. No click felt or heard (See Figure 2. Refer if there is any question of dislocated hip.)

J. No instability noted in hips

K. All digits present and proportionate, not clubbed

L. Hands symmetrical with no simian line (Single line extending across palm.)

M. Nails intact, firm, and flexible

Techniques: *inspection, palpation.*

XIII. Back

   A. Spine straight and mobile

   B. Vertebral processes palpable

   C. No indentations or tufts of hair noted over spine (Pilonidal dimple near the sacrum is common but should be checked carefully to see that there is no opening or sinus and that skin is not irritated.)

   D. Back symmetrical

   E. Scapulas at an equal level when standing (or lying in infant) and when child bends over to touch toes (in older child)

   F. Iliac crests at an equal level

   G. No tenderness noted on pressure or percussion over kidneys

Techniques: *inspection, palpation, percussion.*

XIV. Neurological

   A. Infants

      1. Developmental landmarks reached for age (As measured or observed on screening test such as Denver Developmental Screening Test or a developmental scale.)

      2. Behavior, activity, and degree of alertness appear appropriate for age

      3. Posture, balance, and coordination appropriate for age

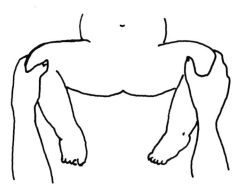

Figure 2.   Abduction of legs.

4. Cry lusty
5. Infant responsive to cuddling
6. Deep tendon reflexes present and symmetrical (The most commonly tested are the patellar, by striking just below knee; Achilles, by striking just above heel with foot pushed up; biceps, by striking thumb against lower point of insertion while child's arm is flexed; and triceps, by striking just above bent elbow. In each case expected response is contraction of muscle that has tendon stimulated. Strike briskly with side of hand, tip of finger, or percussion hammer.)
7. Babinski reflex positive (Up to 18 months the abnormal or positive response of toe fanning and great toe moving up is observed when foot is stroked from lateral part of heel up lateral part of foot and across below toes.)
8. Hand grasp equal (Reflex grasp strongest between 1 and 2 months.)
9. Tonic neck reflex noted (Leg and arm extend on side to which head is turned, flex on opposite side. Reflex lasts up to 5 months.)
10. Moro reflex present (Startle response with extension then flexion of extremities, with arms grasping as around an object. Lasts up to 5 months.)
11. Landau reflex present (Back straight or arched diver fashion when baby suspended over table prone, one of examiner's hands supporting abdomen, other on back. Lasts from 3 to 18 months.)

B. Older child
1. Developmental landmarks reached for age (As measured or observed by comparing with developmental screening test or scale, plus historical information regarding learning achievements.)
2. Behavior, activity, and degree of alertness and cooperation appear appropriate for age
3. Balance steady with eyes open and closed (Tested by such activities as standing, walking, standing with both feet together, on one foot with eyes open and closed, and walking heel-to-toe forward and backward with eyes open.)
4. Fine and gross motor coordination appropriate for age (Tested by such activities as manipulation of toys, drawing, alternatively striking palms of examiner with one hand at a time, touching examiner's finger held before

face then own own nose alternately, touching own nose with eyes closed, hopping, skipping, jumping rope.)

5. Demonstrates ability to spell, do math problems, reason and do abstract thinking (Tested by such activities as asking child to verbally spell two or three words and do some simple math problems mentally, asking to explain a nursery rhyme, familiar story, or proverb.)
6. Demonstrates appropriate short- and long-term memory for age (Tested by such things as asking to repeat a series of numbers; remember a word or phrase during exam; recite alphabet, rhyme, pledge to flag; give address, birthdate, etc.)
7. Deep tendon reflexes present and symmetrical
8. Babinski reflex negative
9. Senses of touch, taste, smell intact

Responses to neurological tests, ability to perform various activities, and quality of responses depend on child's age and individual rate of development. Although there is a wide range of normal responses, referral to references and developmental norms plus the nurse's experience lead to increasing ability to distinguish normal from abnormal responses. Many indicators of neurological function are included in the examination of individual body parts. The examiner should incorporate into the examination routine neurological tests representative of the various areas of neurological function, such as balance, fine and gross motor ability, coordination, reflexes, and memory.

Techniques: *inspection* including toys, *percussion* including percussion hammer.

The following are some suggestions for making maximum use of the outline and other references.

1. Write highlights of the outline on an index card to refer to during practice.
2. Practice examining as many children as possible. Include children of various ages as well as two or more children of the same age.
3. Compare historical data with physical findings.
4. Pursue any unusual finding by seeking additional history on the child and focusing more attention on examination of possibly related areas.
5. At first, write down all findings in the manner in which they appear in the outline. Although this is time-consuming, it leads to rapid learning of many points to check in relation to all body parts.

6.   Think about each normal finding in relation to corresponding possible abnormalities. Use references as necessary.
7.   Periodically study references, looking for more things to check, relationships between physical findings, and answers to questions that come to mind during practice.

CONCLUSION

A nurse's role is to distinguish normal from abnormal, then to decide whether intervention is indicated. If intervention is indicated, the nurse determines what type and the degree of urgency. Judgments become easier and more reliable as skills in examination are more fully developed. Confidence is an important and rewarding outcome for the nurse who learns to do a systematic physical examination.

SUGGESTED READINGS

Alexander, M., and Brown, M. S. 1979. Pediatric History Taking and Physical Diagnosis for Nurses. 2nd Ed. McGraw-Hill Book Co., New York.

Barness, A. 1981. Manual of Pediatric Physical Diagnosis. 5th Ed. Yearbook Medical Publishers, Chicago.

Chinn, L., and Leitch, C. J. 1979. Child Health Maintenance—A Guide to Clinical Assessment, 2nd Ed. C. V. Mosby Co., St. Louis.

Committee on Standards of Child Health Care. 1977. Standards of Child Health Care, 3rd Ed. American Academy of Pediatrics, Evanston, Ill.

Silver, H. K., Kempe, C. H., and Bruyn, H. B. 1980. Handbook of Pediatrics, 13th Ed. Lange Medical Publishers, Los Altos, Calif.

I. Nursing Assessments
Screening for Developmental Problems

D.   Nursing Care of Children with
     Chronic Conditions:
     A Teaching Approach

Rita Lillo, R. N., M. S.

THE GOAL OF THE TEACHING APPROACH presented in this chapter is to help develop independent, self-motivated children and families who can successfully manage a chronic developmental problem. An easily understood theory that can be adapted by nurses to effectively meet the teaching and management demands of families has been developed by Hersey and Blanchard (1977). Called "Situational Leadership Theory," the approach is based on a relationship between the amount of direction (task behavior) and the amount of socio-emotional support (relationship behavior) provided individuals in need.

According to Situational Leadership Theory, as defined by Guest, Hersey, and Blanchard (1977), *task behavior* involves one-way communication; the nurse tells the child or family what task to do, when to do it, and how to do it. *Relationship behavior,* on the other hand, involves two-way communication; the nurse listens to the child and family, provides socio-emotional support in the form of encouragement, positive psychological "strokes," and helping behaviors. Maturity, a major goal of Situational Leadership Theory, is defined by McClelland (1953) as "the capacity to set high but attainable goals (achievement-motivation), and the willingness, as well as ability to take responsibility." In encouraging an individual or family to take mature action, the family's previous education and experience must always be considered. Furthermore, the family's level of maturity should be considered only in relation to a specific task or area in which the nurse wants to influence the child and/or family's behavior. That is to say, children or families cannot be labeled wholly mature or immature, but exhibit differing degrees of maturity in different aspects of their lives. A case illustration follows:

CASE ILLUSTRATION

The referral stated that Bobby, a 6-month-old child with phenylketonuria (PKU), had blood levels indicating poor phenylalanine control for the past month. A review of medical references revealed the following information. Children with PKU have an inborn error of metabolism and are unable to properly metabolize the amino acid, phenylalanine. Abnormal accumulation of phenylalanine apparently prevents normal brain development, with the possible result being mental retardation. Control of PKU, therefore, is entirely dependent upon reducing the dietary intake of phenylalanine. Since this amino acid is present in most foods, a special formula that is virtually phenylalanine free, Lofenalac, was developed by Mead Johnson Laboratories (1958).

In addition to prescribed amounts of the formula, the child with PKU is allowed limited amounts of fruit, vegetables, and cereals that supply the prescribed amounts of phenylalanine necessary for normal growth and development. The intervention goal with Bobby and his family was to control the PKU through diet.

Levels of Maturity

In the process of applying Situational Leadership Theory, the nurse may need to evaluate the maturity level of both the parents and the child, particularly when assessing parent-child interaction.

Bobby's mother, for instance, was able to breast-feed Bobby in the first 3 weeks after birth but was reluctant to encourage the baby to take all the prescribed Lofenalac formula. The first situation of breast-feeding is mature behavior; the second situation, inability to adapt to formula giving, is immature action.

According to Situational Leadership Theory, there are four different maturity levels that the child and/or family may display in terms of accomplishing a specific task. Each level requires use of a different teaching style; thus, a nurse may use several varying teaching approaches with a family, depending on the family's level of maturity in particular situations. The nurse must first assess the child's or family's ability, knowledge, and experience to do a task, and then their willingness or motivation. The following explanations describe the four levels of maturity as related to *ability* and *willingness*:

1. *Low Level Maturity:* The child and/or family do not have the ability to do a specific task and lack the motivation or willingness for involvement. ("Bobby is breast-feeding and looks so healthy. I don't see why he needs a special formula.")
2. *Low to Moderate Level Maturity:* The child and/or family are willing and motivated to be responsible for a particular task, but do not have the ability to do the task. ("I will give Bobby his formula, Lofenalac, but I don't understand how to make it and how to include it as part of his feeding schedule.")
3. *Moderate to High Level Maturity:* The child and/or family have the ability to do the task, but are not motivated to take or continue to be responsible for doing the task on their own. ("Sure, I know Bobby needs to take all of his prescribed formula, but it takes so long for him to take it all. I feel I am forcing him to eat. I don't force my children to eat; besides, I have other things to do for the other members of my family.")
4. *High Maturity Level:* The child and/or family have the willingness and motivation to be responsible to do the task, as well as the ability and knowledge to do it. ("I really felt confident this last month. Bobby took all his prescribed formula and I was able to choose how much and what other fruit, vegetables, and cereals he could have with each

meal. His phenylalanine blood levels and growth measurements indicate he is in good control.")

Clearly, the nurse's goal is to assist individuals in moving toward the highest level of maturity. To accomplish this, the teaching style must be appropriate to the maturity level. The teaching styles that correspond to the four maturity levels, from lowest to highest, include *telling*, to *selling*, to *participating*, and, last, *delegating*.

With low level maturity, the teaching style is in the form of a one-way communication—*telling*—with minimal emphasis on supportive behaviors. The child and family are given information and directions regarding what, how, when, and where to do the task. In Bobby's instance, the mother needs to be told the rationale for restricting phenylalanine, a description of a low phenylalanine diet, diet perscriptions, daily menu plans, replacing of phenylalanine deficits, and how to record the dietary intake. In summary, at this maturity level, the nurse directs and supervises the mother in what to do, and how, when, and where to do the feeding rather than providing support and encouragement.

When the family level of maturity moves from low to moderate maturity, the teaching style that is most helpful is geared to giving directions (e. g., how, when, or where to do the task). In addition, socio-emotional support is necessary, as the child and family are willing to do the task but still lack the ability. This two-way communication is called *selling*. As Bobby's mother begins to take the responsibility to make and give Lofenalac formula and to choose appropriate foods, she will have questions about feeding and formula making and will need help, directions, and feedback, as well as support.

As the level of maturity progresses from moderate to high, the most effective teaching style includes the child and family in the decision-making process in order to decrease resistance in taking responsibility for doing the task. This teaching style includes two-way communication and active listening and is called *participating*. At this maturity level, Bobby's mother is able to make the formula and knows when, where, why, and how to feed him in order to regulate his phenylalanine levels. These tasks can begin to interfere with other family activities; therefore, Bobby's mother will not always be motivated to spend 45 minutes at mealtime encouraging Bobby to eat the right amount of food and formula. The teaching style needed, therefore, is two-way communication, with listening and nondirective counseling. As problems are defined, discussed, and solved, the mother's self-confidence needs to be increased so that she will be motivated to use her knowledge and ability.

The highest level of maturity is best handled by a teaching style that neither gives directions on the how, when, or where of a task, nor finds it necessary to motivate the child and/or family to do the task. The nurse has confidence in the child and/or family to do their own task. This style is called *delegating*. In Bobby's case, when the feeding task is accomplished and his phenylalanine levels are adequate, the appropriate teaching style is to inform Bobby's mother that his blood levels will continue to be monitored every 2 weeks, and if his control is inadequate the family will be notified.

Use of an inappropriate teaching style, or of only one style in all situations, can prevent clients from maturing. If, for example, the nurse uses a telling style for all circumstances, the client may either seek education from another service or become passive and dependent, needing someone to tell him or her what to do and when to do it. Similarly, if the nurse relies exclusively on a selling style, providing extensive direction and support, the client may become psychologically dependent and unable to function on his or her own. Finally, the continuous use of a participating teaching style, by providing too much support, limited education, and minimal structure, may result in a client who has insufficient knowledge of rules or of the various aspects of doing a task. The client is then confused about appropriate action or structure, and performs the task inappropriately.

Effective teaching incorporates flexible, varied styles that meet the demands of a specific client situation. Situational Leadership is a teaching framework to help the nurse understand and share expectations with clients and families. If clients and families know what is expected, they can gradually learn to supervise their own behavior and become responsible, self-motivated individuals.

REFERENCES

Guest, R. H., Hersey, P., and Blanchard, K. H. 1977. Organizational Change Through Effective Leadership. Prentice Hall, Englewood Cliffs, N. J.

Hersey, P., and Blanchard, K. H. 1977. Management of Organizational Behavior. 3rd Ed. Prentice Hall, Englewood Cliffs, N. J.

McClelland, D. et al. 1953. The Achievement Motivation. Appleton-Century-Crofts, New York.

Mead Johnson Laboratories. 1958. Phenylketonuria. Mead Johnson Laboratories, Evansville, Ind.

I. Nursing Assessments
Screening for Developmental Problems

E. Screening for Speech and Language Problems

Kathleen Bryant, M. A.

THE DEVELOPMENT OF SPEECH AND LANGUAGE is part of the normal growth of a child. The growth of communication, like physical growth, proceeds in an orderly manner that may vary in rate but that follows a predetermined pattern. Like all growth, if the development pattern is interrupted, problems in communication may result.

The two essential facets of communication are reception and expression. Reception, the ability to receive messages, depends on an intact auditory system. The ability to code and store the messages for use in a developing language system is thought to be genetic. Expression, the motor act of speech, depends on an intact motor system.

Screening techniques for speech and language problems have been tried and tested for children 5 years and under. Techniques that the school nurse or practitioner can use are informal screening for articulation, language development, voice quality, and fluency of speech, based on knowledge of normal development (see Tables 1 and 2). For the child over 5 years of age, a teacher's and/or parent's complaint about a child's school performance, in these areas is most often relied upon as a form of screening. Such complaints should be followed by referral to an expert so that diagnosis can be initiated.

Following a diagnostic evaluation, the speech/language pathologist can assist the nurse/health care practitioner, parents and teachers to understand the basis for the disorder and can encourage follow-through with therapy. Early intervention maximizes the child's fullest potential for speech, language, and learning.

SUGGESTED READINGS

Bangs, T., and Garet, S. Early childhood education for the handicapped child, birth–3 scale. U. S. Office of Education Grant Project No. OF6-0-9-530-312-456 (618), U. S. Government Printing Office, Washington, D. C.

Bayley, N. 1969. Bayley Scales of Infant Development. The Psychological Corporation, New York.

Bzoch, K. R., and League, R. (eds.).-1971. Receptive-Expressive Emergent Language Scale (REEL). University Park Press, Baltimore.

Chomsky, N. 1972. Language and Mind. Harcourt Brace Jovanovich, New York.

Church, J. 1961. Language and the Discovery of Reality. Random House, New York.

Gesell, A. 1940. The First Five Years of Life. Harper & Row, New York.

Lenneberg, E. H. 1967. Biological Foundations of Language. John Wiley & Sons, New York.

Lewis, M. M. 1959. How Children Learn to Speak. Basic Books, New York.

Menyuk, P. 1971. The Acquisition and Development of Language. Prentice-Hall, Englewood Cliffs, N. J.

Pushau, D. R. 1976. Teach Your Child to Talk. Rev. Ed. Cebco Standard Publishing Co., Fairfield, N. J.

Reilly, A. P. (ed.). The Communication Game. Johnson & Johnson Baby Products Co., Hicksville, N.Y.

Templin, M. C. 1957. Certain Language Skills in Children. The University of Minnesota Press, Minneapolis.

Van Hattum, R. (ed.). 1981. Screening in School Programs—Part I. Seminars Speech Language Hearing, Vol. 2, No. 1. Thieme-Stratton, New York.

Van Hattum, R. (ed.). 1981. Screening in School Programs—Part II. Seminars Speech Language Hearing, Vol. 2, No. 2. Thieme-Stratton, New York.

Zimmerman, I. L. 1979. Preschool Language Scale. Rev. Ed. Charles E. Merrill Publishing Co., Columbus, Ohio.

Table 1.   Speech and language milestones to observe when a child is evaluated

Age	Receptive language	Expressive language
Birth to 3 mos.	1. Is quieted by voice. 2. Reacts to sudden noises. The response may be eye blink, beginning of head turn. 3. Responds to social gestures by smiling.	1. Strong cry. 2. Vocalization of discomfort or comfort sounds. 3. Pre-babbling; the sounds are reflexive.
3 to 6 mos.	1. Recognizes words such as "no, bye-bye, daddy." 2. Turns without other stimulation, when a voice is heard. 3. Locates the source of sounds. 4. Responds appropriately to friendly and/or angry tones. 5. Responds to own name.	1. Initiates vocal play. 2. Laughs aloud. 3. Babbles, using a series of syllables on one breath. 4. Spontaneous smile in response to verbal play. 5. Vocalizes to self in mirror and to toys. 6. Expresses displeasure. 7. Experiments with own voice.
6 to 9 mos.	1. Stops activity when hears "no-no." 2. Responds by raising arms in response to "come up." 3. Shows recognition of family name. 4. Will sustain interest in pictures when a person names them.	1. Develops the sounds of his or her mother tongue. 2. Combines several vowel sounds. 3. Responds to conversation by vocalizing. 4. Uses nonspecific "mama" and "dada" during babbling. 5. Initiates sounds such as a cough, tongue click, or kiss. 6. Develops rhythm.
9 to 12 mos.	1. Obeys simple instructions. 2. Understands gestures. 3. Shows general understanding of the meaning of simple statements questions.	1. By first birthday, has one true word. 2. Says "Mama" or "Dada" specifically. 3. Uses gestures with vocalization.

Table 1. *Continued*

Age	Receptive language	Expressive language
	4. Waves "bye-bye" in response to verbal request. 5. Shows interest in speech over a long period of time.	4. Spontaneously tries to imitate adult sounds. 5. Plays "peek-a-boo."
12 to 15 mos.	1. Plays game of "fetching" for mother. 2. Pats a picture in a book. 3. Increased interest in names. 4. Listens to short nursery rhymes. 5. Shows understanding of new words.	1. Indicates wants by vocalizing and pointing. 2. Says three or four words appropriately, including names. 3. Uses a flow of connected sounds that have inflection and that seem like a sentence.
15 to 18 mos.	1. Carries out two consecutive commands and/or directions. 2. Can point to body parts on a doll. 3. Learns new words by association.	1. Uses 10 words including names. 2. Makes requests by naming objects. 3. Begins to repeat words he or she hears in adult conversation. 4. Leaves off the beginning and end of phrases, e.g., "see you later" becomes "i / u / ler." 5. On one word responses, omits the final consonant.
18 to 24 mos.	1. Follows series of three, simple related commands. 2. Recognizes different sounds. 3. Demonstrates by appropriate responses his or her understanding of action words. 4. Responds to phrases such as "show me." 5. Identifies familiar pictures on request.	1. Uses short sentences—"Daddy go bye-bye." 2. Verbalizes toilet needs. 3. Uses pronouns but has syntax errors. Some pronouns inaccurate. 4. Echoes the last two or three words of a rhyme. 5. Discards jargon. 6. Tells full name. 7. Uses 25% of all consonants.
24 to 36 mos.	1. Carries out three verbal commands given in one utterance. 2. Understands "just one block" as a command. 3. Understands taking turns.	1. Mother understands 90% of his or her communication attempts. 2. Uses noun-verb combinations with correct verb tense.

Table 1. *Continued*

Age	Receptive language	Expressive language
	4. Follows commands using "in, on, under" prepositions.	3. Repeats three numbers, given intervals.
		4. Refers to self by pronoun.
		5. Names siblings on request.
		6. States sex and full name.
		7. Relates his or her experiences.
		8. Recites some rhymes or songs.
		9. Asks for personal help.

A referral is suggested if two items are failed in a child's chronological age category.

Table 2. Development of speech elements

The motor part of speech develops in an orderly sequence. Some children are precocious, while others appear to take the limits of developmental time to achieve sounds. Some children continue to use immature speech patterns after they have reached maturation level for appropriate speech. Maturation level can be determined by asking the child to repeat the age-appropriate words. Stimulation should be used before the child is labeled or referred for articulation therapy. Sounds are tested in the (-1) initial, (-1-) medial, and (1-) final position.

Stimulated Articulation Screen[a]

1.4–2 years	2–3 years
w- as in water	-w- as in mower
m-; -m-; as in mama	-m as in ham
n- as in no	-n- as in penny
h- as in hi	-n as in man
b-; -b-; as in baby	g- as in go
p-; -p-; as in puppy	-g- as in wagon
d- as in daddy	k-; -k- as in cookie
t- as in toe	f- as in fat
	-f as in leaf

3–4 years	4–5 years	5–6 years
y- as in you	r- as in rabbit	-l as in ball
-ng-; -ng as in ringing	-r as in air	-g as in dog
-r- as in carrot	-l- as in bellow	-t- as in rattle
l- as in like	-b as in tub	-t as in hat
-mp as in camp	-ch- as in matches	ch- as in church
-d- as in daddy	-ch as in church	fl- as in flower
c- as in coffee	sh- as in shoe	th- as in thumb
s- as in sit	-sh as in hush	-th- as in nothing
		-th as in mouth
		-ch- as in machine

[a]Reprinted with permission from Templin, M.C. 1957. Certain Language Skills in Children. The University of Minnesota Press, Minneapolis.

II. Hereditary Disorders

Marie-Louise Lubs, Ph. D.

AT LEAST 11 MILLION AMERICANS SUFFER from a genetic disorder. Almost 3 million of these have genetic forms of mental retardation, 1 million have congenital bone or muscle disorders, more than 1 million have handicaps involving hearing or vision, and 6 million have other specific organ defects. The genetic origin of the defects is varied. There can be extra or missing chromosomal material, either in the form of a whole chromosome or a part of a chromosome; or the defect could also be explained by a single mutant gene or by many genes, sometimes in conjunction with environmental factors such as viruses or drugs.

Since the error in the genetic constitution is present in every cell of an individual with a genetic disorder, correction of the error itself cannot be accomplished, and only in a few disorders (for example, those correctable by surgery) can the symptoms of the disease be eliminated or lessened. In view of the serious prognosis of so many genetically determined diseases, increasing emphasis is being given to the development and utilization of methods to screen those individuals at-risk for bearing affected children.

THE CHROMOSOMES

Chromosomes consist of tightly coiled strands of DNA, which is the genetic material. A chromosome can be compared with a string of beads, in which each bead is a gene. Each cell in the human body (except egg and sperm cells) has 46 chromosomes. By treating the cells with different chemicals and stains, it is possible to visualize the chromosomes through a light microscope. In Figure 1 the chromosomes have an identical-looking

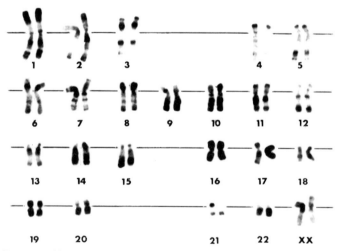

Figure 1.   Chromosomes of normal female conventionally arranged according to length with the exception of the sex chromosome pair.

partner or "homologue." One of the members in each of the pairs is derived from the mother and the other from the father of the individual. These 22 pairs are called the autosomes. The 23rd pair is the sex chromosome pair. In women, this pair consists of two identical large chromosomes looking like the letter X and, therefore, named X chromosomes. They are shown in the lower right corner of Figure 1. Males, however, have a different sex chromosome constitution, as shown in Figure 2. One member of the pair is an X chromosome, as in females, while the other is a small asymmetrical chromosome called the Y chromosome. The Y chromosome must be present in order for the individual to have functional male reproductive organs.

In the formation of egg and sperm cells, a reduction division (meiosis) takes place, so that only one member of each pair will comprise the chromosomal constitution of these cells. Eggs and sperm, therefore, have only 23 chromosomes. All eggs have an X chromosome, half of the sperm cells contain an X, and the other half a Y chromosome. At fertilization, the egg and sperm fuse, forming a zygote with 46 chromosomes that will develop into the embryo. If the sperm cell contained an X, the fetus will be a female, if it contained a Y the fetus will be male. This is shown schematically in Figure 3.

It is not unusual for something to go wrong in the reduction division. Therefore, instead of only one member of each pair making up the constitution of the egg or sperm cell, both homologues will be present or none. This is called a nondisjunction. This abnormal egg or sperm cell will form a

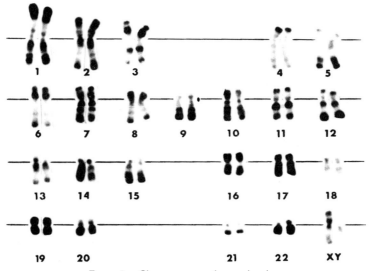

Figure 2.   Chromosomes of normal male.

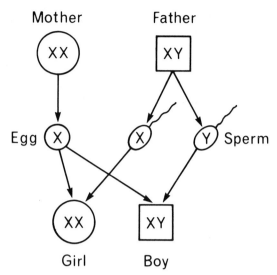

Figure 3.   Sex determination in humans. An X-bearing sperm fertilizing the ovum produces a female fetus, a Y-bearing sperm produces a male fetus.

zygote that is either missing one chromosome, making a total of 45, or has an extra chromosome, a total of 47 chromosomes. All daughter cells from such a zygote will have the same chromosomal defect. Since there are thousands of genes on each chromosome, the effect of nondisjunction is usually disastrous, leading to embryonic death, often at such an early state that the woman never realizes that she was pregnant. (Several chromosomal studies of abortuses have revealed that more than half of first trimester abortuses have extra or missing chromosomes.)

In rare instances, the chromosomally abnormal fetus survives to birth. The infants, as one might expect from the drastically altered number of genes present, generally have multiple major clinical anomalies as well as mental retardation. The exception is an altered number of X or Y chromosomes, where the clinical manifestations are much less severe.

Chromosomal Disorders

Chromosomal disorders are called genetic because they involve a defect in the genetic material. Usually, however, the disorders are not inherited from the parents, but are due to sporadic events in the eggs or sperm of chromosomally normal parents.

Trisomy 21, or Down syndrome, is probably the most common major chromosome abnormality. Such an individual has 47 chromosomes, including an extra small autosome, number 21. The syndrome includes mental retardation and several characteristic clinical features: slanted eyes, protruding tongue, and abnormal fingerprint patterns. Heart disease is also often part of the syndrome. The risk of having a child with Down syndrome increases greatly with increased maternal age (shown in Figure 4). (The risk of other chromosome abnormalities is also somewhat increased with advancing maternal age. The overall risk of a child being born with an extra or a missing chromosome is about 1/200.)

In 95% of Down syndrome cases both parents have perfectly normal chromosome complements. As mentioned, increased age predisposes for nondisjunction at the time of the formation of the egg. Other factors, such as maternal hyperthyroidism or exposure to radiation, have also been implicated. In a very few cases the defect is truly inherited from one of the parents. In those cases, there has been a rearrangement in the chromosomes, called a translocation. This means that a piece of chromosome, in this case number 21, has fused with a portion of another chromosome. This translocation increases the risk of a nondisjunction at the time of the formation of the eggs or sperms. Although the recurrence risk for normal parents with a Down syndrome child is only 1% to 2%, the risk for a parent with such a translocation is probably several times higher, perhaps as high as 10% to 30%. Therefore, in the family with a Down syndrome child, it is important to advise a chromosome analysis, not only to confirm the diagnosis but also to determine if the abnormality is inherited or sporadic.

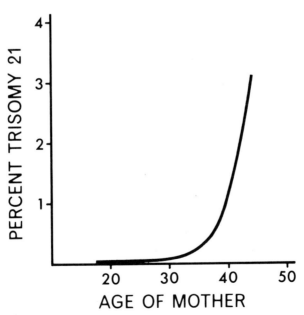

Figure 4.   Frequency of infants with trisomy 21 by maternal age.

Since diagnosis of the chromosomal constitution can be done in the 14th to 16th week of pregnancy, through amniocentesis (Figure 5), all women at-risk should be offered this procedure. Amniocentesis involves removal of about 10–20 cc of the amniotic fluid, which contains some fetal cells. These cells can be analyzed both with regard to chromosome content as well as a number of metabolic disorders. Since older women have a higher risk than the general population, amniocentesis is recommended particularly to pregnant women 37 years or older. Another high risk group is comprised of couples in which one individual is a translocation carrier. A third group that often elects to have amniocentesis consists of women who have already had a child with Down syndrome. Despite the low recurrence risk, such women are often anxious to avoid the trauma of having another abnormal child.

Other chromosomal abnormalities involving the autosomes include trisomy 8, trisomy 13, and trisomy 18. All of these disorders include multiple congenital malformations as well as mental retardation. Numerous cases of partial trisomies (the normal set of chromosomes plus a part of an extra chromosome) or partial monosomies (a part of one chromosome in the set missing) have also been described. The clinical effects are usually extensive, and genetic counseling is advised, including information about prenatal diagnosis of chromosomes of future children—even if the recurrence risk, as in Down syndrome, is low.

The X and Y chromosome abnormalities have less severe clinical consequences. The incidence of newborns with nondisjunction of an X or a Y chromosome is about 1/400 births. Many different sex chromosome constitutions have been described, the most common being: 47, XYY (male), 47,XXY (male), 47, XXX (female), and 45, X (female). (The number indicates the number of chromosomes in each cell, the normal complement being 46, XX and 46, XY.) Usually, the fertility of such individuals is impaired and sometimes, but not always, they are mildly retarded. The most characteristic clinical features found in the 47, XXY male are small testicles, eunuchoid proportions, and sometimes gynecomastia (breast development). The 47, XYY males are usually clinically normal although often taller than average males and are, therefore, usually not diagnosed. They have been found more often in penal institutions than in the general population and it is felt that at least some 47, XYY males have tendencies toward violent and criminal behavior. The 47, XXX women also have normal clinical features. The incidence of mental retardation seems to be higher in this group than in the other three groups mentioned. The 45, X female, finally, always has short stature (never taller than 5 feet), primary amenorrhea, poor breast development, and sometimes a webbed neck, low hairline in the back, and other minor features. Approximately one-third of the cases have heart defects. The 47, XXY male and the 45, X

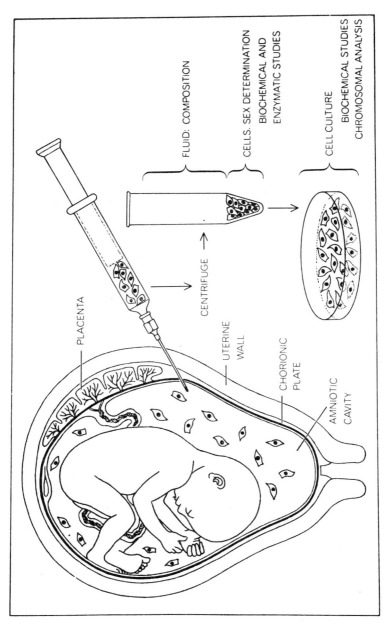

Figure 5.   Amniocentesis. Procedure is usually performed at 12 to 16 weeks of pregnancy. (From Friedman, T. 1971. Prenatal diagnosis of genetic disease. Sci. Am. 225:35. Copyright © 1971 by Scientific American, Inc. All rights reserved.)

female are infertile and are often diagnosed for the first time when they are seen for an infertility workup.

As with Down syndrome, most parents of a child with an extra or a missing X or Y are usually chromosomally normal. The recurrence risk is not known, but probably similar to or only slightly higher than the risk for the general population, which is about 1/400. Although the IQ level of individuals with sex chromosome abnormalities is usually somewhat lower than that of their normal siblings, significant mental retardation is rare. Since there usually are no major abnormalities present, genetic counseling focuses on reassuring the parents both with regard to the clinical prognosis of the affected child and to the low recurrence risk. In the 47, XXY male and the 45, X female the infertility problem is usually the most serious problem the family must face. Secondary sex characteristics, such as breast development and even some menstrual bleeding in the 45, X female, can be achieved if hormone treatments are started in the early teens.

Prevention of Chromosomal Disorders

If a family has had a child with multiple defects found to be due to a chromosomal abnormality, the question of recurrence risk is often raised. It is then essential to study the chromosomes of the two parents to establish whether one of them is a translocation carrier. If this is the case, the recurrence risk is uncertain, but probably 5% to 30%. This is usually considered to be a high risk, and amniocentesis and abortion of affected fetuses should be discussed. If abortion is unacceptable for the family and the husband is the translocation carrier, the possibility of artificial insemination with an unknown donor should be mentioned. (The use of this method is increasing, particularly since adoption, as another alternative, is becoming increasingly difficult because of the fewer number of babies available.)

If the parents are chromosomally normal, the chromosomal constitution in their abnormal child was due to a mutation. Mutations, both on the chromosomal and the gene level, are rare and the recurrence risk is probably less than 1% except for Down syndrome. Even this low risk is considered too high by some couples, particularly in view of the serious consequences. Amniocentesis and abortion of abnormal fetuses are then the only certain means of preventing the birth of a second abnormal child. During genetic counseling, adoption should also be discussed as an alternative.

DISORDERS DETERMINED BY A SINGLE DEFECTIVE GENE

The two homologues in a chromosome pair contain similar genetic material. A gene determining eye color on one homologue is matched by one determining eye color at exactly the same place on the other homologue.

Therefore, genes for all of the different functions are paired, one gene of maternal origin and the other of paternal origin. (Obviously, they are not necessarily identical. It is possible to inherit a gene for straight hair from the father and a gene for curly hair from the mother, for instance.) Such genes that are located at the same place on a chromosome and that code for the same function are called alleles. There is some controversy about how many gene locations or gene loci there are in humans, the estimates varing from 10,000 to 1 million loci. The number of disorders that are attributable to a defect in one single gene locus exceeds 1,000.

Sometimes the characteristic of one allele will dominate in its expression over the allele on the homologue. It is then called a dominant gene. If an individual has a dominant gene on one chromosome homologue, the individual will show the dominant characteristic. However, if both homologues contain the recessive gene, then the individual will have the characteristics of those genes. In other words, it takes only one dominant gene on one of the two homologues to show a dominant characteristic or phenotype, but it takes two recessive genes at the same locus to express the recessive characteristic.

Dominantly Inherited Disorders

Dominantly inherited disorders are characterized by the fact that they are inherited from parent to child. This means that one of the parents usually is affected with the same disorder. Since the parent survived to reproduce, it might mean that the disorder is a mild one. Examples of benign dominant traits are polydactyly (extra fingers), white forelock, and ptosis (droopy eyelids).

Another possibility is that the disorder is variable in its clinical manifestations. A mildly affected parent, for instance, could give birth to a severly affected offspring. An example of a dominantly inherited disorder that is clinically extremely variable is neurofibromatosis, in which the symptoms may include: neurofibromas (anywhere in the body including the brain), scoliosis, mental retardation, malignant tumors, and light brown smooth birthmarks called café-au-lait spots. Sometimes the birthmarks are the only sign of the disease. A third group of dominantly inherited disorders is comprised of those that do not manifest themselves until adult life, perhaps even after the childbearing period. Such a disorder is Huntington's disease, which is a severe nerve degenerative disease starting in the third or fourth decade or even later with tremors, confusion, and altered personality; it ends in complete brain degeneration.

The offspring from a mating of an individual with a dominant disorder and a normal individual is shown in Figure 6. On the average, one-half of the children will inherit the abnormal gene and one-half will inherit the normal one.

Dominant Inheritance

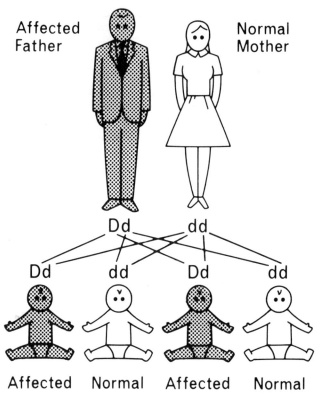

Affected
Father

Normal
Mother

Dd   dd

Dd   dd   Dd   dd

Affected   Normal   Affected   Normal

Figure 6.   Dominant inheritance. Half of the children are affected.

Finally, there are some dominantly inherited disorders that include major congenital malformations and impaired fertility. An example of such a disorder is achondroplasia, which is the most common form of dwarfism, the incidence being about 1/10,000. The clinical features are short arms and legs, although the trunk is normal in size and the head is of normal size but with some bossing of the forehead. Intelligence is normal. The fertility is about 30% of normal, partly because of obstetrical complications in affected women and partly because of social reasons. Some affected individuals die in early childhood and, of those who survive to adulthood, many do not marry or have children. Most cases of achondroplasia, therefore, are not born to an affected parent but are due to new mutations, both parents being normal. The mutation rate in achondroplasia is one of the highest recorded in man—about 1/20,000 germ cells—and seems to increase with increased paternal age. If this dominant gene is present in both homologues, the condition is lethal.

Prevention of Dominantly Inherited Disorders

Few dominantly inherited disorders can be diagnosed *in utero*. Since the majority of disorders are so variable, one would ideally like to determine not only whether the fetus is affected, but also the degree of the phenotypic involvement. If bony abnormalities are suspected, an oblique X ray of the pelvis or ultrasound studies at 20 weeks of gestation might be helpful. Adoption or, if the gene is inherited in the husband's family, artificial insemination with an unknown donor, is the most practical solution at the present time for families who do not want to perpetuate a dominant gene in future generations.

Recessively Inherited Disorders

In recessive disorders, clinically normal parents who carry the gene have clinically affected offspring. The syndromes, therefore, are not directly inherited from parent to child. Two siblings in a family can be affected, however. Males and females are equally often affected.

Recessive disorders are generally much more clinically uniform than the dominant disorders. They are inherited from both parents. The abnormal gene is recessive and the normal gene is dominant. Both parents, although they carry the gene, are clinically normal. The different outcomes of pregnancies involving recessive inheritance are shown in Figure 7. With every pregnancy, there are 3 out of 4 chances to have a clinically normal child and 1 out of 4 that the child will be affected. There is a 2/4, or 50%, chance that the child will be normal, but will carry the defective gene just like the parents. Of the clinically normal offspring, therefore, 2 out of 3 will be carriers.

The most common, severe recessive disorders are: cystic fibrosis, Tay-Sachs disease, and sickle cell anemia. Cystic fibrosis is the most common in the Caucasian population. The disorder affects lungs and pancreas with fibrous overgrowth, and death usually occurs before adulthood. The incidence is about 1/20,000 Caucasian births. At present, there is no method of identifying the normal carrier of the gene (the carrier frequency is as high as 1/23) and there is no prenatal test to identify the affected fetus.

Tay-Sachs disease is common only in Jewish populations of Eastern European origin. The incidence of affected individuals at birth in the New York Jewish population is about 1/5,000, and the frequency of normal individuals who carry the gene is 1/35. The disorder is characterized by developmental retardation, followed by paralysis, dementia, and blindness. Death occurs in the second or third year of life. In this disorder, however, a reliable carrier test has been developed that can diagnose the

Recessive Inheritance

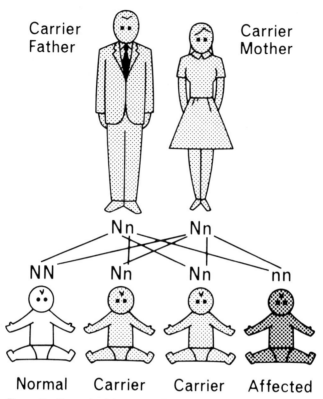

Figure 7.   Recessive inheritance. Parents are clinically normal; one-quarter of the children are affected.

affected fetus in the 12th to 16th week of pregnancy. Several communities have organized screening programs in order to identify all couples who are carriers and who, therefore, have a 1 in 4 risk at each pregnancy of having an affected child.

Sickle cell anemia is a disease in which an abnormal hemoglobin is present in the erythrocytes, causing them to sickle. It is most prevalent in the black population. In U. S. blacks the incidence at birth is 1/400 and the carrier frequency is 1/9. Children with this disorder have severe hemolytic anemia and their growth development is retarded. Another characteristic feature is the occurrence of hemolytic crises, in which blood destruction is increased. Abdominal pains and joint pains are common. Death often occurs in childhood; but some affected individuals reach adult life. In sickle cell anemia, a carrier test is available, and a prenatal test for the disease has been recently developed. Genetic counseling to a couple who are both found to be carriers includes explanation both of the clinical prognosis of an affected child and the 1 in 4 risk at each pregnancy. It is important to emphasize that if the first child is affected it does not guarantee that the next 3 children will be normal. Rather, there is a 1 in 4 chance with each pregnancy.

Phenylketonuria (PKU) is only one of a number of recessively inherited metabolic disorders that have a severe effect on mental development if not diagnosed at birth. Luckily, an inexpensive test for the disorder has been developed. In most states, therefore, laws have been passed requiring every newborn to be tested for PKU. If an affected child is identified, it will be put on a special low phenylalanine diet (phenylalanine is present in protein) for the first years of life. This treatment prevents or greatly reduces the degree of mental retardation that would have followed if the child had been on a regular diet. PKU cannot be identified by amniocentesis, because the mental retardation is caused by a defect in the breakdown of phenylalanine to tyrosine. Since phenylalanine is introduced with food, it is not present until the first feeding after birth. PKU, like most metabolic disorders, is rare. The incidence is about 1/20,000 births and the carrier frequency about 1/70. As in most metabolic diseases, there is currently no reliable method of detecting the carriers.

Prevention of Recessively Inherited Disorders

Most recessive disorders are so rare that screening for carriers, even if a carrier test were available, would be both impractical and prohibitively expensive. Most individuals are identified as carriers only when they have their first affected child. The first case, therefore, is usually not preventable. However, for about 75 rare metabolic disorders, methods of prenatal diagnosis are now available so that a second affected child can be prevented through abortion of an affected fetus. If abortion is unacceptable to the couple, artificial insemination with an unknown donor will lower the risk of a second affected child from 1 in 4 to about 1 in 500 in most cases.

X-linked Recessive Disorders

Numerous genes cause abnormalities on the X chromosome. Most of them are recessive. Therefore, females who have two X chromosomes can be carriers of the disorders and not show any clinical symptoms, just as in the autosomal recessive disorders described previously. Males, on the other hand, who have only one X, will show the defect if the recessive gene is present on their X chromosome. The Y chromosome has no or very few genes homologous with the X chromosome. There will be no normal gene product produced, since there is no homologous normal gene present. The characteristics of X-linked disorders, therefore, are: only males are affected, and inheritance is only through healthy females (no male to male transmission). A normal male and a carrier female can produce the off-spring of four different genotypes as shown in Figure 8.

There is a 1 in 4 risk at every pregnancy to have an affected son, a 1 in 4 chance to have a carrier daughter who is clinically normal like her mother, and a 2 in 4 chance to have a genetically normal son or daughter. It should be emphasized that only the mother in this mating is responsible for the risk, while the father is completely normal. If an affected male mates with a normal female, the possibilities are shown in Figure 9. All daughters will be carriers (and have a 1 in 4 risk in each of their pregnancies) and all sons will be completely normal, since they inherited the normal Y chromosome and not the abnormal X chromosome from their father.

X-Linked Inheritance
(Through Carrier Woman)

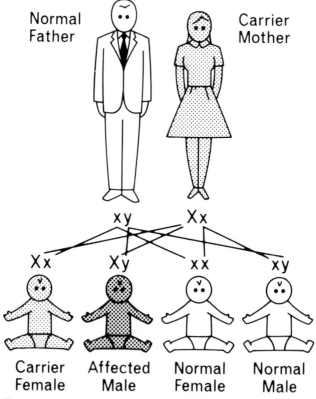

Figure 8.   X-linked recessive inheritance if the mother is a carrier. One-quarter of the children (always males) are affected.

The most common severe disorders with X-linked recessive inheritance are hemophilia A and Duchenne muscular dystrophy. In hemophilia A, available treatments have made it possible for affected males to live more normal lives. The treatments include blood concentrates containing the essential clotting factor, which can be kept frozen and administered at the time of bleeding by patients themselves. The incidence of such severe hemophiliacs at birth is 1/10,000 male births and the carrier frequency is 1/5,000 females. Although the carrier status of the females is established with reasonable certainty by a blood test, a prenatal test to diagnose an affected male fetus is still not generally available. Techniques are being

X-Linked Inheritance
(From Affected Male)

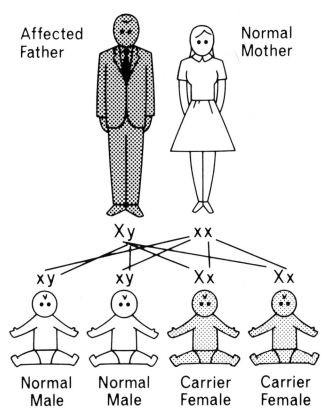

Figure 9.   X-linked recessive inheritance if the father is affected with the disorder. None of the children will be affected, but all daughters will be carriers.

developed that will permit fetal blood sampling through the cord. However, sex can be reliably determined early in pregnancy by looking at the fetal chromosomes. Therefore, at present some couples elect to abort all male fetuses, since only males are affected.

Duchenne muscular dystrophy is a progressive muscle degeneration starting shortly after birth. It affects 1 in 5,000 males. About half of the affected males do not start walking until 18 months or later and they often never proceed past the wobbling gait of a child who just learned to walk. Occasionally, the first 3 years of life are reported to be normal developmentally. Walking becomes more difficult, however, as time goes by. Crutches become necessary and by 10 years of age the boy might be bound to a wheelchair. Mental retardation is sometimes part of the syndrome, as is heart disease, since the heart muscle might be involved in the muscle degeneration. Death usually occurs around age 17. There is no known cure for Duchenne muscular dystrophy. A carrier test has been developed but is less accurate than that for hemophilia A. Many cases are termed sporadic because the family history is negative. This is due to the fact that the mutation rate is comparatively high: one-third of all cases are due to a new mutation in the male fetus and another one-third are due to a new mutation in the mother. In the former case, the recurrence risk is virtually zero, but in the latter case, the recurrence risk is 1 in 4. Therefore, an accurate carrier test performed on the mother is of great value.

Prevention of X-linked Recessive Disorders

Only a few X-linked disorders can be diagnosed in utero. The most important disorder that can be detected prenatally is Hunter's syndrome, or mucopolysaccharidosis type II, a severe metabolic disorder in which affected males have coarse features and progressive mental dementia. This disorder can be diagnosed in the amniotic fluid and prevention of affected siblings of an affected male is possible through abortion. Other X-linked disorders can only be prevented by selective abortion of all male fetuses of carrier females. In the near future, it will probably be possible to separate the X- and the Y-bearing sperm through mechanical or chemical means. The carrier will thus be able to elect artificial insemination with her husband's X-bearing sperm and thus have only daughters. This would obviate the need to abort any male fetuses.

GENETIC ASPECTS OF SOME COMMON CONGENITAL MALFORMATIONS

About 1 infant in 30 has a serious congenital malformation. Although many chromosomal as well as single gene disorders include congenital malformations, the most common major malformations are not inherited in a simple fashion. They are instead caused by several genes and are also influenced by environmental factors. These environmental factors can be placental conditions, implantation site in the uterus, maternal nutritional factors, maternal drug use, viruses, and many other, often unidentified, factors. The etiology of these abnormalities is, therefore, called multifactorial or polygenic. Familial cases have been described, but the recurrence risk is much lower than in single gene disorders. Congenital heart disease, which is present in about 1% of newborn infants, is due to multiple genes about 98% of the time. If a child is born with ventricular septal defect, which is the most common of the malformations, the recurrence risk for other siblings is about 5%. However, if other individuals in the family are affected as well, this recurrence risk increases. If one of the parents is affected, the recurrence risk increases more than if the second individual affected is a more distant relative, such as a first cousin. Therefore, it is very important to obtain a thorough family history and a firm diagnosis on all individuals presumed affected before meaningful genetic counseling can be given. The recurrence risk is also dependent on how common the disorder is in the population. As a rule of thumb, the recurrence risk of a polygenic trait for a subsequent sibling is $\sqrt{p}$, where p is the incidence at birth in the population. This is true only if the family history is negative. In other words, if the incidence is 1/1,000, as is the case with cleft lip with or without cleft palate, the risk of having a second child with the disorder is $\sqrt{1/1,000}$ =1/32 if no other relative is known to have the abnormality. If the woman has a brother with cleft lip but she herself is normal, the risk of her having an affected child is only slightly increased, probably to about 1/150.

Another characteristic of polygenic disorders is the fact that the recurrence risk increases with increased severity of the disorder in the proband. If a child has bilateral cleft lip, the recurrence risk is greater than that for unilateral cleft lip.

Congenital heart disease and cleft lip and palate have been mentioned as two groups of disorders that are polygenically inherited in the majority of cases. Other malformations include central nervous system defects (spina bifida, hydrocephaly, anencephaly), congenital dislocation of the hip, pyloric stenosis, and nonspecific mental retardation. Adult diseases, such as cardiovascular disorders, hypertension, and susceptibility to some forms of cancers, are also inherited as multifactorial traits, as are height, hair color, eye and skin color, and intelligence.

Although the recurrence risks in these multifactorial disorders are considerably lower than those discussed previously, in some cases, such as congenital heart disorders and spina bifida, the burden on the affected individual is great. Modes of prevention include artificial insemination with unknown donor and adoption. Of the disorders mentioned above, spina bifida is the only one that can be detected *in utero*. Amniocentesis is, therefore, indicated at 16 weeks of pregnancy.

THE GENETIC COUNSELING PROCESS

Genetic counseling is best given over a period of time. When a child is born with a birth defect or a serious metabolic disorder, the parents are initially in a state of shock. At this time they should only be informed that genetic services are available and, in addition, inquiries should be made to assure that adequate contraceptive methods are being used. In general, however, the parents' needs at this stage center around support of the child with the problem, and parents are not immediately concerned about the risk for future children. Therefore, regardless if the child died in the neonatal period or survived, a three- to six-month period should be allowed before approaching the parents about genetic counseling. Referral to a genetics clinic should then be made, either by a physician or nurse who discusses this service with the family and encourages them to contact the clinic. The parents may reply that they are not planning to have more children. If there are healthy siblings in the family, however, it is important for the family to know if these children have an increased risk of having children with abnormalities. This is a question not often raised by the parents, but is nevertheless something they frequently worry about. Even if the mode of inheritance is not known or if the family has a problem that is not thought genetic, a visit to the genetics clinic may be useful and relieve much anxiety, since parents often tend to overestimate their recurrence risk.

It is extremely helpful if the child and all medical records are brought to the clinic. If the records are not available or if the diagnosis is not apparent by physical examination, the first visit to the clinic is usually spent gathering information, signing release of information forms, and taking a pedigree. Clinical geneticists are not willing to give genetic counseling without a formal diagnosis by a physician or by themselves. This is because many clinically similar conditions are inherited in different ways with drastic differences in recurrence risks, and explaining all possibilities would not only be confusing but irrelevant to a family's specific problem.

Once the diagnosis is established, the counseling session centers around explanation of the mode of inheritance and the recurrence risk. Since the parents often have preconceived ideas about what this risk may be, some "undoing" of these beliefs is often necessary. The clinical prognosis of an affected child is also an important topic. To many parents, for example, a child with Duchenne muscular dystrophy may seem quite normal at the age of 2. If the grave prognosis is not discussed, parents may mistakenly think either that their child happened to get a milder form of the disease or even that the diagnosis is wrong. Questions are often raised regarding care and rearing of the child; these need to be answered in order for the parents to make informed decisions about family planning.

Ideally, a second counseling session should take place a week or two after the risks and inheritance pattern are first discussed. This session allows additional questions to be answered, and the counselor can clear up any misunderstandings or misconceptions that may have occurred since the first session. The counselor also has an opportunity to reinforce understanding of the recurrence risk. A "one in four" risk may be remembered as a 4% risk, for example, if the counselor is not clear and concise. There is also a tendency over time for the individual to revert to a belief originally held before counseling, but this is a slower process. Over a 2 year period, this effect was shown clearly in a study of 141 families affected by hemophilia or muscular dystrophy. This indicates the need for a long-term follow-up of these families, preferably by health personnel that see them periodically.

THE ROLE OF THE NURSE IN GENETICS

Although the genetics associate with a Master's degree in human genetics has recently become an important figure in genetic programs, many aspects of the service are carried out equally well or better by a nurse, who preferably has some genetics training. The reasons for this are: First, a large number of cases seen in the clinic are referred by nurses, such as local public health nurses and nurses in various health clinics. With some education in genetics, nurses in health programs or even those in private practice could be screening children for genetic disorders. In Dade County, Florida, for example, a feasibility assessment is now being made to evaluate whether a birth defect registry can be developed using nurses as the recorders. Nurses in pediatric as well as specialty clinics would simply record the name and birth date of children with birth defects who are seen by them or the clinic. The names would then be collected periodically and medical charts screened for diagnosis. Such a registry would not only be helpful in offering genetic services to these families, but would be useful in informing families of other related services in the county. Finally, the registry could facilitate state planning of health resources for handicapped children.

Second, nurses may have a role in the genetic clinic itself. With some special training in child development, they may complete a physical examination on the child (and sometimes also on the parents), draw blood for various tests, or perform developmental screening. Such nurses could collect all the background information regarding diagnosis and tests already performed and construct a pedigree. In addition, if the nurse is to follow the family after the visit to the genetic clinic, it is important that he or she be present when the clinical geneticist sees the family, in order to later reinforce what was said in the session or sessions. If a public health nurse is to follow the family, it is helpful for the nurse to have direct contact with the genetic clinic for details of the case as well as the clinical implications of the disease.

A nurse working outside a medical institution can be extremely valuable to a family, both in the first adjustment phase—after the diagnosis and before the genetic counseling—as well as after the counseling, when reinforcement of the genetic information as well as support and encouragement are so important. It is likely that among the many new specialties for nurses that are being developed, a separate specialty curriculum for Genetics Nursing may soon be developed.

REFERENCE

Friedman, T. 1971. Prenatal diagnosis of genetic diseases. Sci. Am. 225: 34–42.

SUGGESTED READINGS

McKusick, V. A. 1969. Human Genetics. Prentice Hall International, London.
McKusick, V. A., and Claiborne, R. (eds.). 1973. Medical Genetics. HP Publishing Co., New York.
Nora, J. J., and Fraser, F. C. 1974. Medical Genetics: Principles and Practice. Lea & Febiger, Philadelphia.
Reed, S. C. 1980. Counseling in Medical Genetics. W. B. Saunders Co., Philadelphia.
Smith, David W. 1982. Recognizable Patterns of Human Malformation. W. B. Saunders Co., Philadelphia.

III. The High Risk Infant
Implications for Development

Annette Lansford, M. D.

A CHILD IS CONSIDERED TO BE at high risk because of adverse genetic, prenatal, perinatal, noenatal, postnatal, or environmental influences that may lead to subsequent development of a handicap or developmental deviation. It is important to note that a handicap is often associated with preceding high risk factors; however, the reverse does not always hold—that is, high risk factors are not necessarily followed by development of a handicap.

The theoretical merit of the high risk concept is based on the premise that by carefully examining a group of infants early in life who may have a greater risk of developmental or physical problems, early identification of those with problems, followed by early intervention, leads to a better chance of minimizing the deviation and promoting the child's normal development and maturing process. Therefore, when an infant has been identified as high risk, a thorough developmental history, physical and neurological examination, and developmental screening should be done at regular intervals.

Below is a list of influences considered to be high risk factors.

FAMILY HISTORY

1. Deafness of genetic origin in parents or siblings.

2. Advanced maternal age. Maternal age has been most strikingly correlated in Down syndrome, which is much more common in the offspring of mothers over 35. Hydrocephaly is also more frequent in babies born to mothers over 35 years of age. In addition, there is a higher incidence of premature birth in mothers who are 40 and older.

3. Maternal age under 18. One study of pregnant women 15 years of age and younger found that one-fourth delivered before 36 weeks. Very young mothers also show a higher risk of having toxemia of pregnancy.

Furthermore, malformations affecting the central nervous system are more frequent in babies born to women who are at the beginning or end of reproductive life.

4. History of previous stillbirths. The combined rate of stillbirths and infantile death for the siblings of children suffering from diplegic cerebral palsy, for example, is approximately twice that expected in the normal community.

5. History of previous children with congenital malformations. A mother who has had one child with congenital malformations runs a considerable increased risk of producing another child with congenital malformations, although not necessarily of the same type. After having one child with spina bifida, a mother has 12 times the standard risk. After having one child with anencephaly, she has six times the standard risk in a subsequent pregnancy. (Anencephaly is a developmental anomaly characterized by complete absence of the brain or the presence of small masses attached to the base of the skull.)

6.   Low socioeconomic class. The percentage of premature births is highest in women of the lower socioeconomic groups.

7.   History of a hereditary, metabolic, muscle, or neurological disease in the family such as phenylketonuria, Duchenne's muscular dystrophy, Tay-Sachs disease, and so on.

8.   Race other than white increases the risk of having an infant with low birth weight.

9.   A short interpregnancy interval also increases the risk of having an infant with low birth weight, as does an out-of-wedlock birth.

PRENATAL

1.   History of maternal rubella or other viral infection in first 4 months of pregnancy.

2.   Toxoplasmosis. This is a parasitic infection, probably caused by protozoa.

3.   Threatened abortion or antepartum hemorrhage. Antepartum hemorrhage or third trimester hemorrhage is an important factor in the prematurity and neonatal death rates, and should always be regarded seriously.

4. Maternal illness during pregnancy, such as pregnancy-induced hypertension, diabetes, and bacterial infections, often result in premature deliveries and low birth weight babies (not infrequently showing intrauterine growth retardation).

PERINATAL

1.   Short gestation (prematurity). Live, born infants delivered before 37 weeks from the first day of the last menstrual period are considered to have a shortened gestational period.

2.   Low birth weight (below the 10th percentile for gestational age). Infants who weigh 2,500 g (5 lbs. 8 oz.) or less at birth are considered to have had either a short gestational period, a less than expected rate of intrauterine growth, or both, and are termed infants of low birth weight.

Prematurity and low birth weight are usually seen together, particularly in infants weighting 1,500 g (2 lbs. 11 oz.) or less at birth, and are associated with a greater death rate and a greater rate of neonatal problems. Though the statistics vary according to which population is surveyed, generally the incidence of low birth weight infants runs from 6% to 16%, about half of which are babies who are not premature but are "small for dates" babies.

Retrolental fibroplasia is a type of toxicity to the retina of the eye associated with excessive exposure of the retina vessels to oxygen. This is primarily a problem of low birth weight babies because of their greater incidence of pulmonary problems and subsequent requirement for oxygen. If the oxygen has been at a high level for long periods of time and becomes toxic to the eye vessels, blindness can result.

Chronic oxygen toxicity to the lungs also occurs, most often in low birth weight infants who have required long-term oxygen therapy. Broncho-pulmonary dysplasia is a condition in which a tremendous proliferation of cells occurs that bulges out into the respiratory bronchioles because of epithelial injury. Infants prone to this dysplasia are often oxygen-dependent at the time of discharge from the nursery and require oxygen for long periods of time before they can gradually be weaned from it.

Low birth weight babies frequently never catch up in height and weight with their normal peers. Most low birth weight babies are significantly smaller than their normal birth weight peers at the end of the first year of life.

The death rate of low birth weight infants who survive to be discharged from the hospital nursery is three times that of full-term infants during the first 2 years of life. Many of these deaths are caused by infections. There is also a high incidence of handicaps, both neurological and mental, among small, premature babies.

3. Moderate to severe asphyxia. Asphyxia, anoxia, and hypoxia are all terms loosely applied to indicate the end result of lack of oxygen from a number of causes. Lack of oxygen is the leading cause of perinatal death or permanent damage to the central nervous system. One cause of fetal hypoxia or asphyxia is the compression of the umbilical cord between the presenting part and the pelvic tissues during labor and delivery. Other causes of fetal anoxia are inadequate oxygenization of maternal blood, low maternal blood pressure, inadequate relaxation of the uterus to permit placental filling, inadequate attachment of the placenta, and placental inadequacy, as in toxemia and postmaturity.

4. Presence of congenital abnormality. It is a general principle that any major congenital anomaly carries with it a risk of mental subnormality. Major congenital anomalies include defects of skeleton and skull, congenital defects of eyes and ears, congenital heart disease, various congenital skin defects, diseases involving muscle, endocrine defects (such as cretinism), other metabolic conditions (such as amino acid diseases), and mixed genetic and chromosomal defects.

5. Polyhydramnios. The presence of polyhydramnios is often associated with prematurity and/or fetal anomaly such as anencephaly, spina bifida, hydrocephaly, or gastrointestinal tract anomalies.

6. Evidence of fetal distress. A diagnosis of fetal distress is made by the use of intrapartum fetal heart monitoring, and refers to underlying baseline changes lasting more than 10 minutes. Another indication of fetal distress is meconium staining. (Meconium is the dark, sticky substance that accumulates in the gastrointestinal tract of the fetus.)

NEONATAL

1. Neonatal hyperbilirubinemia. Bilirubin is a product of red blood cell breakdown and can be toxic to the newborn brain if it reaches high levels. There are several causes of high bilirubin, the most severe being Rh incompatibility. If the bilirubin reaches a high enough level (usually around 20 mg/100 ml in a full-term infant) an exchange transfusion is required. This temporarily delays further red blood cell breakdown in the baby. Any child whose bilirubin level has risen high enough to have necessitated an exchange transfusion is at risk of having brain damage due to bilirubin toxicity. The most severe type of bilirubin central nervous system toxicity is called kernicterus. These babies are usually severely retarded, have cerebral palsy, and have a hearing deficit.

2. An unsatisfactory postnatal state in the infant, particularly when accompanied by any of the following factors:

   a. Pregnancy-induced hypertension. This is a maternal gestational condition that is associated with a greatly increased morbidity and mortality of the mother and fetus. In the most serious form, it can result in maternal convulsions, coma, and death of the fetus. Often, the surviving infants of these mothers show intrauterine growth retardation. The most severe form of toxemia is eclampsia, in which convulsions and/or coma occur in the mother. Babies of toxemic mothers are at much higher risk.

   b. Postmature birth. Postmature births are those in which the babies are born after a gestation of more than 42 weeks. These babies are often small for gestational age and have a higher incidence of neonatal problems. When postmaturity exceeds 3 or more weeks, there is a significant increase in mortality.

   c. Abnormal presentation. Abnormal presentations, which often cause difficult deliveries, are breech, transverse lie, or chin, shoulder, or forehead first. In comparison to cephalic delivery, breech presentation is more likely to be associated with prematurity, low birth weight, growth retardation, congenital abnormalities, obstetrical complications, and increased perinatal morbidity and mortality.

d.   Forceps deliveries. Forceps deliveries can result in a facial palsy (usually only temporary) in the newborn baby. More important, forceps are most commonly used in difficult deliveries, which constitute a high risk factor in themselves.

e.   Cesarean section. Almost all indications for cesarean section as the method of delivery are high risk events themselves.

f.   Maternal diabetes. An increased frequency of intrauterine fetal death sometimes prompts the preterm delivery of infants of diabetic mothers by cesarean section. These babies are more prone to the development of low blood sugar (because the mother's high blood glucose levels have stimulated the baby's pancreas to produce high insulin levels), hyaline membrane disease, hypocalcemia, hyperbilirubinemia, polycythemia, hyperviscosity, and necrotizing enterocolitis. There is also a twofold to threefold increase in congenital malformations observed in infants of diabetic mothers, the most common involving anomalies of the heart and skeletal systems.

3.   Difficulty in sucking or swallowing. The failure to feed well may be the first sign of an infection in the newborn. It also may be an early sign of cerebral palsy or mental deficiency.

4.   Failure to thrive (the failure to gain weight normally, or the loss of weight in infants without a superficially evident cause) that is not explained by simple feeding problems. It is well known that mentally defective children tend to be small in stature. Children with congenital infections, chromosomal abnormalities, and significant neurological impairment such as cerebral palsy, particularly, fail to thrive. Emotional deprivation and physical neglect or abuse, including the withholding of food, are commonly associated with failure to thrive.

5.   Convulsions. These point to a disorder of the central nervous system.

6.   Cyanotic attacks or severe apneic spells. Cyanosis usually indicates respiratory insufficiency, which may be due to primary lung disease or intracranial hemorrhage. If it persists several days, it suggests congenital heart disease.

7.   Phenylketonuria (PKU). PKU is an inherited metabolic disease that, if untreated, causes mental retardation, seizures, growth retardation, and eczema. It can be fairly well controlled by dietary treatment (that is, by giving very little of the amino acid, phenylalanine, which the child cannot metabolize properly). If untreated, the phenylalanine rises to high levels in these children and is quite toxic to their central nervous system.

8.   Abnormal neurological signs in the neonatal period. Examples of this would be poor Moro's reflex, high pitched cry, spasticity or extreme floppiness, poor suck.

9. Severe illness such as meningitis and encephalitis. Meningitis is an infection of the meninges, which are the enveloping tissues around the brain and spinal cord. Bacterial meningitis not uncommonly leaves in its wake defects such as mental retardation, deafness, cranial nerve palsies, and so forth. Encephalitis is an infection of the brain tissue itself.

POSTNATAL

1. History of physical or emotional abuse of the child.

2. Microcephaly (small head size) noted consistently over a period of time.

3. Macrocephaly (large head size) noted consistently over a period of time.

4. Atypical physical appearance, particularly of the face and head. Any child with a peculiar appearance should be assessed for neurological and developmental problems.

ENVIRONMENTAL

1. Single parent.

2. Very young mother (under 15 years). Teenage pregnancies, particularly of the young teenagers, are rising rapidly. Several complications of teenage pregnancy have already been described. As a rule, the younger the mother, the greater the likelihood of a poor pregnancy outcome and the greater chance that both the mother and infant are at risk. With young mothers, there is a marked increase in perinatal deaths and infant deaths. The infant is more likely to be underweight, born prematurely, and have shown signs of fetal distress during labor, manifested by depression at birth.

It has been shown that adolescents as a group, particularly those under age 15, show a consistently poor pregnancy performance. While these problems were at first thought to be biologically related to the adolescent's physical immaturity, it is becoming clear, with the exception of a small pelvis in a very young teenager, that medical complications are more often the result of psychosocial factors. To exacerbate matters, there is a tremendous deficit of prenatal care in this population.

Offspring of adolescent mothers develop less well in childhood. The children at greatest risk are those born to multiparous adolescent mothers (mothers with more than one offspring). Children born of an adolescent mother are more likely to have repeated a school grade than children of older women. Such children also have a notable rate of accidents. Some studies show an increased prevalence of handicapped children in this population as well. Increased child abuse, neglect, and delinquent behavior have been reported among adolescent mothers.

Other risk factors commonly seen in pregnant teenagers, in addition to lower socioeconomic class, are cigarette smoking, use of alcohol and drugs, and poor nutrition, which are not age-related but affect all pregnancies.

Recent research shows that good prenatal care and attention to psychosocial and economic problems of pregnancy can reduce the perinatal deaths and complication rate for pregnant teenagers. The school nurse, along with other team members, can and must become involved with teenagers in discussing parenting, marriage and family planning, the importance of nutrition, and the dangers of cigarette smoking, drugs, and alcohol to the developing fetus. Nurses and other supportive professionals can help the pregnant teenager obtain prenatal care early and regularly.

3. Premature child or very sick newborn who had a long hospital stay. The effects of birth complications on later development can be mediated by the attitudes of the child's caregivers.

4. Large family.

5. Low socioeconomic class coupled with other high risk factors. It has been shown that low birth weight infants born into middle class socioeconomic groups with well-educated parents do well, in marked contrast to low birth weight infants born into a low socioeconomic class, who do significantly less well in both growth and development. Social and economic status appear to have much stronger influences on the course of development than perinatal history.

6. Observed poor mother-child interaction.

7. History of child abuse in a sibling.

8. Historical poor relationship of the mother with her mother.

9. History of psychiatric illness in one or both parents.

FOLLOW-UP OF HIGH RISK INFANTS

Infants who have one or more significant high risk factors in their history should be followed closely in several areas:

1. Growth, height, weight, and head circumference. If the head circumference, height, or weight is rapidly crossing percentile lines on the growth chart, either up or down, the child should be investigated further.

2. Complete physical examination. It is suggested that all premature infants have an ophthalmological examination by an ophthalmologist in the first 6 months of life because of the higher risk of visual problems in this group. It is also recommended that every child who has a history of significant hyperbilirubinemia, therapy with antibiotics that are known to be ototoxic, a family history of deafness, a lack of response to the bell, or delayed language development should have a formal audiogram.

3.   Frequent developmental screenings. This can be done by using the Denver Developmental Screening Test (Frankenburg and Dodds, 1967), the Gesell Infant Scales (Gesell, 1925, 1940), the Developmental Screening Inventory, or similar devices. It is important to evaluate the quality of children's performances on a screening test, as well as whether they pass or fail. Not infrequently children may have an abnormal means of accomplishing a task that must be noted (an example is the hypertonic child who bears weight early, for a pathological reason).

4.   Careful neurological evaluations. In addition to having a traditional neurological examination, the child should undergo other neurological tests by a competent health professional, such as a nurse practitioner, who has knowledge of the normal time sequences of development, including the disappearance of the primitive reflexes and the development of automatic responses. Asymmetrical primitive reflexes, persistence of primitive reflexes after their usual disappearance, or delay in the development of automatic responses are often early indicators of a significant motor problem before gross abnormalities in muscle tone or movement are apparent. It is essential as part of the neurological examination to assess how the child performs in a *functional* way; for example, observe whether the 9-month-old child has a well-developed pincer grasp, or whether the 12-month-old child drags one foot when walking. Such observations often help identify subtle neurological abnormalities that may be interfering with the child's development and are not apparent on the routine neurological examination.

5.   Assessment of the maternal-child interaction. Mothers not infrequently have difficulty in making an attachment to their high risk infant, particularly to those infants who have been sick and required long stays in the nursery or to those with developmental delays. These children are commonly viewed as quite fragile and may not be as responsive or gratifying to their mother, making it difficult for her to relate in a warm, loving, and comfortable manner. As these children often have greater needs for stimulation, it is important to assess the maternal-child interaction on each visit. If distance is noted in the relationship, the professional should attempt to help the mother become more comfortable and more involved with her child.

A pediatrician, an allied health associate, or a nurse can follow the high risk child in a comprehensive manner by checking the above suggested areas frequently during the first 18 months of life. This can be done at the time of routine checks and immunizations, such as 1 to 2 weeks after discharge from the nursery; then every 6 to 8 weeks thereafter until 6 months of age; and then again at 9 months, 12 months, and 18 months. If developmental lags or neurological abnormalities are noted, the child should be referred for a more extensive assessment and early intervention.

REFERENCES

Frankenburg, W. K., and Dodds, J. B. 1967. Denver Developmental Screening Test. J. Pediatr. 71(2)181–191.
Gesell, A. 1925. The Mental Growth of the Preschool Child. Macmillan Publishing Co., New York.
Gesell, A. 1940. The First Five Years of Life. 2nd Ed. Harper & Row, New York.

SUGGESTED READINGS

Babson, S. G. 1970. Growth of low birth weight infants. J. Pediatr. 77(1):11–18.
Battaglia, F. C., and Lubchenco, L. O. 1967. A practical classification of newborn infants by weight and gestational age. J. Pediatr. 71(2):159–163.
Beintema, D. J. 1968. A neurological study of newborn infants. Clinics in Developmental Medicine 28: Heinemann Imported Books, New York.
Cooke, R. E., and Levine, S. 1968. The Biologic Basis of Pediatric Practice. Mcgraw-Hill Book Co., New York.
Dargassies, S. T. 1966. Neurological maturation of the premature infant of 23 to 41 weeks gestational age. In: F. Falkner (ed.), Human Development. W. B. Saunders Co., Philadelphia.
deLone, R. 1979. Small futures: Inequality, Children, and the Failure of Liberal Reform. The Carnegie Council on Children. Harcourt Brace Jovanovich, New York.
Frankenburg, W., and Camp, B. 1975. Pediatric Screening Tests. Charles C Thomas, Springfield, Ill.
Hoskins, T., and Squires, J. E. 1973. Developmental assessment: A test for gross motor and reflex development. Phys. Ther. J. 53(2):117–126.
Osofsky, H., and Schaefer, G. 1978. High risk obstetrics. Clin. Obstet. Gynecol. Harper & Row, Hagerstown, Md.
Paine, R., Brazelton, T. B., Donovan, D. E., et al. 1964. Evolution of postural reflexes in normal infants and in the presence of chronic brain syndrome. Neurology 14(11):1036–1048.
Paine, R. S., and Oppe, T. E. 1966. Neurological examination of children. Clinics in Developmental Medicine, Vol. 20/21. Heinemann Imported Books, New York.
Sameroff, A. J., and Chandler, M. J. 1975. Reproductive risk and the continuum of caretaking casualty. Review of Child Development Research, Vol. 4, pp. 87–244. University of Chicago Press, Chicago.
Vaughan, V., McKay, R. J., and Behrman, R. 1983. Nelson Textbook of Pediatrics. W. B. Saunders Co., Philadelphia.
Warshow, J. 1979. Symposium on fetal disease. Clin. Perinatol. W. B. Saunders Co., Philadelphia.

IV. Vision Screening

James Sprague, M. D.

DEFECTS IN VISION ARE COMMON in children, and vision screening is popular in clinics and health facilities. However, the conditions to look for, the tests to use, and the definition of a correct referral are not agreed upon by experts in the ophthalmologic and optometric professions. The National Society for Prevention of Blindness and most ophthalmologists favor checking monocular visual acuity at distance only (National Society to Prevent Blindness, 1982). The optometric community, on the other hand, tends to favor multiphasic screening to evaluate visual performance in such areas as binocularity, accommodative efficiency, and ocular motor skills, in addition to visual acuity (American Optometric Association, 1979).

Practitioners outside the vision subspecialties frequently feel insecure dealing with eye problems, and the controversy about vision screening is confusing to many practicing ophthalmologists and optometrists. Evaluation of the merit of various philosophies of screening is beyond the scope of this chapter. However, screening techniques are basic and simple; familiarity with their use should help the practitioner feel comfortable working with ocular problems. (For definitions of some of the terms discussed here, see Glossary of Terms at end of this chapter.)

THE VISUAL PATHWAY

The visual pathway (Figure 1) starts at the retina and continues into the optic nerve, which partially decussates in the chiasm. The optic nerve is then known as the optic tract, and it terminates at the lateral geniculate in the thalamus. The tract consists of fibers from homonymous parts of the two retinas. From the thalamus, the visual pathway extends to the occipital cortex via the calcarine radiation. The occipital lobe has three histologically distinct parts, classified by Brodman as areas 17, 18, and 19. Area 17, or the striate cortex, receives the visual radiation (Miller, 1982). Area 18, the parastriate cortex, is thought to integrate the visual impulses. Area 19, the peristriate cortex, coordinates vision with other brain functions, such as speech and hearing.

Visual cognitive function is thought to be based in the angular gyrus on the dominant side, since adults with acquired alexia often have lesions in this area. "Alexia" is usually considered the acquired loss of comprehension of the written word with subsequent inability to read. "Dyslexia" is used more generally for children who are "poor readers." The anatomical reason of dyslexia is not known.

There are acuity problems specific to each stage of the anatomical pathway. Changes in shape of the cornea are responsible for most refractive errors. Opacities in the visual media, such as corneal scars, cataracts, or vitreous opacities may interfere with the formation of a sharp optical

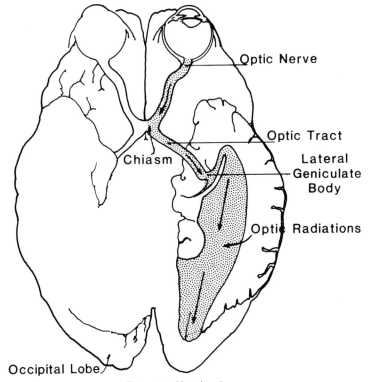

Figure 1.   Visual pathway.

image on the retina. In the child under 6–8 years old, these commonly lead to amblyopia (see below). Retinal and optic nerve lesions interfere with the transmission of the retinal image to the brain. Structural anomalies of the brain may interfere with the optical pathway.

Such lesions interfere with the mechanical transmission of an image to the occipital cortex. The resulting decreased vision should be detected by visual acuity screening. Lesions within the visual association areas of the brain, including those thought to lead to learning disabilities, such as dyslexia, are not detected on routine acuity or strabismus screening.

CONDITIONS IDENTIFIED BY SCREENING

1.   Amblyopia. Amblyopia is usually defined as decreased vision in one or both eyes by two or more lines on the Snellen visual acuity chart in the absence of any obvious ocular pathology. The two principal etiologies are unequal refractive error (anisometropia) and strabismus. In both conditions the affected eye is not used and the visual input is suppressed at the cortical level. Such suppression results in failure of stimulation of the pathway from the eye to the brain and of part of the occipital cortex.

Amblyopia can be reversed with optical correction and patching of the sound eye to force the child to use the amblyopic eye. This treatment, however, is usually effective only before the ages of 6 to 9 years and is most effective prior to 4 to 5 years (Parks, 1975).

2.   Strabismus. In addition to visual acuity, screening programs often include tests for strabismus or misaligned eyes. Straight eyes require normal orbital anatomy, normal extraocular muscles and fascial connections, and normal convergency with accommodation. In addition, equal vision is important even if it is poor, since monocular poor vision often results in strabismus. Finally, the straight-eyed child must have normal fusional ability, which results from a complex sensory motor system. This system centers the object of regard on the macula of each eye and keeps the visual axes of the eye parallel.

Approximately 40% of strabismus cases are congenital, mostly esotropia (crossed eyes). Strabismus with onset in the preschool and school years is usually accommodative esotropia. These patients are either farsighted or over-converge to an accommodative stimulus. The condition may be corrected with glasses, including bifocals, with topical medications, with surgery, or a combination. Intermittent esotropia may become manifest in the preschool and school years, although this condition often starts in early childhood.

The complications of untreated strabismus include amblyopia, loss of binocularity, and psychological maladjustment from the cosmetic defect. Amblyopia is the major treatable complication of untreated strabismus and the comments above about screening for amblyopia with monocular visual acuity apply here.

3.   Refractive Error. There are three types of refractive error: 1) myopia, or nearsightedness, where the patient sees better at "near" than at "far" distance; 2) hyperopia, or farsightedness, where the patient sees better at a distance than close up; and 3) astigmatism, which affects both near and distance vision.

The myopic child typically has difficulty reading the blackboard but has adequate stimulation of the visual pathway because of good near vision. Delayed therapy affects a child's ability to perform at distance, but does not lead to strabismus or to amblyopia. Uncorrected hyperopic children will be blurred for near, and also may be blurred for distance. In addition, they may develop strabismus, specifically accommodative esotropia (Burian and von Noorden, 1972). The child with astigmatism will have poor vision for both distance and near, and, if severely affected, can develop amblyopia, which is typically corrected by proper glasses. The myopic child, therefore, should be identified by distance visual acuity testing, although children with small amounts of myopia may pass screening.

Hyperopic children will have decreased distance visual acuity if their hyperopia is severe, and may have dereased near vision if the hyperopia is mild. This is the rationale for including near visual acuity in visual screening. Children with a large degree of astigmatism will have poor vision at distance, which will be picked up on monocular visual acuity. Children with mild astigmatism may pass routine screening.

SCREENING TECHNIQUES

Vision acuity tests used to check monocular visual acuity vary on the age, developmental status, and cooperation of the child. The most accurate method is to use either Snellen letters or the standardized illiterate "E" game. This test can usually be done with preschool children over the age of 4 years. The cooperative child is given an occluder and shown a chart at a standard distance with "E"s that decrease in size. Since children with amblyopia respond better to single symbols than to symbols in a line, it is preferable to show a child either a full chart or a full line of letters and have an assistant point to the individual symbols that the child is to identify.

The criteria for passing this test vary on the age of the child (Table 1). The eye develops its adult anatomy by the age of 12 months, and only grows slightly from that point on. However, visual acuity frequently does not reach the 20/20 level until the age of 5 or 6 years. Therefore, the screening criteria generally used are 20/50 for 3-year-olds, 20/40 for 4-year-olds, and 20/30 for 5-year-olds.

Criteria for rescreening include:

1. The child who has a two-line difference from expected visual acuity for age. For example, a 5-year-old is expected to see 20/30; if the child is only able to read the 20/50 line, he or she should be referred.
2. The child who has a two-line difference in acuity between the two eyes. For example, if a 5-year-old is able to read 20/40 in one eye, but is able to read 20/20 in the other eye, he or she should be referred as having a possible refractive error or amblyopia.
3. The child who squints during the testing and seems to read the letters more slowly than average. Although this is a subjective impression,

Table 1.   Expected visual acuity level by age

Age	Vision	Usual test
3	20/50	Allen/Picture Cards
4	20/40	Allen/Picture Cards or "E" Game
5	20/30	"E" Game or Snellen Letters

many of these children have refractive errors and should be rescreened.

Younger children or developmentally delayed children may not be able to perform the "E" game, but may be able to recognize the Allen Picture Cards. (See Table 2 for other suggested tests for delayed children.) The child is shown the picture cards, one card at a time, at a 15-foot distance, until he or she has named three of the pictures correctly, or has given the wrong answers. The cards must be well-lighted. These steps are then repeated with the other eye.

The 15-foot testing distance gives a Snellen visual acuity of 20/40, which is appropriate for a 4-year-old child. Criteria for rescreening are: failure to name the pictures at this distance; squinting, which suggests a refractive error; and consistently poorer performance with one eye, which suggests amblyopia.

(The "E" test, Allen Picture Cards, occluder, and spinning toy, along with instructions and scoring forms for these and the cover-cross-cover test are available from LADOCA Project & Publishing Foundation, Inc., 51st Ave. & Lincoln St., Denver, CO 80216.)

SCREENING TESTS: STRABISMUS

Although strabismus is estimated to occur in 1%–2% of normal children, many children with large angle deviations are identified prior to being seen in a screening program. Therefore, the number of screening positives is small.

Larger angles of strabismus can be detected by the corneal light reflex test. The patient is asked to fixate a target either at a distance or nearby, and the position of a light reflex on the cornea is observed. The reflexes should be mirror images. This test is simple, can be done without touching the child, and with little cooperation. However, it may miss small and even moderate angles of deviation.

The Cover-Cross-Cover test (Figure 2) relies on the patient maintaining fixation while the examiner alternately covers the eyes. If the eyes are straight, no movement is seen. If the child is esotropic, the fixating eye will be straight and the other eye turned in. When the fixating eye is covered, the fellow eye turns out to take up fixation, and the previously fixating eye turns in under the cover. If the child is exotropic, the uncovered eye will turn in rather than out.

Screeners performing strabismus tests have difficulty recognizing variations of normal, such as poor fixation, and may not appreciate true abnormals. Therefore, lay screeners should be trained with abnormal children, or videotape presentations, and then achieve reliability during the screening period.

OTHER TESTS

Numerous other tests have been suggested for screening use. There is controversy as to whether they add significantly to overall screening sensitivity (detecting abnormals) without decreasing specificity (referring normals). Moreover, questions have been raised if "abnormals" detected by additional screening tests benefit greatly by therapy, and, in fact, if the children referred require any therapy (Frankenburg and Camp, 1975). These controversial tests, which are not detailed here, include the Plus Lens test, stereo tests, and vision testing machines (Foote and Crane, 1954).

In addition, teachers are sometimes asked to watch for such signs as squinting or rubbing the eyes, or for symptoms such as diplopia (double vision).

EXAMINATION TECHNIQUES FOR
CHILDREN WITH DEVELOPMENTAL DELAY

Strabismus or amblyopia occurs in as many as 40% of children with a developmental delay or mental retardation (Edward, Price, and Weisskopl, 1972). Since the incidence of these problems is so high, many centers specializing in developmental pediatrics routinely obtain an ophthalmological consultation on these children. In addition to documenting visual acuity and the presence or absence of strabismus, the ophthalmologist can also estimate the child's objective need for glasses by cycloplegic refraction and examination of the fundus.

Normal fixation is judged central, steady and maintained; a fixation light should be imaged in the pupillary center, there should be no nystagmus (involuntary movement of the eyeballs) and the child should remain attentive as the target is moved. Fixation is then evaluated with the other eye covered. Some children object to an examiner approaching them. Occlusion can be attempted using an adhesive patch and remaining distant from the child. If the child consistently objects to covering one eye, poorer vision is suggested in the uncovered eye and amblyopic therapy will probably be indicated.

IMPLICATIONS FOR SCREENING

Vision screening should identify preschool children with amblyopia, strabismus, and refractive error, all of which respond best to early therapy. Screening should also identify children with changing refractive errors, usually myopia, who do not perform their best in school because of poor vision. Since screening is designed to identify the asymptomatic patient, a

Table 2. Visual acuity tests for the difficult-to-test child

Test	Type of response	Advantages	Disadvantages	Commercial outlet
Snellen E	Label or point in direction of test target	Short test administration time	Child must know concepts of up, down, right and left and be able to point reliably in all four directions	American Optical Buffalo, NY 14215
		Has both a near point and far point test		Western Optical 1200 Mercer Street Seattle, WA 98109
			Target is 10 or 20 feet from child for far testing	Bernell Corp. & Others 422 E. Monroe Street South Bend, IN 46601
Sjogren Hand	Label or point in direction of test target	Short test administration time	Child must know concepts of up, down, right and be able to point reliably in all four directions	American Optical Buffalo, NY 14215
		Has both a near point and far point test		Western Optical 1200 Mercer Street Seattle, WA 98109
			Target is 10 or 20 feet from child for far testing	Bernell Corp. & Others 422 E. Monroe Street South Bend, IN 46601
Lawson Chart	Label colored pictures pictures of food items	Short test administration time	Requires accurate verbal labeling	Milton Roy Co. Sarasota, FL 33578
		Not directional in response	Target is 20 feet from child	
			Colors may provide extraneous cues	

Test	Response	Characteristics	Notes	Source
HOTV (Lippmann)	Match or label letters H-O-T-V	Short test administration time Not directional in response	Has far point chart only Target is 10 feet from child	Good-Lite Co. 1540 Hannah Avenue Forest Park, IL 60130
Lighthouse Flashcard	Label or match pictures: house, apple, umbrella	Short test administration time Not directional in response Has both near point and far point tests	Target is 10 feet from child Threshold is based on the first incorrect response	New York Association for the Blind 111 E. 59th Street New York, NY 10022
Allen Picture Cards	Label or match pictures	Not directional in response	Target is 12–20 feet from child	Western Optical 1200 Mercer Street Seattle, WA 98109 Bernell Corp. & Others 422 E. Monroe Street South Bend, IN 46601
Parsons Visual Acuity Test	Direct pointing response to pictures: hand, cake, bird	Not directional in response Has both near and far point tests Both tests are given at 13 inch distance	Longer test administration time Requires more screener expertise Cost of materials is greater (?)	Bernell Corp. & Others 422 E. Monroe Street South Bend, IN 46601

Parsons Vision Screening Project for the Difficult-to-Test, Parsons Research Center, University of Kansas Bureau of Child Research, Parsons KS 67357

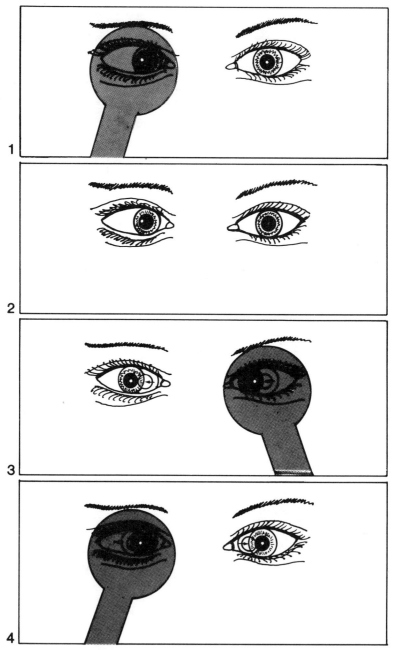

Figure 2.   Cover-cross-cover test.

child who complains of poor acuity or who reads well only from the front of the room, should be referred, regardless of the result of screening.

Most children injured at school are seen by a physician. However, checking the visual acuity of a child with facial injury may give the school nurse an indication of how urgent the referral should be. Usually good visual acuity in an injured eye suggests that major ocular injury has not occurred.

Routine screening should be performed during the preschool years and then at intervals during school. One method is to screen children in 1st, 3rd, 5th, 7th, and 10th grades, as well as any new students recently enrolled.

REFERENCES

American Optometric Association. 1979. Guidelines on Vision Screening. American Optometric Association, St. Louis.

Burian, H., and von Noorden, G. 1972. Binocular Vision and Ocular Motility. C. V. Mosby, Co. St. Louis

Edward, W. C., Price, W. D., and Weisskopl, B. 1972. Ocular findings in developmentally handicapped children. J. Pediatr. Ophthalmol. Strabismus 9:162–167.

Foote, F. W., and Crane, M. M. 1954. An evaluation of vision screening. Except. Child. 20:153–161.

Frankenburg, W. K., and Camp, B. W. 1975. Pediatric Screening Tests. Charles C Thomas, Springfield, Ill.

Miller, N. R. 1982. Walsh & Hoyt's Clinical Neuro-Ophthalmology. 4th Ed. Williams & Wilkins Co., Baltimore.

National Society to Prevent Blindness. 1982. Children's Eye Health Guide. Publication No. 202. National Society to Prevent Blindness, New York.

Parks, M. M. 1975. Ocular Motility and Strabismus. Harper & Row, Hagerstown, Md.

Reinecke, R. D., and Simons, K. Amblyopia screening and stereopsis. In: New Orleans Symposium on Strabismus. C. V. Mosby, Co. St. Louis.

GLOSSARY OF TERMS

Amblyopia   Decreased vision in one or both eyes without ocular disease. Usually due to strabismus or refractive error.

Anisometropia   A difference in the refraction of the two eyes.

Astigmatism   Irregular refractive power of the cornea or lens so that light from a point source is not focused at a point.

Esotropia   Convergent strabismus, the nonfixating eye deviates inward (crosseyed).

Exotropia   Divergent strabismus, the nonfixating eye turns outward (wall-eyed).

Hyperopia   Farsightedness; sees better at distance.

Myopia   Nearsightedness; sees better at near.

O D   *Os dextra*, right eye.

O S   *Os sinistra*, left eye.

Refractive Error   The defect in the power of the cornea or lens to bring an image into focus on the retina, usually corrected by glasses or contact lenses.

Snellen Chart   A standard chart for checking visual acuity. The numerator shows the testing distance, usually 6 m (20 feet). The denominator is the distance from the patient at which the letters or symbols subtend an angle of 5 minutes of arc.

V. Early Identification and Intervention for Auditory Problems

Marion Downs, M. A.

SCREENING FOR HEARING LOSS IN EARLY INFANCY and through school age has been mandated for Early Periodic Screening, Diagnosis and Treatment (EPSDT) programs, and is strongly recommended for all health and education agencies. Fortunately, nurses and other health care professionals are in a good position to utilize a range of methods to screen for early hearing problems.

A large number of screening options are available and within reach of any agency or program that deals with infants and young children. The screening techniques that have been developed satisfy, in general, the prescribed requirements for efficient programs. Efficiency, of course, is technically expressed in terms of specificity and sensitivity. Specificity refers to how well the test identifies normal individuals. Sensitivity refers to how well the test identifies abnormal individuals. The problem is that in order to obtain true measures of sensitivity and specificity one must subject the entire population being screened to a criterion test—in this case, a professional audiological assessment by an acknowledged expert or experts. There is only one report of this having been done for newborn hearing screening—a report from Israel (Feinmesser and Tell, 1957). The Israeli study followed some 85% of 17,000 infants who were examined for high risk factors and who were given hearing screening tests. In the U. S. the difficulty of getting a large normal population to return for testing seems insurmountable, because there are insufficient numbers of babies returning to public health clinics or other public agencies that routinely test for hearing.

No reports in this country on newborn screening studies even approach the thoroughness of the Israeli study. There are impressive figures, however, on the Crib-O-Gram technique, the brain stem evoked response (BSER) and the High risk register (HRR). The yield in these screens is so much higher than any projected estimate that one can hardly doubt their high sensitivity and specificity even if the entire population did not receive a criterion test.

IDENTIFICATION OF CONGENITAL DEAFNESS AT BIRTH

Several acceptable options are available at present for hearing screening in the newborn nursery. There seems to be a technique for every budget, ranging from the economical high risk register to the fairly expensive brain stem evoked response audiometry. Clearly, the availability of these options makes it mandatory for any hospital or public health department to institute some type of newborn screening procedures.

The High Risk Register

There has been general agreement that a small number of high risk categories will produce an acceptable yield of infants with hearing loss. The list of categories that has been recommended in a 1982 statement by a National Joint Committee on Infant Hearing (consisting of representatives from the American Academy of Pediatrics, the Academy of Otolaryngology—Head and Neck, the American Speech-Language-Hearing Association, and the American Nurses Association) includes:

1. A family history of childhood hearing impairment
2. Congenital perinatal infection (e.g., cytomegalovirus, rubella, herpes, toxoplasmosis, syphilis)
3. Anatomical malformations involving the head or neck (e. g., dysmorphic appearance including syndromal and nonsyndromal abnormalities, overt or submucous cleft palate, morphologic abnormalities of the pinna)
4. Birthweight less than 1500 g
5. Hyperbilirubinemia at a level exceeding indications for exchange transfusion
6. Bacterial meningitis, especially *H. influenzae*
7. Severe asphyxia, which may include infants with Apgar scores of 0–3 or who fail to institute spontaneous respiration by 10 min and those with hypotonia persisting to 2 hours of age

These categories may be identified in different ways for different institutions, the first and most basic being a simple procedure applicable to state public health departments. The second applies to individual hospital programs.

State Public Health Department Procedure   The at-risk categories can be compiled by public health departments in a very simple manner because four of the high risk categories are usually available on the infant's birth record. These categories are the bilirubin count, the head and neck defects such as cleft palate, the birth weight of the child, and the Apgar score. Thus, a simple reference to the birth record will produce four of the categories for risk.

The other categories can be obtained by an interview conducted by the nurses in the hospital, who will ask for family history of childhood deafness and for history of rubella during pregnancy (see Table 1 for sample interview form). Meningitis will be evident from the child's record. This information will be reported to the public health department to form a central register for all babies who are at risk for hearing loss.

In instances where such programs have been initiated (H. Weber, personal communication) the state health department has given training to audiologists, and has then referred high risk infants to these audiologists for follow-up testing. The Colorado State Department of Health's program, for example, has produced a yield not unlike that reported in programs using some of the more sophisticated methods of identification, so it would appear that the procedure is highly acceptable. The expense of

Table 1. Sample questions for mother's interview for high risk register

Do you know if the baby has any relatives who could not hear well before the age of 5? Think hard about all of your family and the baby's father's family.	Yes _____	No _____
Did you have German measles, rubella, or a rash with fever during your pregnancy?	Yes _____	No _____
Do you have any reason to worry that your child could have a hearing loss? If yes, why?	Yes _____	No _____

such a program is minimal, but it does require a supervisor's time to compile the register and arrange for the follow-up.

Individual Hospitals Procedure   The seven-category register can be compiled by nurses, audiologists, or trained volunteer personnel (Northern and Downs, 1970). A central office is usually necessary to keep the records of the register and to mail letters or telephone parents of infants who are on the register, who are then asked to return to the hospital for follow-up testing during their children's first few months of life. The previously mentioned statement prepared by the Joint Committee recommends follow-up by 2 months of age, but no later than 6 months of age.

The designated personnel can conduct the interviews of the mothers that will ascertain family history and rubella history. In addition, these personnel can search both the child and the mother's records for the presence of any of the other high risk categories. A sample form for the chart review is shown in Table 2.

The known yield from such a program is one deaf child in 40–60 children in the high risk register (Downs, 1978). In the general population this is a yield of 1 in 500, which indicates that the technique is satisfactory in terms of numbers identified.

In a hospital, the expense of such a program can be minimal (Downs, 1978), the greatest cost being the maintenance of a central register and the cost of mailing follow-up letters to parents. The follow-up testing may be borne by the hospital if so desired, or it may be charged to the parents. (Most hospitals add a $5–$10 charge to newborn nursery expenses to cover the cost of the high risk register.)

Crib-O-Gram

The Crib-O-Gram is an automated system for screening an infant in the newborn nursery. It consists of a motion-sensitive transducer placed under the crib mattress, an associated amplifier, an automated timing device, a strip chart recorder, and a loudspeaker. At preprogrammed intervals the machine turns itself on, records a minimum of 10 seconds of baseline crib activity, presents a two-second 90 db stimulus peaking at 3000 Hz and records crib activity during a stimulus presentation (Simmons, 1975).

Table 2.   Sample items for high risk register interview in hospitals

Is birth weight less than 1500g?	Yes _____	No _____
Was 5-minute APGAR total or less?	Yes _____	No _____
Abnormalities of head or neck:		
Cleft palate?	Yes _____	No _____
Cleft lip?	Yes _____	No _____
Abnormal or malformed ears?	Yes _____	No _____
Was unconjugated bilirubin over 20 mg.% or did baby have exchange transfusion?	Yes _____	No _____
Did baby have meningitis?	Yes _____	No _____
Did baby have multiple apneic spells in nursery?	Yes _____	No _____

Simmons (1975) reports identifying 1 deaf child in 30 or 40 failures in the intensive care unit where these instruments have been utilized. This represents one in 300–400 in the general population and, again, is an acceptable yield. With the exception of the initial expense of purchasing the instrument, states Simmons, use of the equipment involves a low cost ratio per child identified.

Brain Stem Evoked Response Audiometry

As reported by Hecox and Galambos (1974) and others, the usual Brain Stem Evoked Response (BSER) technique is to attach standard electroencephalograph (EEG) electrodes to the scalp at the vertex and the mastoid region and to place an earphone over the ear that will deliver clicks at approximately 37 per second to the ear. The electrophysiological responses to these clicks are extracted from the amplified EEG signal by an averaging computer, and the BSER tracings are displayed on a strip recorder. The records consist of a sequence of waves in which waves I, III, and V stand out prominently at high intensities; as intensity drops, their amplitudes diminish and their latencies increase. To make an audiological diagnosis, one finds the weakest stimulus that produces wave V for the approximate threshold, then establishes the wave V latency obtained at each intensity.

Several instruments for BSER procedures have been developed, ranging from a screening instrument reported by Peltzman (1980) to the standard BSER instrumentation. The options for application of BSER are:

1.   To test the entire newborn population. This would involve considerable expense and would perhaps not be cost-effective, as at least 500 babies would have to be tested in order to identify 1 with a hearing loss.

2.   Testing in the intensive care unit exclusively. This is not recommended, as children in the regular nursery who may be at risk for deafness would not then be identified. In one year's screening pro-

gram at the University of Colorado Health Sciences Center, it was found that of 8 babies who were identified as having hearing impairment 7 had been in the regular nursery, one in the intensive care unit.

3. Testing with BSER of babies in the intensive care unit, plus follow-up of those who are on the high risk register. Such a combination of high risk register plus BSER screening is perhaps the most effective of all screening protocols. Where expense is no object, this is the protocol that should be utilized for the most effective screening. Even with this protocol it is still necessary to arrange follow-up audiologic testing of the high risk infants. Some of the potential causes of hearing loss may result in a later-appearing hearing loss. For example, some hereditary deafness does not manifest itself until some time after birth, and the deafness from maternal rubella also can appear at a later time.

The early identification of congenital deafness allows intervention procedures to be initiated at the most optimal time for the development of language concepts. As Greenstein et al. (1976) have shown, the earlier that a hearing loss is identified and training begun, the better will be the speech and language skills of the child.

IDENTIFICATION OF ACQUIRED HEARING LOSS

Like screening for congenital deafness at birth, screening for acquired hearing loss can be accomplished at several levels of cost effectiveness, of sensitivity and selectivity, and of acquired competencies. The techniques vary with age and with the kind of facility that sponsors the testing. The range is such that any facility, be it a public health clinic, physician's office, or audiology clinic, can initiate some type of hearing screening to fit its needs.

In addition to actual hearing screening, impedance testing—or "tympanometry"—is recommended as an adjunct to all screening of the infant and older child. The tympanometer is an instrument that reveals the status of the middle ear by testing the "impedance," or resistance, of the eardrum to a tone that is delivered through an ear insert. The insert is positioned in the ear canal by means of a sealed ear mold, and air pressure is forced in and out to vary the resistance of the drum. The result is a measurement of the resistance that shows whether there is fluid behind the drum. Studies have shown that tympanometry has a 96% correspondence with good pneumatic otoscopy done by experts (Paradise, Smith, and Bluestone, 1976).

The only limitation of tympanometry is that with children under 7 months of age it can misidentify some ears with middle ear effusion, or otitis media. One study (Paradise et al., 1976) showed that for infants under 7 months more than 50% of the ears with otitis media were missed by tympanometry. The normal ears were identified correctly. However, with this limitation in mind, tympanometry is recommended as an integral part of any hearing screening program.

Birth to 5 Months

The principle underlying screening for birth to 5 months is that babies in this period are constantly assaulted by what is to them noise of a loud and unfamiliar nature. They are unable to sort out what should be meaningful to them from the background of generalized ambient noise that surrounds them. Therefore, they cannot be expected to attend in any observable way to the particular sounds that are chosen to be used for testing. All they can be expected to do at this age is to respond reflexively to sudden loud sounds that are presented. Because the stimuli that must be used to obtain a reflex need to be quite loud, one can make only gross determinations of the hearing level of infants at this age through screening techniques. Where more sophisticated instrumentation is available, such as brain stem evoked response audiometry, small numbers of babies may be screened. However, BSER is contraindicated for screening older infants because most often they need to be sedated in order to have the test applied.

Three types of screening tools—noisemaker testing, electronic instruments, and a questionnaire—will be discussed in relation to screening at this age. The tools may be used in either public health clinics or physicians' offices.

1. ***Noisemaker Testing.*** Noisemakers can be selected that give a sudden loud noise over 75 dB, or the loud horn from a commercially-available Hear-Kit can be used to produce startle reflexes. The reflexes consist of: a Moro's type startle, or jump, in which the whole body makes a visible startle reflex; an eyeblink reflex or auropalpebral response in which there is a definite blinking of the eyes, which may or may not be accompanied by startle response of some type. A noise with a very sudden onset is required to produce this kind of reflex, so one must be careful to select the right kind of noisemaker.

2. ***Testing with Electronic Instruments.*** Instruments that have been suggested for newborn behavioral screening will be appropriate for use at this age. One such instrument is the Leridan audioscreen, produced by Leridan Associates, 520 Barker Pass Rd., Santa Barbara, Calif. This emits a high frequency, narrow band of noise that can be presented at 90 dB or 100 dB for the purpose of producing a startle.

3.   *Hearing and Communication Questionnaire (Table 3).*
The mother can be asked the questions, on the Hear Kit questionnaire, as shown in Table 3, which are graded to various age levels. The application of such a hearing questionnaire is necessary to distinguish the hearing questions from those related to general development. The reason for this distinction is related to the following questions on the standard communication scales that assume a relationship to hearing:

a.   *Does the baby turn to a sound?* One characteristic of deaf infants is that they are unusually visually alert, and attend to movement in their peripheral vision. Therefore, if the mother reports that her child turns around to an interesting sound or when his name is called, the question must be asked if she is sure that the sound is out of his peripheral visual field.

b.   *Does the baby babble and increase his or her vocalizations when talked to?* One of the erroneous assumptions that has been made in the past is that a deaf infant does not babble or make sounds like a normal hearing infant. However, until the age of 6

Table 3.   Sample questions to ask the mother at well-baby examination

2 Months		
Have you had any worry about your child's hearing?	Yes ＿＿＿	No ＿＿＿
When he's sleeping in a quiet room, does he move and begin to wake up when there's a loud sound?	Yes ＿＿＿	No ＿＿＿
Does he smile at you when you smile at him?	Yes ＿＿＿	No ＿＿＿
4 Months		
Does he try to turn his head toward an interesting sound, or when his name is called?	Yes ＿＿＿	No ＿＿＿
Does he laugh and giggle without being tickled or touched?	Yes ＿＿＿	No ＿＿＿
6 Months		
Does he lift up his head and chest with his arms?	Yes ＿＿＿	No ＿＿＿
8 Months		
Does he enjoy ringing a bell or shaking a rattle?	Yes ＿＿＿	No ＿＿＿
Can he pick up two objects, one in each hand?	Yes ＿＿＿	No ＿＿＿
10 Months		
Does he try to imitate you if you make his own sounds?	Yes ＿＿＿	No ＿＿＿
12 Months		
Is he beginning to repeat some of the sounds that you make?	Yes ＿＿＿	No ＿＿＿
Can he say "mama" or "dada"?	Yes ＿＿＿	No ＿＿＿

The full questionnaire to 2 years of age is available with the Hear Kit from BAM World Markets, Box 10701 (Dept. BHK), University Park Station, Denver, CO 80210.

months, deaf infants sound exactly like normal infants; they
babble just as much; they increase their vocalizations when the
parent appears and coos at them just as the normal child; and
only an expert phonetician can identify the subtle qualitative differences in the babbling sounds that the deaf child makes.
Therefore, great care has been taken in the Hear Kit questionnaire not to assume that the baby's vocalizations are any index
of his ability to hear.

c. *Does the baby say "mama" at 1 year of age?* A misleading indicator is the mother's report that her baby says "mama" at around
the age of 1 year, and that therefore the baby must be hearing.
Oddly enough, the mothers of most deaf children make such a
report, and it is universally true that a profoundly deaf infant will
appear to be saying "mama" at around 1 year of age. Actually
what he or she is saying is "amah," which is the most primitive
sound that can be made, involving the almost animal-like "ah"
vocalization plus the coming together of the lips. It has been
postulated that one of the reasons for the development of this
sound is that in infancy the baby is carried close to the mother,
and feels the vibrations or hears low frequencies of her voice,
and is thus stimulated to perpetuate the sounds. At any rate, the
sounds soon drop off, and nothing remains but the "ah" vocalization in a strident voice.

5 Months to 2 Years

By 5 months the infants' faculties are well enough organized to begin to
search for a particular sound in their environment, particularly if that
sound has become meaningful to them, or if they have been conditioned to
respond to it. Again, it is important to understand the various levels of
testing procedures that are available for this age group, as well as their cost
effectiveness and the level of confidence that one can apply to their use.
The available options are appropriate for either public health clinics or
physicians' offices.

Noisemaker Tests   Public health nurses in England for over 35
years have been screening the hearing of infants using noisemakers originally recommended by the Ewings (Ewing and Ewing, 1944). A standardization of the noisemaker tests, called the Sytcar Hearing Test (Sheridan,
1957), is currently being used in England and Israel (Feinmesser and Tell,
1976). In the early 1950's a similar procedure was proposed by the Maryland State Public Health Department (Hardy, Dougherty, and Hardy,
1959). A modification of these techniques has been developed by Downs
(1981).

Levels of Confidence   Only two studies are available that identify the level of confidence of noisemaker tests. The first is the Feinmesser and Tell (1976) report, mentioned at the beginning of this chapter, that followed 17,000 babies from birth to age 3. A modification of the Ewings' test, the Stycar Hearing Test (Sheridan, 1957), was performed by regular clinical nurses especially trained and briefed for this purpose. The sensitivity of this test was demonstrated to be 59%, indicating that almost 30% of the positive conditions may be missed with this test. However, depending upon the circumstances, this sensitivity may be acceptable.

Another noisemaker test was shown to have a much greater sensitivity than the Stycar, namely the BOEL test, developed in Sweden by Dr. K. S. Junker (Mencher, 1978). This test was reported in a study by Huber, Stangler, and Routh (1978) to have 86% sensitivity in identifying children who had otitis media.

For the nurse who is willing to practice zealously and perfect necessary skills on many infants, a simplified procedure using noisemakers has been suggested by the author (Downs, 1981). A guide to the procedure and a set of measured noisemakers designed specifically for such testing are included in the Hear Kit (see Table 3).

Tympanometry   For the older infant and child, tympanometry is an extremely useful, accurate tool. It is not a foolproof technique, however, and a great deal of training and experience is required for accuracy. One of the most common errors is to press the ear insert against the wall of the ear canal, thus producing a tympanogram that indicates fluid in the ear. This error can occur with both a screening tympanometer with hand-held insert, or a clinical, head-band type.

Another source of error is when the child is crying hard or fighting the insertion. Every effort should be made not to alarm the child about the test. A little patience is required in first gently placing the insert and then letting the child become accustomed to it before the seal is secured. The person administering tympanometry should have thorough training in the procedure, which must include spot checks in its use by an expert.

Because hearing screening does not identify all the ear pathologies in children, tympanometry should be an integral part of every screening program for older ages as well as in infancy. The author recommends that the guidelines suggested by the American Speech-Language-Hearing Association be followed (see Table 4).

Conditioned Visual Response Audiometry   A large number of clinicians have developed screening tests based on conditioned visual response audiometry (VRA). This technique has been described in clinical use as appropriate for children over 6 months of age (Wilson, Moore, and Thompson, 1976). The technique includes the presentation of an attractive visual stimulus along with an auditory stimulus, thereby conditioning a

Table 4. Middle-ear screening criteria

Classification	Results of initial screen	Disposition
I. Pass	Middle-ear pressure normal[a] or mildly positive/negative[b] and acoustic reflex present.[c]	Cleared; no return.
II. At-Risk	Middle-ear pressure abnormal[d] (and acoustic reflex present); or acoustic reflex absent (and middle-ear pressure normal or mildly positive/ negative).	Retest in 3–5 weeks. a) If tympanometry and acoustic reflex fall into Classification I, PASS. b) If tympanometry or acoustic reflex remain in Classification II, FAIL and refer.
III. Fail	Middle-ear pressure abnormal and acoustic reflex absent.	Refer.

From: American Speech-Language-Hearing Association. 1979. Asha 21:238–288.
[a] Normal: Pressure peak in range ±50 mm H O.
[b] Mildly Positive/Negative: +50 to +100 mm H O/-50 to -200 mm H O.
[c] Present: Pen or meter needle deflection judged to be coincident with the reflex eliciting stimulus at levels of 100 dB HL for contralateral stimulation, 105 dB SPL for ipsilateral stimulation at 1000 Hz.
[d] Abnormal peak outside the ranges described for Classification I.

child to look for the visual stimulus when he or she hears the auditory signal. H. Weber (personal communication) has modified this technique for use in well-baby clinics. Two loudspeakers are positioned on poles on either side of the chair where the mother sits with the child on her lap. An attractive toy is placed on the instrumentation panel that controls the signals and is held in front of the baby. The tester activates the auditory signal at a loud level and when the child looks, the tester reinforces with a flashing light on a doll. Once conditioning has been established the tester reduces the signal to a predetermined screening level, usually around 20 dB, and presents the signals on alternate sides. The stimuli consist of warbled pure tones and a woman's voice speaking to a baby.

Hearing and Communication Questionnaire Apply the appropriate questions from the Hear Kit questionnaire (see Table 3.)

Follow-up

The ideal referral for children who do not pass the at office or clinic screening is to a center where an otologist can examine the child's ears and an audiologist can test the child's hearing in a standard sound room. Even if the high risk children are passed at their office or clinic visit, they should continue to be screened at every succeeding visit, for the danger of developing a hearing loss in these children is always present.

Exceptions are infants in the high bilirubin category and those in the small birth weight category. Once a professional has determined that there is perfectly normal hearing in such a child at 3, 6, or 9 months, there is no reason to recheck the hearing regularly, other than what is normally done for non-high risk children.

SCREENING FOR THE PRESCHOOL AND SCHOOL-AGE CHILD

It is vital to the child's cognitive development that he or she hear well during the early years of life. Studies have shown that even mild hearing losses can cause learning problems (Bond, 1935; Downs,1975; Ling, 1972; Holm and Kunze, 1969; Luke, 1965; Scottish Council for Research in Education, 1956). Ninety percent of the hearing losses of children who reach school age are caused by otitis media, and can be remedied medically or surgically.

A small number of sensorineural losses will not have been discovered during the first 2 years of life. These may only number about 10% of all the hearing problems in children, but they are important because of the severity of the handicaps they cause. Two screening tools, described below, are presently available to nurses.

Guidelines for Pure Tone
Hearing Screening of the Young Child

Any agency that attracts preschoolers in large numbers should undertake a hearing screening program. These agencies include: 1) doctors' offices; 2) public well-baby clinics; 3) neighborhood health centers; 4) Headstart programs; 5) public preschool programs; and 6) child care centers.

Pure Tone Screening Tests for the 2- to 3-Year-Old

1. Selection of a quiet room for the testing should be made carefully, keeping in mind the building noises and the traffic in the area. (Ideal screening conditions call for commercial soundtreated booths, but realistically most clinics cannot afford this purchase.)
2. Check the hearing of your own ear or that of another person whose hearing has been previously tested and is known to be normal. If those thresholds have not changed more than 5 dB, the instrument should be in good calibration.
3. Play-conditioning procedure for testing the 3- and 4-year-old child includes the following:
    a. Have available a pegboard, a ring tower, plain blocks, or other simple toy that is motivating to young children.
    b. With headphones on your ears, take a block (or a peg, etc.) and hold it up to one ear as if listening. Make believe you hear a sound, say: "I hear it," and put the block on the table.

   c. Put the phones on the child's ears and hold his hand with the block up to his ear.

   d. Sound a 50-dB tone at 1000 Hz and guide his hand to build the block tower. Repeat once or twice and then see if he can do it alone. If he can, proceed to the next step.

   e. Set the hearing level at 25 dB and repeat the test. Sweep through the other frequencies (1,000 Hz, 2,000 Hz, and 4,000 Hz.).

   f. Rescreen any child who fails to respond to any one frequency in either ear.

   g. Refer for a threshold audiogram the child who still fails to respond at even one frequency.

Tympanometry (See above description.)

SUMMARY

Hearing screening techniques are available for children of any age in a hierarchy of sophistication and expense. For newborns, the high risk register, the Crib-O-Gram, the brain stem evoked response, audiometry, and behavioral screening have been sufficiently studied to be recommended for application.

For the older infant, the array of available hearing screening tests for clinics or physicians' offices includes noisemaker tests, visual reinforcement audiometry, and tympanometry.

The preschool and school-age child should be screened with pure tone audiometry, using play conditioning techniques for the younger 3- to 5-year-old preschoolers. Tympanometry is highly recommended as an adjunct to the screening.

Every clinic, hospital, and physician's office has at its disposal well-researched methods for hearing screening that fall within any budget. Therefore, the omission of such screening from examination protocols can no longer be tolerated.

REFERENCES

Bond, G. L. 1935. Auditory and speech characteristics of poor readers. Teachers' contribution to education #657. Teachers College, Columbia University, New York.

Downs, M. P. 1975. Hearing loss, definition, epidemiology and prevention. Public Health Reviews 4:3–4.

Downs, M. 1978. Report of the Colorado newborn screening program In: G. T. Mencher and S. E. Gerber (eds.), Early Diagnosis of Hearing Loss, Grune & Stratton, New York.

Downs, M. P. (1981) The Hear-Kit Manual. Hear-Kit, BAM Marketing, Denver.

Ewing, I. R., and Ewing, A. W. G. 1944. The ascertainment of deafness in infancy and early childhood. J. Laryngol. Otol. 59:309–338.

Feinmesser, M., and Tell, L. 1976. Evaluation of methods for detecting hearing impairment in infancy and early childhood. In:G. T. Menchor (ed.), Early Identification of Hearing Loss: Proceedings. S. Karger, Basel, Switzerland.

Greenstein, J. M., Greenstein, B. B., McConville, K., and Stellini, L. 1976. Mother-Infant Communication and Language Acquisition in Deaf Infants. Lexington School for the Deaf, New York.

Hardy, J. B., Dougherty, A., and Hardy, W. F. 1959. Hearing responses and audiometric screening in infants. J. Pediatr. 55:382–390.

Hecox, K., and Galambos, R. 1974. Brainstem auditory evoked responses in human infants and adults. Arch. Otolaryngol. 99:30–33.

Holm, V. A., and Kunze, L. H. 1969. Effect of chronic otitis media on language and speech development. Pediatrics 43:833–838.

Huber, C. J., Stangler, S. R., and Routh, D. K. 1978. The BOEL test as a screening device for otitis media in infants. Nurs. Res. 27:178–180.

Joint Committee on Infant Hearing. 1982. Position statement 1982. Pediatrics 70(3):496–497.

Ling, D. 1972. Rehabilitation of cases with deafness secondary to otitis media. In:A. Glorig and K. S. Gerwin (eds.), Otitis Media, pp. 249–253. Charles C Thomas, Springfield, Ill.

Luke, J. 1965. A comparative investigation of language abilities among children with limited auditory impairment. Unpublished master's thesis, Colorado State University, Ft. Collins.

Menchor, G. T. (ed.). 1976. Early Identification of Hearing Loss: Proceedings. S. Karger, Basel, Switzerland.

Northern, J., and Downs, M. 1978. Hearing in Children. 2nd Ed., Williams & Wilkins Co., Baltimore.

Paradise, J. L., Smith, C., and Bluestone, C. D. 1976. Tympanometric detection of middle ear effusion in infants and young children. Pediatrics 58:198–206.

Peltzman, P. 1980. Paper presented at the International Audiology Society, Kracow, Poland.

Scottish Council for Research in Education. 1956. Hearing Defects in School Children. University of London Press, London.

Sheridan, M. D. 1957. Manual for the Stycar Hearing Test. Mere, Upton, Park Slough, Bucks, National Foundation for Educational Research in England and Wales.

Simmons, F. B. 1976. Automated hearing screening test for newborns: The Crib-O-Gram. In:G. T. Menchor (ed.), Early Identification of Hearing Loss: Proceedings. S. Karger, Basel, Switzerland.

Wilson, W. R., Moore, J. M., and Thompson, G. 1976. Soundfield auditory thresholds of infants utilizing visual reinforcement audiometry (VRA). Paper presented at the American Speech and Hearing Association Annual Convention, Houston.

VI. Sensorimotor Integration in Children

Patricia Komich, O.T.R.

OUR UNDERSTANDING OF CHILD DEVELOPMENT as well as the growth of the central nervous system has changed vastly in the past few decades. At one time, very young children were simplistically considered to possess only limited ability to discriminate among aspects of the world around them or develop complex skills at an appreciable rate, and to relate passively to people and their environment. It is now known that infants are capable not only of discrimination processing in several areas, but can integrate several functions into skillful acts, and be extremely active in searching out or responding to stimuli in their environment.

Where development was once described and measured solely in the broad terms of gross motor, fine motor-adaptive, language, and personal-social function, these areas are now being broken down into more specific functions. Fine motor-adaptive, for example, can be further delineated into subareas of sensorimotor, visual-perceptual, and perceptual motor function.

The components of the central nervous system are identified via levels of hierarchy in control (spinal, midbrain to cortical) or by specific types of function (motor, sensory, language, or visual). The more important and complex aspect of integration of the central nervous system components can now be appreciated. In the normal functioning brain, the central nervous system can be viewed as an information-processing mechanism that screens, analyzes, interprets, organizes, and selects information available in the external and internal environment. This is thought to be a continuous process that is in turn modified by the reactions made by the individual. Reactions are adaptive and made meaningful when all systems function to interpret, organize, and select stimuli in an integrated manner. Behavior can then be seen to move from reflexive to purposeful in increasingly complex patterns.

When there is dysfunction or damage in the central nervous system, one may see disruption not only in specific areas but, more significantly, in the integration of several areas. Thus, it is important to know the components of different functions, their normal developmental sequences, and how they interrelate with other areas.

The development of sensorimotor function, visual-perception, and fine motor coordination occur simultaneously and are interdependent. When well integrated, these areas help develop what is frequently referred to as perceptual motor function.

Perceptual motor function can in turn be viewed as a base for higher level skills such as self-care activities, prewriting, and prereading activities. Most perceptual motor development is best observed in the development of play behaviors. The sections that follow briefly outline developmental sequences of subareas of perceptual motor function. Neuromotor development and gross motor function (indicating reflex and vestibular function) are not included here but are discussed in the chapter on gross-motor function.

SENSORIMOTOR DEVELOPMENT

Tactile, or Haptic Function

Tactile sensation begins to develop *in utero* and is the most predominant sensation at birth. While not refined in terms of discrimination, the awareness of touch, pressure, and temperature allows the child to respond to his or her environment on a reflexive basis by orienting toward (rooting/-grasp) or avoiding stimuli (self-protective withdrawal-pain).

Tactile stimulation given during caring for children, particularly in the neonatal period, enhances their awareness of themselves and their physical (bodies) boundaries. It also provides them a basis for pleasure and trust in being touched and encourages them to reach out and explore the environment through touching.

The oral area is the most sensitive to tactile stimulation and plays the leading role in a child's investigation and discrimination of features of the environment during the first few weeks and months.

As development of visual and motor systems allows for more control and movement, tactile exploration and discrimination are enhanced. Reflex grasp and touch avoidance initiated by tactile stimulation mature and are modified to develop more sustained tactile contacts of self and the environment.

As arm control and grasp are improved, manipulation of objects is sustained and tactile perception becomes more discerning. In the early months it is suspected that the focus of tactile perception is to explore self (face, feet), surface, and textures. Hard-soft, rough-smooth, verbal labels will come much later, but the tactile experience establishes a meaningful association to be connected with visual and verbal cues. For most children, haptic perception (the sense of touch and active exploration and fingering of objects by hand) plays a joint or even secondary role with visual perception in development of object recognition and discrimination. For the blind child, however, haptic perception assumes a leading role. Formal studies of haptic development identify the child of 2½–3½ years as able to recognize familiar objects, but clinical observation of blind children indicates this is possible at 8 months.

Proprioception

The most important co-function in developing sensorimotor awareness and discrimination is that of proprioception. Proprioception is the sense by which muscular motion, weight, and position are perceived. When muscles are contracted or stretched and/or joints are bent, straightened, pulled, or compressed the individual receives internal (own body) awareness of that process. Information is received whether the action is passive or active.

Infants begin to receive much passive proprioception from being handled and placed in various positions. In this initial period, proprioception and tactile sensations allow them to actively snuggle into a holding position. Reflexive and random body movements are felt (without aid of vision) and gradually repeated until voluntary control is exercised.

Vision later plays a role in guiding motor movements of the head, trunk, arms, and fingers, but tactile and proprioception sensation establish the basis for planning and executing motor activity. One must know (feel) where one is to begin with, know in what direction and with how much force one is moving, and when the goal has been achieved. Proprioception provides the base for such awareness in the form of constant sensory-feedback.

Visual Perception

While visual perception eventually assumes a dominant role in processing sensory information in the environment, its beginnings are dependent on subcortical sensory processes. Input from vestibular-proprioception and touch systems is required for development of vision from a crude sense of movement and dark-light contrast to a sophisticated perception of spatial orientation and detail form.

Initial visual attention and tracking is reflexive in nature and best oriented to slow-moving stimuli with dark-light contrasting edges. Rapid development in terms of acuity, fixation, and tracking in turn enhances depth perception, figure ground perception, and appreciation of solidarity and texture. As visual explorations become better controlled and the infant can sustain his or her attention on objects from different perspectives, form recognition is made by comparison and association. Higher-level discriminations of detail, size, position, and spatial orientation follow. Gradually, visual perception ability not only transfers data to other systems for richness of information (by sight we know if something is soft, light, or rough), but translates line symbols into thought (reading) or guides motor movements for writing.

Development of Hand Function

The development of controlled hand function emerges as motor behavior. Tactile and proprioception responses and visual attention mature and integrate from reflexive to voluntary action. Progress can be observed in gradual changes of controlled reach, and in refinement of grasp patterns to prehension, voluntary release, and finally isolated finger control.

Gross bilateral use occurs initially, followed by control of unilateral movement with transference of objects from one side to another. As control of both sides is refined, a period of bilateral use or interchange occurs. Finally a lead or dominant hand emerges and the other hand acts as an assistant or holding tool while the lead hand does precise manipulations. Hand preference for refined manipulations usually occurs between the second or third year, when specific tool use is beginning (eating with a spoon). Delay in establishing a preferred hand frequently occurs in children with a delay in fine motor control.

PLAY BEHAVIORS REFLECTING PERCEPTUAL-MOTOR DEVELOPMENT

Phase I—Reflexive/Trial-Error Response (Approximately 1-3 Months)

During Phase I, reflexive behaviors initiate activity and responses are brief. Each area is active in responding but not well integrated, that is, the child looks to see, touches and moves to feel, and grasps on reflex. The child is gradually able to sustain responses in each area and then begins to combine behaviors by reaching for visual stimuli or visually attending to hand movements.

Phase II—Simple Manipulation (Approximately 3-6 Months)

During Phase II, there is rapid development in each area and in integration between them. Visual attention, tracking, and discrimination are increased. Tactile exploration of the body and surfaces in the environment is more frequent, and feedback from movement varies the intensity and direction of movements. These combine to provide control in reaching, grasping, and transfer of objects from one hand to another. Simple motor schemes of mouthing, banging, squeezing, and shaking objects occur. Emphasis for the child during this period is not on the object itself as much as it is on the processes of reaching, grasping, and mouthing.

Phase III—Manipulation and Exploration (Approximately 6-12 Months)

Now that basic functions of visual, sensory, and motor actions are established, attention focuses in Phase III on elaborating and refining control of movement as well as exploring the properties of objects. The child begins to hold objects longer for sustained visual inspection. He or she selects movements that elicit appropriate responses from objects, such as squeezing a rubber toy and shaking a noisy toy. Refined manipulation includes prehension of small objects and poking with individual finger control to move the action parts of objects. Improved tactile and proprioception functions enable the child to modify intensity and direction of movements when handling objects of different weight or density. The child begins to recognize a vast array of objects, uses them appropriately (bottle, cup), and begins to combine them in new ways. The child can empty containers, stack or pile by trial and error, and begins to fill objects into a container as he or she gains control of release. The child enjoys imitating those adults actions that he can perform, and begins to imitate new actions. Repetitions of motor acts and experimentations of these motor behaviors on a variety of objects is the hallmark of this period.

Phase IV—Simple Construction
(Approximately 14 Months 3 Years)

In Phase IV the child begins to phase out the predominance and rapid growth of sensory and motor functions and begins the greater elaboration of visual perception and refined perceptual-motor manipulation. Simple take-apart and put-together activities and toys are the most favored. As prehension and voluntary release are mastered, empty and fill activity is expanded. The child can stack blocks higher and higher. He or she can take pegs out and put them in, put lids on cans, rings on a stick, and string beads. Because visual perceptual discrimination of shape and size has developed, the child can now do simple puzzles (basic shape and single piece forms) and nest a series of 3 size cups. The child also enjoys imitation of activities he or she observes around the house, such as washing the car with mother or dad or sweeping the rug.

Phase V—Imagination-Construction
Play (Approximately 3-4 Years)

There is now an increasing emphasis on imaginative play, that is, acting out familiar actions that have taken place in the past (driving to the gas station or store) and roles of daily life (play house). The importance of imaginative play in relation to perceptual-motor function is that by "play-acting" it is known the child is able to recall and plan motor sequences. Manipulation is further improved and the child enjoys toys that tax his or her dexterity as well as perceptual discrimination ability. Thus, construction toys that also require matching of shape, size, and/or color are varied (peg patterns, hammer nail, puzzles, Lego-blocks). Toys such as Lego blocks also allow for imaginative building. For example, the child will frequently build something first and then name it.

Phase VI—Pre-School Manipulative and Perceptual-
Motor Reproduction Skills (Approximately 4-6 Years)

During this stage of fine motor dexterity and perceptual motor function, the child is able to sustain attention for longer periods, gain greater command of individual finger control, and use tools such as pencils, crayons, and scissors. The degree to which the child enjoys and is skillful in this area determines his or her readiness for writing and possible reading activity. Hand preference is usually established by now, and leads to a refinement in tool control. If there is a delay in establishing a preferred hand, it is highly likely that use of tools will also be delayed. As coloring in of pictures teaches the child to control movement of the crayon in spatial direction, drawing of pictures teaches the child to translate visual images into motor planning and motor acts. Cutting and pasting also requires a high degree of bilateral integration, visual-spatial, and visual motor planning. Manipulation and reproduction of geometric shapes into meaningful representations as well as designs is the prerequisite to recognition and reproduction of abstract symbols for communication (reading and writing).

SCREENING AND REFERRAL

With the current increase in demand for early screening and identification of developmental delays, professionals in health and education must utilize good observational skills. Standardized screening tests, such as the Denver Developmental Screening Test (DDST) (Frankenburg and Dodds, 1967), provide a sampling of developmental levels in several areas (gross motor, fine motor-adaptive, language) with established norms. Through their use, one gains an appreciation of relative strengths and weaknesses in a child's overall development.

Other standardized tests, such as the Beery-Buktenica Developmental Test of Visual-Motor Integration (Beery, 1967), examine one specific ability area (copy design). Many standardized "school readiness" tests sample several areas of skill (visual recognition and discrimination, copy design, and auditory discrimination) that are considered important in academic success.

Screening tests should be selected that are appropriate to the age and level of the child being screened. The screener should be familiar with the norms and items of a test for a given population in order to appreciate the differences between delay in performance versus dysfunction. It is important to know the behavioral and psychosocial development of children in order to support the child and elicit the best performance. Obtaining a good developmental history from the parent should provide detailed information regarding past development and current behaviors. This should assist the screener to determine if there is need for further evaluation.

One of the most important criteria for assessing screening tests is whether the child is able at present to functionally perform daily activities on a par with his or her peers. Failing a specific item or falling below a specific score is less critical than the fact that a child is unable to perform many of the tasks that his or her peers are asked to perform. When a child is unable to participate in joint efforts and activities, it is important to be able to determine the cause. Referral for in-depth evaluation should be made to an appropriate professional. If a child is school-age, utilizing school specialists who have the most expertise in the area of concern may be the best place to begin. They, in turn, can refer the child to other experts if necessary. In the areas of fine motor, visual perception, and perceptual motor skills, one needs to refer to a therapist, such as an occupational therapist, who is accustomed to working with children who have motor, developmental, and sensorimotor delays. Such an individual has been specifically trained to provide testing in reflex assessment of perceptual motor and functional motor skills. A test frequently used by occupational therapists for children over the age of 5 is the Ayres Southern California Sensory Integration Test Battery (Ayres, 1980.) This set of standardized tests was designed to test children from ages 5 to 11 in visual-perception, fine motor, sensory discrimination, and visual motor integration skills. The administration and interpretation of the tests require specialized training and should only be performed by individuals who have had such training.

If the child has an overt motor problem with specific difficulties in motor control or coordination, referral to an occupational therapist or physical therapist who is well versed in neurodevelopmental testing and treatment is most appropriate. Neurodevelopmental testing and treatment is a theoretical approach that helps the tester understand how neuromotor development evolves, identifies the specific deviations from the norm, and assists the child to adapt and function at his or her highest potential. It is important to remember that whenever a child is referred for specific evaluation, the findings of any isolated test are meaningful only if they relate to the whole. The interpretation of findings must be correlated with the overall development of an individual child, with his or her background experiences and environment, with his or her past rate of development in different areas, and, in addition, should enable one to determine the child's strengths or weaknesses in a particular area. Interpretation of findings should also be related to the functional abilities or disabilities one might expect in that specific child.

When a child has not passed age-expected levels on a screening test and is referred for in-depth evaluation, one must determine whether the child's performance is: 1) immature; 2) demonstrates a specific dysfunction; or 3) whether there is retardation. The child's performance, though developmentally delayed for his or her chronological age, may be appropriate for his or her overall developmental age.

Immaturity

When a child's performance is delayed in many areas, but is still within normal limits—that is, less than a year delay—the child may simply be immature, and may not have any specific type of dysfunction. The cause of the child's immaturity may simply be that the child's development is slow. It may be that his or her exposure to the types of activities being tapped has been impoverished because of psycho-social or economic factors. The child may not need specific therapy or remedial programming, but simply more exposure to the tasks in which he or she is deficit, or may merely need an extended period of time in order to demonstrate normal maturation. It must be remembered that all children show some variance of development in accomplishing specific tasks. All children cannot be expected to walk, finger-feed, or even use scissors for cutting at a specific chronological age. Most children's performance may range 6 months above or below the general expected age norm for any specific task. This is particularly true for the child who has entered kindergarten or first grade without a preschool experience. If the child begins to achieve such expectations within a relatively brief period, one can feel more comfortable that it is a problem of immaturity rather than specific dysfunction.

Specific Dysfunction

When a child's profile in screening or in in-depth testing indicates that some areas of function are adequate for chronological age, but other areas are depressed and/or the child has historically been slow in achieving them, one can begin to support the finding of a specific dysfunction. Frequently, this type of child is considered to have, at the school level, a learning disability because specific areas of function do not permit him or her to learn as rapidly as others in the program in which the child is enrolled. Often this child can demonstrate a capacity to learn and understand in other areas of function that are adequate for age level. It is critical to identify this type of child and refer the child for specialized training in deficit areas in order to improve his or her overall performance.

Retardation

Some children show marked developmental delay that is greater than a year behind chronological age. Such delay in performance is found in many areas, including motor, language, and visual perceptual. It is important to identify this child as having overall developmental delay that is considered within a retardation level, so that the child's performance can be assessed and the developmental delay not regarded as a specific type of dysfunction appropriate for the child's overall developmental level. For example, many children with moderate to severe retardation will show delay in motor, visual-perception, and perceptual motor skills. These children may not need specific intervention for their perceptual motor delays, but rather a general developmental program that will assist them to continue to progress, even though at a much slower pace than their chronological age peers.

SCHOOL-AGE CHILDREN: INDICATIONS OF
FINE MOTOR AND PERCEPTUAL-MOTOR DIFFICULTIES

The identification of sensorimotor and perceptual-motor problems in the school-age child has become "popular" in recent years, almost to the point of over-emphasis. From the time the child enters kindergarten until third or fourth grade, anyone not achieving in reading, writing, or mathematics is considered to have perceptual problems and to be learning-disabled. This, of course, is false. The child may simply be immature, retarded, have a perceptual motor or emotional problem, or have been subjected to inadequate teaching.

Having a fine motor or perceptual motor problem does not necessarily make a child learning-disabled. The classification depends on the child's other skills, capacity to adapt, frustration tolerance, family's understanding and support, and the skill levels of the other children in the child's class.

The teacher is often the first to suspect a problem. When it is noticed that a child is not learning to write, read, or do mathematics as well as his or her peers, but seems to be "smart," the teacher is often puzzled. She may describe a child as "never finishing paperwork on time," or as one "whose writing is sloppy." She may feel the child is poorly motivated or a behavior problem. Sometimes the child may be seen as clumsy or aggressive on the playground. This is the time when screening is appropriate. Frequently, the school nurse is asked to test the child's general gross motor, vision, and hearing abilities. Psychological testing may also be requested to determine the child's overall cognitive abilities and/or to determine if there is a great discrepancy between verbal and performance skills. When screening is completed, findings must be reviewed and a decision made as to whether further testing is required.

The sections following briefly discuss common problems seen by a teacher or the school nurse in reviewing a child's behavior, either in screening or in the classroom. The problem areas are not all-inclusive, but are meant to suggest that when several indicators are noticed in a particular child, further screening or referral is probably merited.

Functional Vision

Acuity   The first line of investigation for any question of visual or perceptual problems is to determine whether visual acuity is adequate and whether there is good binocular vision. Excessive eye rubbing by the child or squinting when looking at distant stimuli are additional indicators for visual acuity screening.

Visual Tracking   It is also important to determine whether a child's ability to visually attend a target and to follow a moving target with smooth pursuit is adequate. The child should be able to keep track of an object in a horizontal, vertical, and circular pattern. These procedures are usually included in the nursing visual screening assessment program. The importance of not only the acuity, but the tracking seems most relevant in terms of children's ability to visually follow lines of print in reading and to keep their place, not only in the book, but in looking from the blackboard to the paper. A question of any deficits in this area merits a referral for more thorough ophthalmological examination. This is particularly important in the early school years, as this is a period of rapid growth and adjustment of functional vision. The most critical aspect of the visual tracking component is that the child be able to visually track a target with a minimum of head-turning. If there is not maintenance of head position with the eyes essentially moving, the efficiency in tracking will be limited. It is important that the eyes, in horizontal tracking, do not lose pursuit and/or jerk either at the midline or in the peripheral field. Consistent difficulty in this area is an important indicator for more detailed ophthalmological evaluation.

Visual Perception   It is not easy to determine all the components of visual perceptual discrimination. The most frequent aspects or indicators of a problem are usually found by the teacher in classroom performance if the child has trouble recognizing detailed discrimination of form, discriminating left/right orientation of letters, or discriminating visually similar words. The younger child, perhaps the kindergartener, may show a marked delay in recognition of color and size discrimination, as well as poor performance in completing multiple piece puzzles.

It is common for a child in kindergarten or even in the first few months of first grade to have difficulty in discriminating right/left orientation of similar letters. The problem at this time may reflect simply a matter of immaturity or inexperience. If difficulties discriminating positional changes persist past the first 6 months of first grade, screening or more in-depth evaluation is indicated, particularly when the child appears to be developing in other areas.

Another indicator of visual-perceptual discrimination difficulty is when the child frequently loses his or her place in copying words or sentences from the blackboard or when reading from a textbook. There may be a problem in eye tracking, but it may also be that the child's visual discrimination and memory are immature and that he or she cannot hold visual information long enough to read and scan the material properly.

A second indicator or potential problem area in visual-perceptual discrimination is the ability to visualize spatial rotations. A child who has good functional ability in this area, for example, knows left/right on himself, and can determine what is left and right in a reversed position, or the left/right side of a person in front of him. This is usually accomplished by the age of 7 or 8 years. A more simplistic aspect of this ability is demonstrated when the child, in solving puzzle pieces, realizes that an upside-down piece in front of him could be rotated and placed in the puzzle right side up in front of him. Spatial rotation ability is a precursor to writing abilities. Children learning to write first visualize where to start writing and on what side of the paper. They must be able to space the words in the right sequence and in the right spatial proportions in order to get the correct number of words or sentences on a line before coming to the end of the page. The problem most commonly seen in this regard by classroom teachers is the child who is unable to organize paperwork in reference to top/bottom/side/middle. The difficulty emerges in pasting activities as well as in writing tasks.

Poor Writing

The most frequent referral concerning children in the area of fine-motor and perceptual-motor skills is that of poor writing. This is a broad category that is discussed here in terms of the sub components that need to be identified in order to understand the dynamics of a child's poor writing ability. The assessment is best made in an in-depth evaluation by an occupational therapist; however, the components are included here to assist the school nurse or teacher in determining whether a problem may exist.

Fine Motor Coordination

1. *Posture.* The child's general posture in a sitting position at the desk should be sufficient to enable good head and trunk control and good stability at the shoulder and elbow, thereby allowing freedom of movement at the wrists and fingers. A child who has excessive high tone or low tone, who must lean on the desk and on his or her elbows, and/or has poor head position or fatigues quickly, will not have sufficient background posture control to free hand use for writing tasks. When there are problems in some of these basic components, one frequently sees the child, if not shifting the paper in order to write, shifting his or her total body while trying to draw or write words along a line or in different places on the paper. This behavior is common in later preschool and kindergarten classrooms. The paper also often slips to the floor, because the hand not writing does not assist in holding onto the paper.

2. *Lack of Hand Dominance in a Child Approaching First Grade or Beyond.* It is uncommon for a child not to have established a hand preference by first grade, at least for writing tasks. A preference is necessary for the child to refine movements in pencil control. Many children who have difficulty in refining gross to fine motor skills persist in this lack of hand dominance.

3. *Specific Pencil Grasp.* The child entering first grade should be demonstrating a dynamic tripod posture in holding the pencil. That is, the pencil is grasped distally, or near its point; precise opposition of thumb, index, and middle fingers maintains a hold on the pencil; and movement is

beginning to be localized from the wrist toward the joints of the fingers. When it is difficult for a child to maintain this posture, in which movements essentially occur in the fingers of the hand, we see most movement coming from the wrist and total arm. While such movement is normal for the kindergarten and first grade child, it should be resolved by the time the child is in second grade. A delay in this progression will make rapid and precise movement problematic for a child, likely causing much shifting of the trunk and upper arm, or shifting and rotation of the body or paper to compensate for lack of movement in the fingers. It is frequently seen in children who are unable to make fine patterned movements of thumb and finger opposition, or finger ab/adduction patterns. Some children may make these patterned movements in one hand, but are unable to do this simultaneously in both upper extremities. Problems in these areas are indicators of poor mechanical fine motor movements and will lead to difficulty in line quality in the child's writing or drawing and also to an early fatigue period. One may see the child's writing adequate in the beginning of the writing activity, but after five minutes the child begins to move slowly, loses control of line quality and "sloppy writing" occurs.

Perceptual Motor Reproduction Skills   Writing problems in this area stem not from difficulty in fine motor control, but rather in the ability to plan movements.

1. *Inability to Copy.*   A child has difficulty copying basic designs or letters, even though he or she can visually discriminate among them or recognize them. The problem occurs in the child's inability to know in what direction to make the movements or sequence of movements in order to reproduce that design. The child may be able to imitate someone else make these movements, but be unable to initiate the movement himself. This leads to writing or copying difficulties, whether the child is copying a design at close range on his desk or from the blackboard. The more severe problems of this nature are identified at the kindergarten and first grade levels when the child had difficulty learning to write his or her name, an early task that is learned and becomes rote. Some children do learn this rote aspect of writing, but encounter further difficulty when required to write all of the alphabet or multiple words or sentences. The reversal of small case letters such as *d* and *b*, *p* and *g* are the most frequent letter writing errors. There may be a motor planning problem for some children when making the transition from printing to cursive writing, in which the perceptual motor match of where and how to make the connections between letters in sequences is extremely difficult. For some children who are having a minor difficulty in this area it may appear that the child is simply slow in being able to complete the task. It is the effort that it takes for the child to process the information and execute it that is likely taking the child such a long time.

2. *Other Spatial or Directional Concept Errors.*   Such errors occur, for example, when a child knows how to make a letter correctly, but when using it in a word, the sequence of letters is out of order, despite the fact that he knows how to spell the word. Or the child may have trouble planning the spatial arrangement of words on the page so that he "runs out of space on a line" before finishing a word. The child may also have difficulty modifying or making his letters a uniform size. Obviously, all children have these problems in the beginning stages of writing, and these errors will be frequent in the kindergarten/first grade level, but persistence beyond the end of first grade is likely to indicate some type of perceptual motor problem.

3. *Translate Verbal Commands onto Paper.*   One of the more high-level and integrative of processing problems in the perceptual motor area is that of writing or drawing from a verbal command. In this task, the child must process an auditory message into a visual image and then into a motor act. For example: From an auditory command, the child receives an auditory signal to draw a circle. The child must change this auditory stimulus into a visual image of a circle and then change that visual image into a motor pattern or sequence of motor movements. As the child progresses and must encode auditory symbols for letters, words, and sentences, the entire process becomes more discriminating and more rapid; for many children, however, accomplishing all of the skills involved in this activity is extremely difficult.

SUMMARY

When a child is identified as having trouble with learning in school, particularly in terms of reading, writing, and spelling, the teacher must endeavor to identify the problems she suspects the child is having. She can do this through observation of activities and paperwork, through screening procedures of basic visual or motor difficulties, or through referral to the nurse for further assessment.

Once the child's apparent specific difficulties have been identified, the teacher and the school nurse can observe the child independently or together for screening and can 1) make sure that visual acuity is adequate, 2) make certain that eye mobility and motility are within normal limits, 3) check visual perceptual motor skills, and 4) check fine motor skills.

Indicators to watch for when administering the Beery Developmental Test of Visual-Motor Integration (Beery, 1967) to a child that might suggest visual motor/perceptual motor reproduction difficulties or fine motor coordination difficulties (*in addition to the total score*) include: 1) how the child holds the pencil, 2) in which hand the pencil is held, 3) how the child proceeds to reproduce the design, 4) whether the child has a tendency to shift his or her body, rather than making finer movement adjustments with his or her hand in drawing, 5) whether the child has a tendency to switch hands from page to page, and 6) whether the child's total score is more than a year behind that of his or her chronological age. (See also "Red Flag" concerns in Table 1.) Once the teacher and school nurse combine their findings, they can decide whether more extensive testing should be performed by special education support services, an occupational therapist already in the school system, or an outside agency.

Table 1. "Red Flags"—concerns for further evaluation
The following items should be checked by the teacher or nurse. When a number of findings occur in conjunction with developmental delay, referral for in-depth evaluation should be considered.

Visual Perception
Does not look at or briefly track a moving target (4 months); does not look at object held in hand (6 months)
May persist in fixating on lights (6 months)
Absence of eye contact with adult or objects
Inability to find a small piece of food on high chair tray
Does not anticipate feeding at sight of spoon, bottle, or cup
Infant does not look for toys as they roll or fall out of sight
Does not like simple one-piece puzzles or form boards (2 years)
Does not like to "look at picture books" or point to specific objects in picture (2 years)
Not interested in color, size, or shape in manipulation of play material (4 years)
Is not able to match color, size, or shapes (3 years)
Is not able to match letters, recognize name (school age)
Persists in confusing letter reversals past first grade
Delay in reading—word or letter confusion
Poor in copying from blackboard—loses place, skips words
Does not like to be blindfolded in games

Tactile Discrimination
Dislikes being cuddled or hugged
Dislikes being touched unexpectedly
Demonstrates excessive need to touch
Demonstrates self-stimulating behavior
Prefers mouthing of objects to tactile exploration beyond 8 months
Does not like to touch certain textures (rough-sharp)
May not feel pain easily or may be over-reactive
Does not like certain kinds of material in clothing

Vestibular Function
Exhibits more than the usual amount of rocking, jumping, and spinning, or likes fast movement more than most children
Dislikes swinging, bouncing, or being tipped upside down
Dislikes climbing on play equipment or balance
Can move quickly but not slowly

Table 1. *Continued*

Fine Motor—Grasp of Prehension and Manipulation
Asymmetry in function
Extreme of muscle tone (hyper/hypotonia)
Persistence of "fisted" hand postures
Delay in hands to mid-line (after 4 months)
Persistence of reflex grasp—delay of voluntary grasp
Delay in transfer of object from one hand to the other (after 6 months)
Delay in prehension after 1 year
Immature control or release after 18 months (cannot build block tower)
Lack of clear hand preference in routine feeding activity such as spoon use (by 3
    years)
Persistent delay in establishing hand preference (by 6 years)
Poor opposition of thumb to finger tips in successive pattern—both hands at one
    time (6 years)
Persistence of pronator grasp of pencil (beyond 5 years)

Perceptual Motor Function
Delay in reaching for objects
Delay in visual inspection of object while holding it
Lack of variation or manipulative pattern (shake, drop, bang, squeeze)
Delay in empty-fill play
Delay in stacking objects
Unable to complete single piece puzzles or basic shapes at 2½ years
Lack of interest in simple construction-type toys at 3 years
Dislike of paper-pencil/crayon activity for even brief time (4 years)
Unable to copy or imitate geometric shapes at age level
Poor in cutting or pasting tasks as compared to peers
Unable to dress or complete buttons at age level
Frequent shift of hand used as lead—or equal use
Inability to plan sequence of motor movements required in a manipulative task
Reversal of letters beyond first grade
Poor pencil grasp control—too tight—loose or awkward posture
Shifting of paper or body in coloring or drawing tasks (after first grade)

REFERENCES

Ayres, A. J. 1980. Sensory Integration and the Child. Western Psychological Ser-
    vices, Los Angeles.
Beery, K. 1967. Developmental Test of Visual-Motor Integration. Follett Publishing
    Co., Chicago.
Birch, H. G. 1981. Brain Dysfunction in Children. In: P. Black (ed.), Etiology, Diag-
    nosis, and Management. Raven Press, New York.
Frankenburg, W. J., and Dodds, J. B. 1967. Denver Developmental Screening
    Test. J. Pediatr. 71(2):181–191.
Gilfoyle, E., Grady, A. P., and Moore, J. 1981. Children Adapt. Charles B. Slack,
    Thorofare, N. J.

VII. Motor Development in Infants and Children
Assessment of Abilities and Detection of Abnormalities

Linda Lord, R. P. T., M. P. H.

NORMAL MOTOR DEVELOPMENT PROCEEDS in a regular, cephalocaudal progression, from mass, reflexive movements to specific voluntary movements. This orderly sequence is governed by the maturation of the brain and is dependent upon an intact nervous system.

The newborn baby exhibits innumerable reflexive patterns that later blend into voluntary patterns of movement and become unrecognizable as the reflexes themselves. These reflexes and early reactions are patterns of movement that are automatic responses to touch or movement and are the basis for voluntary movement. They are necessary for the initiation of movement, for the development of the postural system, and for avoidance of noxious stimuli.

Normal infants are flexor tone predominate and move toward developing increased extensor tone in their first year of life, as evidenced in their ability to hold up their heads, extend their trunks and legs, and then walk. Extensor tone develops first in the neck and shoulders, and is demonstrated by the infant's ability to prop on his or her forearms around 2 months of age. Full extension of the trunk and legs does not develop until the infant reaches 5 to 6 months of age. At this time infants are capable of the pivot prone position, allowing them to swivel around using their stomachs as a pivot point. As the brain matures, primary reflex responses give way to more mature secondary balance and righting reactions. The normal infant then develops the basic motor patterns including head and trunk control, sitting balance, coordination of the arms and then hands, ability to locomote by crawling or hitching, pulling to stand, and walking. These basic patterns of movement, in different combinations, evolve into more complex motor skills later seen in the 3 to 4 year old.

As knowledge of developmental disorders improves, there is an increasing need for physicians, nurses, and therapists to know the developmental motor milestones and the reflexes and patterns of movement on which these milestones are based in order to recognize as early as possible the deviations from normal. The need for early identification of abnormal movement patterns and delays in development in order to offer stimulation or therapeutic intervention for infants has been stressed for many years. Improved screening abilities are essential for *all* allied health professionals because of the increased number of individuals providing well- and sick-child care. Health professionals may find that using a developmental screening tool, such as the Denver Developmental Screening Test (DDST) (Frankenburg and Dodds, 1967), in conjunction with the reflex testing chart featured in Table 1 will give a more complete picture of an infant's or child's development. Noting that a reflex is or is not present without relating this finding to the developmental status of the infant does not allow one to make a full determination concerning the infant's abilities or needs. When the examiner understands the relationship between the presence of a reflex pattern and the development or lack of development of motor milestones, the examiner's data are of greater significance in describing an infant's individual development and level of functioning. (See Tables 2 and 3 for the major reflexes and their relationship to normal and abnormal development.) It is also extremely important for the examiner to be aware of the quality of a child's motor performance and to develop keen observational skills in order to detect more subtle problems. The preschool or school-age child who is described as awkward, clumsy, or incoordinated may have sensory motor problems that could have been remediated through therapy as an infant or toddler. The terms "awkward or clumsy" are often used to describe children with "soft" neurological signs or minimal brain dysfunction. These children frequently have problems with balance, poor strength, slightly abnormal muscle tone, difficulty with execution of rhythmical patterns of movement (skipping, jumping jacks, clapping rhythms), and poor spatial orientation and body awareness. They often look unstable, fall frequently, and have difficulty with their own body "boundaries," bumping into things and others. Awkward children frequently have inadequate sensory feedback and poor utilization of sensory information so that their motor performance is incoordinated. In order to detect more subtle motor problems in children by improving observational skills, a list of questions and statements has been developed to help guide examiners in their observations (see Tables 4 and 5).

For the best possible documentation of a child's development it is important to follow that child over a period of time. If, on any one visit, delays in motor development are noted, if strong reflex patterns appear to interfere with functioning, or the child's movements seem incoordinated, a close scrutiny of these areas at the next visit is warranted. Should these delays continue over a 2-month period, referral to a developmental evaluation clinic where a team of professionals could assess the child should be considered.

Adolescents who exhibit extreme awkwardness, or those who tend to be inactive and/or unwilling to participate in gym class, sports, or social dancing may also have a history of motor delays and difficulties. A review of descriptions of a child's early motor performance, plus his or her own personal history of abilities and problems may help determine the need for therapy at this stage. Adolescents and adults can certainly benefit from physical or occupational therapy for sensory motor and postural problems, although the results may not be as dramatic as might have been noted earlier.

Orthopedic and posture screening is critical for the entire pre-adolescent and adolescent population, but is especially important in the adolescent with motor problems, who is particularly at risk for developing back deformities and postural problems related to unequal use of the two sides of the body, deficient muscle tone, and a poor postural system. The most common back deformities identified in this population include scoliosis, kyphosis (hump back of upper spine), and lordosis (sway back affecting the lower spine).

SUMMARY

A careful look at a child's early motor development, movement patterns, righting and protective reactions can give a health professional a good idea of how a child's nervous system is functioning, can help identify problems early, and anticipate the need for intervention. Children with significant motor delays, and very abnormal muscle tone and reflex development may later show signs of cerebral palsy, mental retardation, or other brain dysfunction. Children with awkward movements,—"soft neurological signs"—that are more subtle or mild delays may later show signs of minimal brain dysfunction and school learning problems. All of these children can benefit from intervention from home stimulation programs and occupational and physical therapy input. They should, therefore, be referred for appropriate therapy. (See Table 6 for a listing of possible indicators of brain dysfunction.) The purpose of intervention is not to enable the child to become a competitive athlete, but rather to enable the child to gain more information about his or her environment through participating as fully as possible in peer related and school activities.

REFERENCES

Frankenburg, W. K., and Dodds, J. B. 1967. Denver Developmental Screening Test. J. Pediatr. 71(2):181–191.
Trembath, J. 1979. The Milani-Comparetti Motor Development Screening Test. Meyer Children's Rehabilitation Institute, University of Nebraska Medical Center, Omaha.

SUGGESTED READINGS

Fiorentino, M. R. 1972. The influence of primitive reflexes on motor development. In: Normal and Abnormal Development. Charles C Thomas, Springfield, Ill.
Milani-Comparetti, A., and Gidoni, E. A. 1967. Routine developmental examination in normal and retarded children. Dev. Med. Child. Neurol. 9(5):631.
Paine, R. S., Brazelton, T. B., Donovan, D., Drobaugh, J. E., Hubbell, J., and Learns, E. M. 1964. Evolution of postural reflexes in normal infants and in the presence of chronic brain syndromes. Neurology 4:1035.

Table 1. Reflex testing—newborn to 12 months (// = most accepted range; --- = upper or lower limits); L = left; R = right; P = prone; S = supine)

Note: For optimal test results, the infant should be alert and quiet and the examiner should be aware of the child's head position at all times during reflex testing.

Primitive Reflexes—Brain Stem		New-born	1 mo.	2 mos.	3 mos.	4 mos.	5 mos.	6 mos.	7 mos.	8 mos.	9 mos.	10 mos.	11 mos.	12 mos.
1. Sucking		//	//	//	//	//	//	//	---	---				
2. Rooting		//	//	//	//	//	//	---	---	---	---	---		
3. Foot grasp	L	//	//	//	//	//	//	//	---	---	---	---		
	R	//	//	//	//	//	//	//	---	---	---	---		
4. Hand grasp	L	//	//	//	//	//	---	---	---	---	---	---		
	R	//	//	//	//	//	---	---	---	---	---	---		
5. Asymmetrical tonic neck reflex (ATNR)														
Supine (posture)	L		//	//	//	//	---	---						
	R		//	//	//	//	---	---						
Supine (tone)	L		//	//	//	//	---	---						
	R		//	//	//	//	---	---						
Quadruped[a]	L													
	R													
6. Crossed extension														
Partial	L	//	//	---										
	R	//	//	---										
Full	L	//	//	---										
	R	//	//	---										
7. Tonic labyrinthine	P	//	//	//	//	//	---	---	---	---	---	---		
	S	//	//	//	//	//	---	---	---	---	---	---		
8. Symmetrical tonic neck reflex (STNR)														
Head extension							//	//	//					
Head ventroflexion							//	//	//					
9. Stepping		//	//	//	//	---								

143

Table 1. *Continued*

		New-born	1 mo.	2 mos.	3 mos.	4 mos.	5 mos.	6 mos.	7 mos.	8 mos.	9 mos.	10 mos.	11 mos.	12 mos.
10. Placing		//	//	//	//	//	//	//	//	//	//	//	//	//
11. Positive supporting														
Extension	L	//	//	//	//	···	···	···	···					
	R	//	//	//	//	···	···	···	···					
Extension flexion	L				//	//	//	//	//	//	//	//	//	//
	R				//	//	//	//	//	//	//	//	//	//
12. Moro's														
Complete	L	//	//	//	//	//	//							
	R	//	//	//	//	//	//							
Partial	L							···	···					
	R							···	···					
Midbrain Righting Reactions														
13. Head vertical	L		···	//	//	//	//	//	//	//	//	//	//	//
	R		···	//	//	//	//	//	//	//	//	//	//	//
14. Body righting on body rotation	L					//	//	//	//	//	//	//	//	//
	R					//	//	//	//	//	//	//	//	//
15. Landau														
Head					//	//	//	//	//	//	//	//	//	//
Head and thorax								//	//	//	//	//	//	//
Head, thorax, and legs										//	//	//	//	//
Protective Reactions														
16. Downward legs	L					//	//	//	//	//	//	//	//	//
	R					//	//	//	//	//	//	//	//	//
17. Sideways arms	L							//	//	//	//	//	//	//
	R							//	//	//	//	//	//	//
18. Backward arms	L									···	//	//	//	//
	R									···	//	//	//	//
19. Parachute	L										//	//	//	//
	R										//	//	//	//

Reference: Trembath, J. (1979). The Milani-Comparetti Motor Development Screening Test. Meyer Children's Rehabilitation Institute, University of Nebraska Medical Center, Omaha.
[a] No norms for this.

Table 1. *Continued*

KEY FOR REFLEX TESTING
Primitive Reflexes—Brain Stem

1. *Sucking reflex*—Finger placed on lips results in immediate sucking motion of lips; jaw drops and lifts rhythmically.

2. *Rooting reflex*—Corner of mouth lightly stroked outwards results in lower lip dropping at that corner. On continuation of this contact to cheek, tongue moves towards stimulus and head turns to follow it.

3. *Foot grasp* (Supine)—Pressure given to the ball of the foot with examiner's finger results in the toes grasping. (Standing)—Stimulation of the sole of the foot by contact with the table results in toes grasping.

4. *Hand grasp* (Supine)—Placing a finger in the infant's hand from the ulnar side results in fingers closing over the examiner's finger.

5. *Asymmetrical tonic neck reflex (ATNR)* (Supine)—Rotation of the head to the side (90°) results in flexion of the arm on the skull side and extension of arm on face side. If no motion occurs, note increase in flexor tone on skull side and increase in extensor tone on face side. (Quadruped)—Check for this reflex in the same manner in the quadruped position, when the child can maintain the all-fours position (at approximately 7 months).

6. *Crossed extension* (Supine)—Extend one leg with pressure at the thigh. At the same time, stroke the sole of the foot of the extended leg. Fully present if opposite leg flexes and abducts, then extends and adducts. Partially present if opposite leg flexes and extends.

7. *Tonic labyrinthine* (Supine)—Placement of the body in the supine position results in extension of the upper and lower limbs with minimal flexion of these extremities. When this is strong, the increase in extensor tone is also evidenced by difficulty in placing the arms and legs in flexion. (Prone)—Placement of the body in the prone position results in flexion of the upper and lower limbs and minimal extension of these extremities. When this is strong, the increase in flexor tone is also evidenced by difficulty in placing the arms and legs in extension.

8. *Symmetrical tonic neck reflex (STNR)*—Place infant in the quadruped position. Passive extension of the head results in increased extension of the arms and flexion of the hips. Passive ventroflexion of the head results in increased flexion of the arms and extension of the hips.

9. *Stepping reflex*—Holding the infant under his or her arms in the standing position and leaning the infant forward results in automatic walking steps that are rhythmical and demonstrate a heel strike.

145

Table 1. *Continued*

10. *Placing reaction*—Holding the infant under his or her arms in the standing position so that the dorsum of the foot brushes the edge of the table results in the foot being lifted and placed upon the table top.

11. *Positive supporting reaction*—Holding the infant under his or her arms to bounce infant on his or her feet elicits extension of both lower limbs, with plantar flexion of feet. This reaction may also elicit extension of both lower limbs, followed by flexion of the hips and knees.

12. *Moro's reflex*—Holding the infant in a semi-sitting position by supporting his or her back and head, allow the head to fall backwards (20° to 30°) by releasing support of the head. This produces a sudden extension and abduction of upper extremities, with opening of the hands, followed by flexion to the midline.

Midbrain Righting Reactions

13. *Head vertical*—Holding infant upright under his or her arms and tilting him or her 45° laterally results in bringing head back to the midline. Test both sides.

14. *Body righting on body rotation* (Supine)—Passively rotate the shoulder or hip. This results in segmental rotation of shoulders, trunk, and pelvis.

15. *Landau reaction* (Prone)—Suspend infant by holding him or her under upper thorax. This results in: a) first stage Landau, extension of head above shoulder level; b) second stage Landau, extension of head and thorax; and c) third stage Landau, extension of head, trunk, hips, and legs.

Protective Reactions

16. *Downward legs*—Holding infant under the arms, lift infant up and rapidly lower him or her toward the table. This results in extension, abduction, and external rotation of the legs.

17. *Sideways arms* (Protective extension)—Place infant in sitting position. Pushing him or her sideways off balance will result in abduction of the opposite arm with extension of elbow, wrist, and fingers.

18. *Backward arms* (Protective extension)—Place infant in sitting position. Pushing him or her backward results in: a) Full reaction—backward extension of both arms; and b) Partial reaction—trunk rotation with backward extension of one arm.

19. *Parachute*—Hold infant at the waist, up-end and move him or her rapidly downward toward the table. This results in immediate extension of arms with abduction and extension of fingers as if protecting the head.

Table 2. Primary reflexes and their relationship to normal and abnormal fine motor and gross motor

Primary reflexes	Normal	Abnormal
Hand Grasp—tactile Stimulation of the palm elicits reflexive closure over the object.	Part of the total flexion pattern noted in the first 3 months of life. Should disappear with the development of increased extensor tone.	Retention of reflex prevents voluntary grasp and release of objects and development of mature grasping patterns (pincer grasp) (10–12 months).
Moro's Reflex—head Head and shoulders are raised from table and head is dropped back suddenly. Arms and fingers abducted, extended and externally rotated, followed by return to flexion.	 This reflex persists approximately 0–4 months. Should disappear with better head control and protective reactions forward in sitting.	Persistence past 4 months of age may prevent the infant from developing good sitting balance, forward protective reactions in sitting, and the parachute reaction.
Postural Reflexes Asymmetrical tonic neck reflex (ATNR): Turning of the head by examiner evokes extension of arm on the face side, flexion of the arm on the skull side (fencer's posture). Legs often affected in the same manner as the arms.	Noted in the first 4 months of life, but never an obligatory response in a normal infant, nor should it interfere with activities such as turning over or getting hands to mouth. Serves to create an awareness of two sides of body and beginning of eye-hand coordination.	Too strong a reaction or retention of reflex prevents getting hands to midline (3 months), rolling back to side (3–4 months), hand-to-mouth activities, and symmetrical movements of the limbs if head is turned.

Table 2. *Continued*

Primary reflexes	Normal	Abnormal

Tonic labyrinthine reflex

a. Prone or face-lying position in and of itself produces flexor tone in all extremities.

a. Normal flexor tone noted in newborn (fetal position). Begins to disappear with development of extensor tone (2–5 months).

a. Retention of reflex prevents head extension in prone and ability to assume on elbows position (2 months), pivot prone and Landau reaction requiring full extension (5–6 months).

b. Supine or back-lying position in and of itself produces extensor tone in all extremities.

b. Allows development of extensor tone for kicking in supine and total extension (opposite of fetal positioning).

b. Retention of reflex may cause opisthotonic posturing (total extension with arching of the back) in severe cases. May prevent getting hands to midline and mouth because of retraction of the scapulae (2–3 months), rolling supine to prone (3–5 months), raising head in anticipation of being picked up (5 months), playing with feet when backlying (5 months).

Positive Supporting Reflex

Child held vertically under arms and bounced on balls of feet.

In first 2–4 months, reflex extension of legs and some weight bearing are noted.

Between 5–7 months, extension of legs is followed by flexion and kicking responses. This becomes a more voluntary standing response from 6 months on.

Rigid extension with planter flexion is almost never seen in a normal infant after the first 4 months of life.

Rigid extension with scissoring is usually an abnormal response at any age.

Retention of this reflex will prevent normal reciprocal movements of the legs necessary in walking.

Retention of this reflex may cause toe walking when the child begins to walk, and interfere with balance reactions in standing.

149

Table 3. Secondary reflexes and their relationship to normal and abnormal fine motor and gross motor

Secondary reflexes	Normal	Abnormal
Automatic Head Righting		
a. When held supported under stomach, head extends at least in line with rest of body.	a. Newborn to 2 months. Head in line with body or above. Important beginning stages of head control. This is an automatic, not a learned response.	a. Cannot raise head in line with body but flexes over examiner's hand. Demonstrates poor optical and labyrinthine righting and is delayed in head control.
b. When held in sitting, infant holds head steadily.	b. Between 2-4 months, infant shows increased ability to hold head steadily. This is an automatic, not a learned response.	b. Inability to keep head in midline even momentarily (head falls to side, forward, or backward with no correction by infant) indicates delay in head control and weakness in muscles and/or retention of primary reflexes.
c. When held in vertical position under arms and tilted sideways, head returns to midline to correct for body position.	c. Between 4-6 months, infant shows increased ability to bring head to midline. Responses become increasingly faster with the older infant. This is an automatic, not a learned response.	c. Child will show poor head and trunk control, and difficulty with sitting balance without his automatic head righting response.
Landau Reaction Suspend the child by holding face down under upper thorax.	1st stage—1-3 months. Extension of head above shoulder level. 2nd stage—3-6 months. Extension of head and thorax. 3rd stage—6-12 months. Extension of head, trunk, hips, and legs. Full extension at this age (6-12 months) indicates the ability to maintain the upright posture.	Rigid extension of head, trunk, and legs in the first 2 months may be early signs of hypertonicity. Flexion of the trunk over the examiner's hand instead of extension may indicate abnormal hypotonia. 

Protective Reactions (appear in response to a sudden displacing force and are in the same direction as the force).

1. Sitting

   a. Forward—child's balance in sitting is suddenly disturbed forwards by pushing the child from the back.

   b. Lateral—child's balance in sitting is suddenly disturbed by pushing the child sideways.

   c. Backwards—child's balance in sitting is suddenly disturbed by pushing the child from the front.

(Normal responses to movement, not learned skills.)

a. Forward—arms will immediately move forward and the child will prop on arms (4-6 months). This response will improve with age.

b. Lateral—arm on side closest to supporting surface will reach out to catch the child (6-8 months). This response should be equal on both sides and improve with age.

c. Backwards—arm will reach backwards to break the anticipated fall, with rotation of the trunk and forward flexion of the legs (8-12 months). This response usually is present before walking can be anticipated.

a. No response in an attempt to protect oneself at expected age will delay sitting and walking and may be indicative of retention of some primary reflexes.

b. Unequal protective responses, that is, elicited to one side and not the other, may indicate one-sided involvement such as a hemiparesis or a strong asymmetrical tonic neck reflex.

c. Consistently slow responses in any direction are usually reflected in a child's delayed motor development.

151

Table 3. Continued

Secondary reflexes	Normal	Abnormal
2. Parachute or Protective Extension Forward Child is held by waist, is up-ended and moved quickly toward the table or floor.	Child's upper limbs and fingers abduct and extend as if to protect his head. Fully developed parachute is anticipated by 9 months, but a partial reaction can be seen by 4–5 months. 	No reaction by 5–6 months is of concern. Child may retract arms in response, and this may be indicative of a poorly integrated Moro or other primitive reflex. Some delays in sitting, crawling, and walking may be noted if parachute reaction is not present by 9 months. 

Table 4. Observation form—sensorimotor development (newborn–6 years)

Newborn–3 months

1. *Infant at rest—supine or back-lying position.*
   a. Head is often held to one side or the other, but can be held in the midline when placed, at approximately 2 months.
   b. Arms and legs tend to stay flexed toward the body with little *full* extension or straightening of the limbs noted.
   c. Arms and legs should move equally well, as observed when the infant stretches and kicks. Movements of the arms and legs are close to the body and not usually in full arcs.
   d. Hands are often fisted, though some opening can be seen.

2. *Head control.* Pull to sit or when held at adult's shoulder.
   a. Initial head lag when pulled to sit, disappearing by 3 months.
   b. Infant is able to control head best when held in the sitting position.

3. *Infant on stomach or in prone position.*
   a. Infant should be able to clear nose and move head side to side.
   b. Observe beginning of better head control and shoulder stability as the infant begins to support self on elbows.
   c. Watch for crawling movements of the legs.

3–6 Months

1. *Supine or backlying position.* Infant tends to hold a more symmetrical posture with head held in the midline and attention focused on hands, which he or she plays with a great deal.

2. *Head Control.* Infant tends to hold head steadily when moved from stomach to back, to sitting, to being held at an adult's shoulder.

3. *Prone or stomach-lying position.* Observe if infant has developed some shoulder stability.
   a. Can infant rest on elbows and look around at toys and people in the environment?

4. *Independent locomotion.* Look for stability and control as infant moves.
   a. Does infant roll with control and some directional sense?

Table 4. *Continued*

3-6 Months

    b. Does infant push up on straightened arms, alternating between on elbows and straight arm positions?

    c. Can infant reach for an object with one hand while resting full weight on other arm?

    b. Does infant pivot on stomach in a circle? (6 months)

    c. Does infant raise self up by arms and move forward inch by inch?

6-9 Months

1. *Independent locomotion.* Observe movement patterns, for example, pulling to stand, walking holding on. How does infant perform these—with effort, unsure of self, or easily?
   a. Does infant belly crawl or crawl on hands and knees using arms and legs in a coordinated and alternating pattern?

2. *Sitting balance.* Observe how infant supports self in sitting, and infant's balance and stability.
   a. Can infant sit alone momentarily? (5-6 months)
   b. Does infant sit well with good control, holding trunk or back straight.
   c. Can infant sit and play with toys, and move limbs without upsetting his or her balance?
   d. Can infant sit and get to and from sitting independently? (9 months)

9-12 Months

1. *Independent locomotion.* Observe infant's balance and control as he or she moves.
   a. Crawls reciprocally, one hand, opposite leg.
   b. Crawls hands and feet.

2. *Reaction to movement.*
   a. Does infant enjoy "roughhouse" play?
   b. Does infant enjoy being danced with and tossed in the air?

   c.   Scoots on bottom.

   d.   Walks holding on.

   e.   Walks independently, with a wide-based gait, arms in a high guard position.

Observe infant's ability to maneuver about his or her environment.

   a.   Does infant "get stuck" under furniture?

   b.   Does infant have trouble sitting down after pulling himself or herself to stand?

12–18 Months

1. *Independent locomotion.*

   a.   Does child walk independently with only occasional falls?

   b.   Does child crawl upstairs or walk up and downstairs with help?

   c.   Can child walk backwards with good balance?

   d.   Can child stand up from the middle of the floor without pulling up on furniture?

18–21 Months

1. *Independent locomotion.* Observe child's balance and stability when walking and moving.

   a.   Does child seem to walk easily, and stop and start with control?

   b.   Does child balance well—for example, stoop to pick up objects without falling?

   c.   Does child have good balance and stability in that he or she can squat in play?

   d.   Can child seat himself or herself in a small chair, and climb into an adult-sized chair?

Table 4. *Continued*

  e. Can child balance on one foot well enough to kick a ball?
  f. Can child walk backwards pulling a toy?
  g. Can child run, though he or she tends to do so with a stiff-legged pattern?

21-24 Months
1. *Independent locomotion.*
  a. Can child carry a large object while walking?
  b. Can child walk up and downstairs with his or her hand on the railing?
  c. Can child push and pull large toys, or boxes, or an adult-sized chair?

24-30 Months
1. Observe the child's balance and control when moving.
  a. Can child run well without much falling, and adjust to various ground surfaces (grass, concrete, uneven gravel, etc.)?
  b. Does child have enough balance and stability to walk on knees, walk on tiptoes, and jump?
  c. Does child walk with a mature heel-to-toe gait?

30-36 Months
1. Observe the child's balance and control when moving.
  a. Can child jump up and down several times without losing his or her balance?
  b. Can child run with ease, stopping and starting and avoiding obstacles?
  c. Can child distance jump without losing his or her balance?

d. Can child stand up from the floor without having to turn over to hands and knees and push up?

36-42 Months

Balances on each foot, jumps keeping both feet together, distance jumps, walks upstairs alternating feet without using railing, pedals tricycle.

42-48 Months

Hops on one foot, gallops well, turns somersaults, can walk on a line.

48-54 Months

Walks up and downstairs alternating feet, enjoys animal walks (duck walk, bear walk, crab walk), plays imitative games with arms or other body parts and imitates rhythm or finger plays, can catch a bounced ball.

54-60 Months

Pumps swing, balances on either foot with good control, can sit up from lying on back without use of hands or rolling to the side.

60-72 Months

Hops with good endurance, skips alternating feet, jumps rope, rides two-wheel bicycle, catches a ball with good control, dribbles a ball well, can walk backwards on a line.

Table 4. *Continued*

Preschool and Kindergarten

(for use at school and in home environment)

1. Look at *how* the child moves around the room—walking, running.

   a. When walking, does the child move easily, with a natural swing to his or her arms, and without a limp or exaggerated movements of the legs?

   b. When walking or running, can the child start and stop with good control and avoid bumping into objects or other children?

   c. If he or she starts to fall or trip, does the child show abilities to catch or balance himself or herself?

2. Look at how the child uses his or her whole body in activities.

   a. Does child use both sides equally well?

   b. Does child's head seem to lead his or her body all the time or does child's body appear to work together?

   c. Does child seem dependent upon vision to guide all his or her movements, or does child move sideways, backwards, etc., with ease?

3. Does the child show good stability in that the child can support himself or herself well on arms or hips for:

   a. Wheelbarrow walking.

   b. Crawling around and in and out of obstacle courses.

c. Turning a somersault.

d. Walking on knees.

4. Look at how the child deals with large pieces of equipment such as playground equipment.

   a. Does child seem overly hesitant or fearful about certain movements or activities?

   b. Does child climb to the top and then have trouble planning movements to get down?

   c. Does child show proper judgment about activities?

   d. Does child climb and run without falling a great deal?

5. Does child enjoy gross motor activities, or tend to avoid individual or group participation in motor games?

6. Look at the way the child uses his or her hands in manipulative tasks and his or her use of materials.

   a. Does child use both hands together, not *avoiding* the use of one?

   b. Has child established a hand preference or does he or she keep switching hands?

   c. How does the child respond to various textures and tactile stimulation? Does child enjoy or avoid messy activities such as finger painting, playdough, playing in wet sand?

Table 5.   General physical findings

1. Observe the child's appearance:
    a. Body proportions
        —head size appropriate to body
        —arm and leg lengths
    b. Growth and impression of health status
    c. Any physical handicaps
2. Observe the child's movement and activity:
    a. Inactive . . . very active
    b. Fluctuations in activity and circumstances of activity
    c. Characterization of movements (gross and fine motor)—
        jerky, smooth, tremulous, stiff, too loose or floppy
    d. Tolerance to movement
    e. Fatigue level

Table 6.   "Red Flags"—concerns for later development

Following is a listing of "red flag" concerns in the newborn period through school age that may possibly indicate brain dysfunction and may necessitate further evaluation.

1. Newborns generally show symmetrical and equal movements and development—thus asymmetrical findings such as fisting on one side and not the other, or a grasp reflex on one side and not on the other, should be of concern.

    Asymmetrical Moro's responses or asymmetrical spontaneous movements of the arms and legs may indicate hemiparesis.
2. Absence of primary reflexes listed in Table 1 may indicate poor cerebral development or damage.
3. Lack of spontaneous movements of the head or limbs may indicate paralysis or weakness.
4. Extreme jitteriness may be an early sign of hypertonicity or a sensitive child. This child will need special handling, with mother given extra support.
5. Extremes of muscle tone, either hypotonia (floppy baby) or hypertonia (stiff baby).
6. Scissoring of the legs may indicate increased tone or a strong positive supporting reflex and /or crossed extension reflex.
7. Excessive fisting—too strong a grasp reflex may interfere with normal opening of the hands at rest and prevent voluntary use of the hands.
8. Excessive activity level or a child who is moving all the time may indicate poor sensory integration.
9. The "lazy" or inactive child who does not move into or out of positions often or pursue toys out of reach may indicate poor sensory motor abilities or a child who may look "awkward" in later years.
10. "Rejection" of cuddling or holding may be indicative of poor sensory integration.
11. The child who resists participation in group motor games may be an awkward child with poor sensory motor abilities.
12. The child who tends not to actively use school playground equipment or withdraws from active games may have problems with sensory integration. School-age children with motor problems often have difficulty with peer relationships because of a hesitancy to involve themselves in motor activities.
13. Children who fatigue easily may have sensory motor problems and depressed muscle tone and joint stability.

VIII. Neurological Assessment in Developmental Diagnosis

Lawrence Bernstein, M. D.

CLINICIANS AND FAMILIES frequently face the predicament of a developmentally delayed or learning-disabled child whose difficulties cannot be explained by any particular disease process. The child is slow in walking, but has no discernable orthopedic problem. He is not speaking properly, but has not been noted to have suffered specific brain damage. He has difficulty reading and writing, but otherwise seems normal. He is not growing properly, but has no cardiac, renal, endocrine, or other systemic disorder. He has poor attention or simply will not follow directions, but is evidently bright, and, therefore, is thought to be obstinate and disobedient. In all of these situations the question that plagues the parents and caregivers is "Could there be an organic problem, a nervous system dysfunction underlying the child's difficulties?" At this point, the family is frequently referred to a neurologist for consultation.

ROLE OF THE NEUROLOGIST

Elsewhere in this volume various authors have described the physical examination, as well as screening procedures for genetic, visual, hearing and speech, and neuromotor problems. What, then, does the neurological examination potentially offer? First, one must recognize that the neurological examination attempts to sample at a particular time the overall integrity of the nervous system. The neurologist not only tries to determine whether a problem exists, but endeavors to identify where in the system the problem is occurring. Then, using his or her knowledge of the patient's history and of the natural course of disease processes, the neurologist tries to establish what kind of pathological or developmental process might explain the child's problem.

The kinds of questions neurologists seek to answer in conducting an examination of a child with a potential impairment would include the following:

1. Is the nervous system intact but functioning abnormally, as one might see in a seizure disorder, metabolic disorder, or drug intoxication?
2. Is the nervous system structurally damaged? If so, is the damage focal, as in a tumor or abscess, or is it diffuse, as in a dysgenetic process, an arteritis, or an infection?
3. Is the underlying pathological process static—that is, once the damage has been done, does it stop there? Or is the process progressive and liable to cause more damage?
4. Is the process remediable, as in a subdural hematoma or hydrocephalus?
5. Are the individual's problems the developmental repercussions of an otherwise static process? That is, are the existing dysfunctions a

measure of the way the nervous system has functionally compensated during its development subsequent to a static lesion?

6. Is the nervous system completely intact, with the individual's difficulties resulting from nonadaptive or nonoptimal learning?

7. How well does the clinical picture mimic the course of known disease processes? This last question undoubtedly colors the neurological examination most significantly, since suspecting a particular disease process will lead one to look for its particular pattern of abnormal findings.

THE EXAMINATION

The cerbral cortex may be thought of as the body's chief executive—it makes the decisions, explores past decisions, and anticipates future needs and desires. The basal ganglia, thalamus, cerebellum, and deep nuclei are the cortex's chief advisory committees. They look at the state of the organization (body) in relation to its internal and external environment and help coordinate change. The myelinated, white matter nerve tracts are the chain of communications. The peripheral nerves, including the cranial nerves, carry information toward the brain from the sensory receptors and then transmit orders back to the front-line muscles, glands, and sensory processors (see Figure 1).

Tables 1 and 2 outline some basic levels of neural organization, the components of the neurological examination that test their integrity, and the abnormalities accompanying their dysfunction. Table 2 can be supplemented by referring to the neurological and neuromotor examinations outlined in Chapter 1, Part C and Chapter 7.

The disease processes to consider when a child is developmentally delayed include:

1. Cerebal palsy
2. Hydrocephalus
3. Minor motor or psychomotor seizure disorder
4. Neuromuscular problem
5. Degenerative disorders
6. Minimal brain dysfunction and/or learning disabilities

(For definitions of terms contained in the discussion of each of the above processes, see the Glossary of Terms at the end of this chapter.)

Cerebral Palsy

This group of disorders may frequently underlie instances of developmental delay. Although often a result of perinatal hypoxia or cerebral hypoperfusion, cerebral palsy may stem from any of a number of perinatal insults.

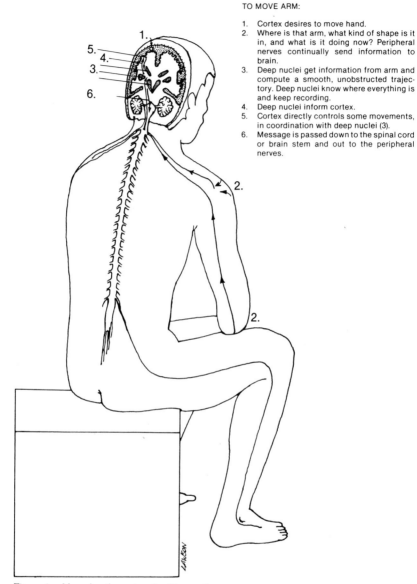

TO MOVE ARM:

1. Cortex desires to move hand.
2. Where is that arm, what kind of shape is it in, and what is it doing now? Peripheral nerves continually send information to brain.
3. Deep nuclei get information from arm and compute a smooth, unobstructed trajectory. Deep nuclei know where everything is and keep recording.
4. Deep nuclei inform cortex.
5. Cortex directly controls some movements, in coordination with deep nuclei (3).
6. Message is passed down to the spinal cord or brain stem and out to the peripheral nerves.

Figure 1. Neural pathway involved in moving arm.

Frequently an etiology is not established. Nonetheless, the tissue damage is by definition always static and never progressive. In most cases, since the insult is acquired early, near the time of birth, the clinical symptoms will continue to evolve as the child's nervous system matures. The functional impairments may be purely motor, entirely sensory, mainly cognitive, or a combination of all of these. When the central nervous system has been severely damaged, the child's dysfunction will be readily apparent. However, with more mild injury, the clinical signs may be quite subtle. In a young, preverbal infant or child, one is first concerned with the motor system and should look for a delay in acquired motor milestones or the persistence of primitive reflexes. Absent or diminished spontaneous movements, especially if occurring asymmetrically (either between the two sides of the body or between the upper and lower extremities), may be a sign of cerebral palsy. These asymmetries will be noticed when one examines the developmental and primitive reflexes of infancy. For example, the Moro's reflex may show a less functional movement of one arm than the other; or the stepping reflex of one leg may be absent. Other abnormal signs include: hypotonia of the trunk or decreased or increased deep tendon reflexes; upgoing toes on plantar stimulation (the Babinski reflex); postural abnormalities; rapid, nonrhythmic, jerking movements of the upper extremities indicating choreiform cerebral palsy (these may not be apparent until after 6 or 8 months in a motorically delayed child); or ataxia. Not infrequently, strabismus (a lazy eye or crossed eyes) and/or a seizure disorder may accompany cerebral palsy, and a head circumference below the third percentile may signify brain damage with resulting poor brain growth. The onset of hand preference prior to 1 year of life is in itself highly suggestive of hemiparetic cerebral palsy.

Remember, the examiner is looking for delayed or abnormally acquired motor development. A loss of acquired skills may signify a progressive lesion of the nervous system that will require further investigation and possible treatment. If the lesion is static, the child's development can be followed by the health care provider with the assistance of a physical or occupational therapist, as needed. These individuals must bear in mind that a child who initially appears to have damage of the motor system alone, may later have difficulty with language, cognitive, and emotional development when competencies in these areas are expected to emerge.

Hydrocephalus

Hydrocephalus may be the cause of developmental delay in children of all ages. However, as with most processes that affect the nervous system, the child's age will determine the clinical picture. In infants and young children in whom behaviors and skills are being acquired rapidly, one may see primarily a delay, retardation, abnormality, arrest, or regression in the acquisition of milestones. In the older child who has already developed a variety of skills, one may mainly see behavior changes or a loss of acquired functions.

Hydrocephalus may result from a dysgenesis (abnormal development) of the nervous system or may develop after a meningitic illness.

Table 1. Levels of neural organization

Levels of organization	Functions	Test for:	Findings should include:
Cortex	Mental status; intellect; fine motor; sensory integration; planning organization	Alert, explores environment; language comprehension; speech; reading; naming; intellect; visuomotor and graphomotor skills; stereognosis; graphesthesia; mood; affect; behavior	Decreased alertness; Decreased interest, impulsivity; Decreased or abnormal affective interactions; Intellectual deterioration; Decreased stereognosis, graphesthesia; Incoordination, spasticity; Corticospinal pattern of weakness; Increased deep tendon reflex (DTR) and Babinski reflex
Basal ganglia	Involuntary movements; muscle tone	Well integrated quality to body movements and postures	Chorea; Athetosis; Ballistic movements; Akinesia; Dystonia
Thalamus	Sensory and motor integration	Abnormal appreciation of pain, temperature, joint position, vibration, visual perception, and auditory perception	
Cerebellum	Balance; coordination	Tandem gait, heel-shin; rapid alternating movements; sequential movements (foot tapping, hand patting, vocalizations—puh-tuh-kuh or ba-na-na); retrieve objects; trace lines; touch between points	Abnormal gait; Incoordination; Scanning speech; Poor visual pursuit

Structure	Function	Examination	Findings
Cranial nerves (Brain stem)	Sensory, motor, autonomic, including special sensory function (taste, smell, vision, hearing)	Vision; smell; hearing; pupillary light reflex; conjugate eye movements; facial movements and expressions; bite; suck; swallow; gag; tongue movement shoulder shrug; neck turning	Anosmia; Blindness, diplopia; Abnormal extraocular movements; Difficulty chewing, sucking; Abnormal facial movements; Deafness; Vertigo, Dysequilibrium; Dysphagia; Decreased gag; Weak sternocleidomastoids; Decreased taste; Respiratory difficulties
Spinal cord	Ascending sensory information; descending motor control; autonomic neurons and controls	Muscle bulk, tone and strength; sensation—all modalities; bowel and bladder control; deep tendon reflexes; Babinski reflex	At or below level of lesion; Pain; Paresthesias; Weakness; Incoordination; Increased DTRs; Decreased bowel and bladder control
Lower motor neuron and peripheral nerve	Sensory input; final motor pathway; autonomic fibers	Muscle bulk, tone and strength; sensation—all modalities; sweating and vasomotor tone; bowel and bladder; deep tendon reflexes	Findings may be distal and symmetrical; or focal in single or multiple nerve distribution; Paresthesias; Weakness; Decreased sweating; Decreased vasomotor tone; Absent DTRs; Decreased sensation
Muscle		Muscle bulk, tone and strength; deep tendon reflexes	Weakness (Proximal greater than distal); Muscle atrophy; Pseudohypertrophy; Diminished DTRs; Sensation and autonomic function both intact

Table 2.   Motor development in infancy and childhood

In the absence of orthopedic difficulties, presence of the reflexes below is indicative of the intactness of the motor system. The examiner should look especially for asymmetrical involvement between the right and left sides of the body, the upper and lower extremities, or the involvement of single extremities.

Primitive Reflexes:

Flexor tone	0–4 months
Moro's reflex	0–5 months
Tonic neck	0–5 months
Grasp: hand	0–5 months
foot	0–5 months

Acquired and Persistent Reflexes:

Head control	0 months (Persists)
Pincer grasp	4 months (Persists)
Body righting	4 months (Persists)
Parachute	5 months (Persists)
Handedness:	not before 1 year

Milestones

Rolls over	2–4½ months
Sits alone	4½–8 months
Stands alone well	9½–14 months
Walks	11–14 months
Pedals trike	21–36 months
Hops on foot	3–5 years

Processes such as tumors, abscesses, subarachnoid hemorrhage, or a subdural hematoma may ultimately be responsible. In all cases, however, there is ultimately the presence of excessive cerebrospinal fluid in the ventricles and subarachnoid spaces of the brain. This places some or all of the brain tissue under increased mechanical pressure that in itself may produce damage. When hydrocephalus follows an increase in intracranial pressure, one may initially see generalized symptoms. In an infant or young child, these might be lethargy or irritability, while the older child may complain of headache or nausea. In either situation, there may be vomiting. The specific findings the examiner should be cognizant of include:

Enlarged Head Circumference   An enlarged head circumference disproportionate to body size or familial head size. Usually this will be greater than the 97th percentile and in some instances will not be apparent until after the 24th week of life, when many pediatricians routinely discontinue head circumference measurements. Occasionally the head circumference may be below the 97th percentile but is increasing at a rapid rate and growing across percentile lines. This, as well, is highly suggestive of a hydrocephalic process.

Skull Shape   Skull shape may provide a clue to underlying pathology. Parietal bulging is seen in subdural hematomas and porencephalic cysts. Obstructive hydrocephalus may produce bilateral frontal bulging and the "setting sun" sign of downward eye deviation. On skull X rays the posterior fossa may be small with aqueductal stenosis or enlarged with Dany-Walker cysts. Split cranial sutures may be palpated in infants or diagnosed on skull X rays in children, and the anterior fontanel may be tense and bulging in infants.

Slow Motor Development   Slowed acquisition of motor milestones, especially those involving the legs. In older children, gait disturbances and ataxia may be present. Spasticity may be present.

Cranial Nerve Signs   Any cranial nerve signs, including papilledema.

Personality Changes

If hydrocephalus or an increase in intracranial pressure is suspected of causing a developmental delay, a number of confirmative tests such as a Computerized Axial Tomography (CAT) Scan should be administered as soon as possible. This should be done in consultation with a physician.

Minor Motor and Psychomotor Seizure Disorders

Occasionally a seizure disorder may accompany a child's developmental delay. This may only be an expression of the underlying damage responsible for the delay—as in cerebral palsy—and may not in and of itself producing the delay. Frequently, overt seizure activity may intensify developmental problems, especially those impairing intellectual development. In some cases, what appears to be a developmental delay may be the clinical manifestations of the seizure disorder itself.

The clinical manifestations of seizure activity are frequently obvious. There is rarely any difficulty recognizing the generalized tonic-clonic convulsion with its accompanying loss of consciousness. Similarly, the individual with focal motor seizures is easily identified and treated. This is not so in situations in which brain seizure activity expresses itself in behavioral alterations; here, seizures may go unnoticed for long time periods. The school-age child is variously labeled "lazy, inattentive, sleepy, retarded, or just uncooperative," and the infant or young child is described as intellectually or motorically delayed.

The kinds of convulsive disorders that can be easily missed by the casual observer include:

Infantile Spasms   Infantile spasms usually begin between 3 months and 18 months of age. They present as a Moro-like response with a sudden loss of head and neck tone accompanied by a myoclonic jerking of the arms toward the midline. They may occur more frequently when the child awakens from a nap, and recur up to 50 or 100 times a day. The electroencephalogram (EEG) shows a typical pattern, the child's overall development is frequently delayed, and underlying cerebral pathology is the rule.

Akinetic Spells   Akinetic spells have a somewhat similar appearance to infantile spasms, but they occur in an older child. These episodes are characterized by a sudden, momentary loss of posture or muscle tone. A young child may nod his head or slump forward in his chair, while the standing child may slump to the floor. Loss of consciousness is usually only momentary.

Petit Mal   Petit mal of the classical variety usually occurs between 5 years and 9 years of age. The attacks are sudden in onset, often without any aura, and may recur frequently throughout the day. These spells arrest the individual's consciousness for 5 to 10 seconds, thereby altering attention and perception. They may be accompanied by a slight loss of muscle tone or minor movements such as lip smacking or facial twitching. The child is often unaware of these episodes and the EEG has a characteristic 3/second spike-wave discharge.

Atypical Petit Mal   Atypical petit mals are clinically similar to true petit mals and are frequently distinguished only by history and the EEG. Often these spells have no accompanying movements, but occasionally they are accompanied by eye or extremity movements. They are highly correlated with some preceding cerebral insult.

Psychomotor Epilepsy   Psychomotor seizures most often occur in later childhood or adolescence. They are associated with abnormal activity in the temporal lobes of the brain and are characterized by a behavioral alteration of which the individual is unaware. During these episodes the individual may frequently respond to the environment in a limited way. An aura in which the child experiences fear, stomach upset, a "strange" feeling, or some other complex sensory phenomenon is followed by a lapse of consciousness accompanied by purposeless movements such as lip smacking, picking at clothes, tapping, or walking off aimlessly. These movements are usually stereotyped and repetitive. If the child is restrained during these episodes, he or she may strike out or resist in a poorly organized way. The total seizure episode may last several minutes. The EEG pattern may be helpful in identifying this specific type of seizure disorder. Overall, it may be said that episodes of staring, inattention, poor comprehension, head nodding, postural disturbance, minor twitches or jerking movements, or senseless or stereotyped automatic behaviors should alert one to the possibility of a seizure disorder. Although observable seizures may accompany developmental delay, in many instances less obvious seizures may simply pass for a developmental delay. Again, the EEG may be very helpful in specifying what subtype of seizure disorder is present. This may be crucial for the proper choice of anticonvulsant therapy. Moreover, since some seizures may be the expression of an underlying pathological process such as a subdural hematoma, an abscess, or a tumor, the EEG—and, when indicated, the CAT scan—may aid in identifying the etiology of the disorder.

Neuromuscular Problem

As with minor motor seizures, diseases of the muscles and nerves may, on occasion, express themselves as delays in motor development. The ages of onset of these disorders are variable, ranging from the newborn period through the teenage years and beyond. The causes of these disorders encompass the entire range of pathological processes. When an infant or young child exhibits primarily weakness or in infancy primarily delay in motor milestones, muscle or peripheral nerve disorders should be considered. These may be accompanied by muscle atrophy or pseudohypertrophy, as well as muscle pain and absent or diminished deep tendon reflexes. Frequently, a history of similar affliction in other family members may be revealed. Although these are generally uncommon disorders, some of the more frequent types of condition are described below:

Werdnig-Hoffmann Spinal Muscular Atrophy   Werdnig-Hoffmann disease may present at birth or in the first years of life. It is a disorder of the motor nerve cells of the spinal cord and no current treatment is known. Infants are usually very floppy at birth. If the illness presents later, infants show a plateau effect in gaining new motor milestones and then begin to lose acquired motor skills, but the intellect remains intact.

Duchenne Muscular Dystrophy   Duchenne muscular dystrophy occurs in males usually between 3 years and 6 years of age. It is gradual in onset and the child may exhibit difficulty in arising from the floor, climbing stairs, or running. There is muscle pseudohypertrophy and, as in all the dystrophies, there should be no sensory abnormalities. Mild intellectual impairment may be present and cardiac problems are frequently seen.

Facioscapulohumeral and Limb-girdle Dystrophies   Facioscapulohumeral and Limb-girdle dystrophies are both autosomal disorders, the former dominant and the latter recessive. They present between 5 years and 12 years of age and produce weakness primarily in those areas that their names imply.

Myasthenia Gravis   Myasthenia gravis, an autoimmune disorder of the neuromuscular junction, may occur in childhood after the first year, but is rare. It may be characterized by generalized weakness, drooping eyelids, abnormal eye movements, difficulty swallowing, and respiratory difficulty.

Dermatomyositis   Dermatomyositis is an insidious disorder that may occur at any age beginning at 2 years. It is characterized by weakness that is generalized but prominent proximally. The child may appear listless or lethargic and complain of muscle aches or tenderness. He or she may have a number of accompanying skin rashes that may go undetected to the untrained eye.

***Charcot-Marie-Tooth and Dejerine-Sottas Hereditary
Sensorimotor Neuropathies*** Charcot-Marie-Tooth disease and
Dejerine-Sottas disease are two examples of hereditary sensorimotor neuropathies. They both begin in the first decade, frequently by 3 years or 4
years, and produce delayed motor milestones. Initially, gait difficulties may
be seen. Weakness may eventually progress into the hands as well.

All of the above examples of neuromuscular disorders are mentioned
to alert the examiner that some individuals with delayed motor milestones
or diminished acquisition of milestones may have underlying muscle or
nerve disease. A family history or some peculiarity of the total picture
should arouse suspicions and prompt one to seek a medical consultation.

Degenerative Disorders

The progressive dementing disorders of childhood are rare and for the
most part untreatable. They are mentioned here primarily to alert the examiner to early detection and confirmation, so as to allow appropriate
family support.

These disorders are characterized by the loss of or failure to develop
age-appropriate motor and intellectual milestones. The earlier the onset of
the disorder, the greater the failure to acquire expected behaviors. The
later the onset, the greater the tendency for milestones to plateau or deteriorate. In older children this means that the first signs one sees may be
behavioral aberrations or language abnormalities. As the disease progresses, the full spectrum of abnormal neurological signs may be expected. These disorders are frequently inherited and often have accompanying systemic abnormalities.

Minimal Brain Dysfunction,
Hyperactive Syndrome, and Learning Disabilities

Not infrequently when a child enters school he or she will be identified as
having a behavioral or learning problem. Often such children will have had
some mild delay previously in the acquisition of their motor or language
milestones. They were clumsy children, slow to sit or walk, or did not begin
to speak until 3 years of age or later. On the other hand, they may have
always been physically active in a seemingly misdirected, unorganized fashion; they were often unable to follow or understand directions. Perhaps
they were only withdrawn, shy, and verbally nonspontaneous, or con-
versely very verbal, but socially inappropriate. All of these descriptions
and more might easily be incorporated within the rubric of minimal brain
dysfunction, or MBD. MBD is a conglomerate, over-inclusive term whose
borders are, unfortunately, hazy. Children who are thus labeled ordinarily
have either behavior problems, learning disabilities, or most commonly a

combination of both behavior and learning problems. Implicit in the term MBD is that the underlying cause of the child's problem(s) is at least part biological. Socio-emotional factors from the environment may precipitate, intensify, or complicate the child's difficulties, but are never thought to be solely responsible. Most strikingly, the qualifier "minimal" is employed to signify that in most instances, no specific, classical brain pathology is known to be responsible for the symptoms and signs, though the brain is certainly thought to be the culprit.

The most noticeable behavioral component of the MBD syndrome *when it occurs* is hyperactivity. A young child who is continually on the go, often in a helter-skelter fashion, is a difficult child to care for, and stands out unmistakeably from "normal" children. Today, however, it is more fashionable and probably more accurate not to be obsessed with a child's hyperkinesis, but to look for other behavioral components. Any combination of the above may accompany the hyperactive-inattentional syndrome. Other characteristics would include: emotional immaturity, impulsivity, poor attention and concentrating abilities, difficulty following directions, and immature organizational capabilities. These children often are refractory to (do not respond to) punishment. On many occasions a child will have the hyperactive-inattentional syndrome without the hyperkinesis, or will have outgrown the hyperkinesis, leaving the inattention, distractibility, and impulsivity. More often, the child will have accompanying learning problems ranging from language comprehension difficulties, naming problems, poor articulation, reading and spelling dysfunction, to math, visuo-spatial, and writing handicaps. These children are not considered retarded and, in fact, their disabilities are usually neither as severe nor as global as those seen in retarded individuals. The areas of poor social, motor, or cognitive function are interspersed with areas of seemingly normal performance. In some cases, one may see an exceedingly bright child with only a single area of dysfunction, such as an attentional problem. Children are labeled as having a problem or being problem children when they cannot adequately compensate with resources that they possess for talents that they lack.

Careful observation and neurological examination of MBD children will frequently reveal the above-mentioned behavioral characteristics as well as a variety of "soft" neurological signs. These so-called soft signs are subtle attenuated versions of the more classical neurological signs that are accepted as signifying damage to specific areas of the nervous system. Where a classical hemiparetic posture is taken to represent damage to the contralateral corticospinal system, a subtle weakness or clumsiness on one side of the body or a mild unilateral hyperreflexia in an otherwise healthy individual is only suggestive of damage or dysfunction of the corticospinal system. In addition, in MBD children, one may see developmental immaturities of the motor system in which motor patterns characteristic of younger children are still present in the older child.

When a learning problem is suspected as part of the clinical picture, the child should receive educational and intellectual testing. An Individualized Education Plan (IEP) may need to be developed addressing the special education needs. A structured environment with limits and a warm but firm interacting teacher or parent is necessary for the impulsive, inattentive, hyperkinetic child. Once these have been instituted as far as possible, one may wish to try to further improve the child's attentional capabilities with a trial of a stimulant medication such as methylphenidate. When appropriately used, up to 70% of attentionally deficient children may respond to these medications. They may, however, cause an upset stomach and adversely affect appetite and sleep patterns. Drowsiness may also occur in responders receiving too high a dosage. The stimulant medications should, therefore, be carefully monitored. In addition, the MBD population is one in which the examiner may need to consider obtaining an EEG if there is any question of a concurrent seizure disorder.

PREVENTION AND IMPLICATIONS FOR HEALTH CARE PROVIDERS

The neurological approach to the developmentally disabled child attempts to determine whether an organic disturbance of the nervous system is contributing to the child's problems. Once a problem is identified, the neurologist endeavors to place it within the context of the individual's medical background, social and family history. With the aid of the examination, the examiner formulates what areas of the nervous system are dysfunctional to explain the child's condition and what disease processes could cause such a situation. Commonly, if a neurological impairment is part of the developmental problem, prevention of disease is no longer possible at the time of detection. However, early detection can certainly diminish morbidity and the amount that an individual will suffer from the disease. Early detection may further prevent a host of attendant problems that families and caregivers are confronted with as a result of illness. Therefore, nurses and other health care providers should consider obtaining a neurological consultation for a child when any progressive neurological problems are suspected. Further complications may thus be avoided and appropriate therapeutic intervention instituted.

SUGGESTED READINGS

Barlow, C. F. 1978. Mental retardation and related disorders. Contemporary Neurology Series. Vol. 17.

Heilman, K. M., and Valenstein, E. 1979. Clinical Neuropsychology. Oxford University Press, New York.

Menkes, J. H. 1974. Textbook of Child Neurology. Lea & Febiger, Philadelphia.

Paine, R. S., and Oppe, T. F. 1966. Neurological examination of children. Clinics in Developmental Medicine. Vols. 20, 21.

Prensky, A. (ed.). 1976. Pediatric neurology. Pediatr. Clin. North Am. Vol. 23.

Volpe, J. (ed.). 1977. Neonatalneurology. Clin. Perinato. 4:1.

Weiner, H., Bresnan, M., and Levitt, L. 1977. Pediatric Neurology for the House Officer. Williams & Wilkins Co., Baltimore.

GLOSSARY OF TERMS

Akinesis   Inertia, immobility, difficulty getting started moving.

Anesthesia   Loss of sensation.

Anosmia   Loss of sense of smell.

Aphasia   Inability either to properly use or understand language.

Aqueductal Stenosis   Narrowing or obstruction of the narrow passage in the brain stem through which cerebrospinal fluid must flow.

Ataxia   Inability to coordinate movements.

Athetosis   Condition marked by writhing movements.

Atrophy   Wasting away.

Autonomic Neurons   Conducting cells of the nervous system that regulate vital organ systems, such as the heart, intestines, bladder, as well as sweating and blood flow.

Ballistic Movements   Flinging, explosive movements.

CAT Scan   Computerized Axial Tomography Scan. Computerized Xray showing structural detail in soft, nonbony tissues.

Chorea   Nonrhythmic, jerking movements of extremities.

Choreiform Cerebral Palsy   Motor disorder characterized by fluctuating muscle tone and nonrhythmic, spontaneous, darting movements of the fingers, hands or feet.

Corticospinal Pattern of Weakness   Diminished strength of shoulder elevation and wrist extension in the upper extremity; and hip flexion and ankle dorsiflexion in the lower extremity.

Dandy-Walker Cyst   A congenital membrane or cyst, behind an abnormally formed cerebellum, which may block flow of cerebrospinal fluid.

Diplopia   Blurred or double vision from nonconjugate eye movements.

Dysgenesis   Abnormal embryological development.

Dysphagia   Difficulty in swallowing.

Dystonia   Abnormal posture of trunk, extremity, or facial musculature.

Graphesthesia   Ability to identify symbols by touch when they are "written" on the skin.

Hemiparetic Cerebral Palsy   Motor disorder affecting predominantly one side of the body.

Hydrocephalus   Literally "water on the brain"; usually an abnormally enlarging head size caused by an abnormality of cerebrospinal fluid production, resorption, or flow.

Hypoperfusion   Insufficient blood flow to nourish a tissue.

Obstructive Hydrocephalus   Hydrocephalus (see above) resulting from a block in the flow of cerebrospinal fluid.

Papilledema Abnormal appearance of the optic nerve and retina, suggesting increased intracranial pressure.

Paresthesia Abnormal sensation, e. g., tingling.

Porencephalic Cysts Abnormal fluid-filled cavity or out-pouching of the brain.

Posterior Fossa Compartment at the back of the skull containing the cerebellum and brain stem.

Static Nonprogressive, self-limited.

Stereognosis Ability to identify an object by palpation alone.

Subarachnoid Hemorrhage Bleeding over the brain or spinal cord within the cerebrospinal fluid space.

Subdural Hematoma Blood clot over the surface of the brain or spinal cord.

Tandem Gait Manner of walking as if walking a tightrope with each foot alternately placed immediately in front of the other.

Vertigo A sense of spinning, dizziness.

IX. Detection and Referral of Dental Problems in Children

Paul S. Casamassimo, D. D. S., M. S.
Beverly A. Entwistle, R. D. H., M. P. H.

THE FIRST STEP IN PREVENTING severe dental conditions in children who are developmentally disabled is to familiarize dental and dental hygiene students and practitioners with the roles of other health professionals in the community, and to increase understanding and communication between private and public health delivery systems.

The second step is the education of nondental professionals about dental development, dental health factors, and dental care delivery considerations. This second goal is the object of this chapter.

OROFACIAL AND DENTAL DEVELOPMENT

Development of the Teeth

The first sign of tooth development (Figure 1) occurs at about 5 or 6 weeks *in utero*, at which time the teeth begin as slight thickenings on the embryonic jaw epithelium that soon invaginate into underlying mesenchyme. The teeth will develop within the bone of both maxilla and mandible.

The process of tooth development is continuous. At any moment from the fifth week *in utero* until early adult life, a primary or permanent tooth is developing (Table 1). For simplicity of discussion, tooth development is divided into four major stages: 1) growth; 2) calcification; 3) eruption; and 4) attrition. The first two stages occur while the tooth is encased in the jaw. The last two stages occur in the mouth.

Growth   The growth stage has been further divided into 5 phases: *initiation*, which is the appearance of the tooth bud; *proliferation* or the growth of the primitive bud to larger size; *morpho-* and *histodifferentiation*, during which the shape of the tooth and the specialized cells needed for growth develop; and *apposition*, when the matrix that will become the calcified portion of the crown is deposited.

Calcification   During calcification, the organic matrix of the developing tooth changes to the hard consistency associated with erupted teeth. At this stage, the crown of the tooth as it will appear in the mouth has been determined.

Both the growth and calcification stages are sensitive to environmental and genetic influences. For example, in the environmental area, maternal rubella, infant fever, medications such as tetracycline, and vitamin deficiencies or excesses can affect the developing teeth. Children who receive tetracycline in infancy may have irreversible staining of permanent teeth which calcify during that time. Chronic renal disease, which alters calcium and phosphate balance, may create defects in tooth shape. On the other hand, fluoride ingestion during tooth growth and calcification can increase resistance to future dental caries. Excessive amounts of fluoride, however, can cause white chalky staining or severe brown fluorosis.

DENTAL DEVELOPMENT

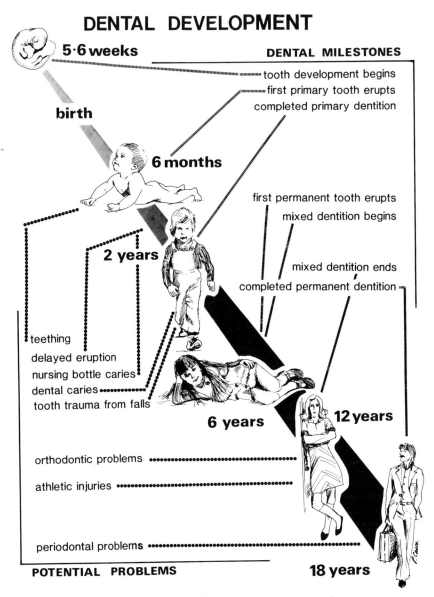

Figure 1.   Dental development.

Regarding genetic disturbances, genetic disease can cause absence of some teeth or presence of extra teeth. Enamel pitting can accompany various syndromes. Defective structure of the dentin may occur in osteogenesis imperfecta. Abnormalities in shape and size are often found in Down syndrome.

Table 1. Chronology of the human dentition

Tooth		Hard tissue formation begins	Amount of enamel formed at birth	Enamel completed	Eruption	Root completed
Deciduous dentition						
Maxilla	Central incisor	4 mos. *in utero*	Five-sixths	1½ mos.	7½ mos.	1½ yrs.
	Lateral incisor	4½ mos. *in utero*	Two-thirds	2½ mos.	9 mos.	2 yrs.
	Cuspid	5 mos. *in utero*	One-third	9 mos.	18 mos.	3¼ yrs.
	First molar	5 mos. *in utero*	Cuspids united	6 mos.	14 mos.	2½ yrs.
	Second molar	6 mos. *in utero*	Cusp tips still isolated	11 mos.	24 mos.	3 yrs.
Mandible	Central incisor	4½ mos. *in utero*	Three-fifths	2½ mos.	6 mos.	1½ yrs.
	Lateral incisor	4½ mos. *in utero*	Three-fifths	3 mos.	7 mos.	1½ yrs.
	Cuspid	5 mos. *in utero*	One-third	9 mos.	16 mos.	2¼ yrs.
	First molar	5 mos. *in utero*	Cusps united	5½ mos.	12 mos.	2¼ yrs.
	Second molar	6 mos. *in utero*	Cusp tips still isolated	10 mos.	20 mos.	3 yrs.
Permanent dentition						
Maxilla	Central incisor	3–4 mos.		4–5 yrs.	7–8 yrs.	10 yrs.
	Lateral incisor	10–12 mos.		4–5 yrs.	8–9 yrs.	11 yrs.
	Cuspid	4–5 mos.		6–7 yrs.	11–12 yrs.	13–15 yrs.
	First bicuspid	1½–1¾ yrs.		5–6 yrs.	10–11 yrs.	12–13 yrs.
	Second bicuspid	2–2¼ yrs.		6–7 yrs.	10–12 yrs.	12–14 yrs.
	First molar	At birth	Sometimes a trace	2½–3 yrs.	6–7 yrs.	9–10 yrs.
	Second molar	2½–3 yrs.		7–8 yrs.	12–13 yrs.	14–16 yrs.
	Third molar	7–9 yrs.		12–16 yrs.	17–21 yrs.	18–25 yrs.
Mandible	Central incisor	3–4 mos.		4–5 yrs.	6–7 yrs.	9 yrs.
	Lateral incisor	3–4 mos.		4–5 yrs.	7–8 yrs.	10 yrs.
	Cuspid	4–5 mos.		6–7 yrs.	9–10 yrs.	12–14 yrs.
	First bicuspid	1¾–2 yrs.		5–6 yrs.	10–12 yrs.	12–13 yrs.
	Second bicuspid	2¼–2½ yrs.		6–7 yrs.	11–12 yrs.	13–14 yrs.
	First molar	At birth	Sometimes a trace	2½–3 yrs.	6–7 yrs.	9–10 yrs.
	Second molar	2½–3 yrs.		7–8 yrs.	11–13 yrs.	14–15 yrs.
	Third molar	8–10 yrs.		12–16 yrs.	17–21 yrs.	18–25 yrs.

From Logan, W.H.G. and Kronfeld, R. 1933. Development of the human jaws and surrounding structures from birth to fifteen years. J. Am. Dent. Assoc. 20:379. (Slightly modified by McCall and Schour 1953. Noyes Oral Histology and Embryology. 7th Ed. Lea & Febiger Publishers, Philadelphia.)

Developmental problems occurring during growth and calcification are important because they are usually irreversible and must be treated with dental restorations. Alterations in the number, size, shape, color, or consistency of teeth suggest problems in growth or calcification.

Eruption   Tooth eruption is a complex process that is mediated by both local and systemic influences. Factors such as trauma or infection can delay eruption, as can certain diseases and hormonal deficiences such as hypophosphatemic rickets or hypothyroidism. Genetic disorders such as Down syndrome and achondroplasia are also associated with delayed tooth eruption.

The first tooth usually erupts at 6 months of age, but can erupt as late as 12 months without concern. A child whose first tooth erupts late may or may not experience eruption delays throughout life. Of concern is the child with an eruption delay 6 months beyond the usual time of eruption. Of similar concern is the child with other general delays who has delayed eruption, as well as the child with known genetic or other disease and delayed eruption. Early identification of eruption delays makes management easier because the majority of problems occurring during eruption are often reversible.

Attrition   A seldom considered stage in the development of the dentition is *attrition*, which refers to the functional wearing away of the tooth. Teeth normally undergo attrition over years of use. Teeth that are structurally weak tend to erode faster. Dentinogenesis imperfecta, a developmental disturbance of the dentin often occurring with osteogenesis imperfecta, makes teeth brittle and subject to rapid wear. Bruxism, or night grinding, is an example of abnormal wear of normal teeth. Primary teeth have a short life span and can show signs of attrition early in childhood. Permanent teeth should be free of wear into adolescence.

Dental developmental problems can occur at various stages of tooth development (Table 2). Exfoliation of the primary teeth is considered a part of the eruptive stage. Delays in exfoliation are possible in conditions such as Down syndrome and hypothyroidism. Delayed loss of primary teeth can cause similar delays in permanent eruption that may or may not be reversible. Retained primary teeth also may lead to malocclusion or crowding of the permanent teeth.

Development of the Jaws and Face

At birth, the brain case has reached about 63% of adult size and accounts for one-fourth of the overall body size of the newborn. The development of both the maxilla and the mandible during early life is minimal. The cranium grows to about four-fifths of its adult size by 1 year of life.

The space available for teeth is determined early in life. Between the time of eruption of the last primary tooth and eruption of the permanent

Table 2. Developmental stages in the life of a tooth: potential problems of excess and deficiency

Developmental stages	Problems of excess	Problems of deficiency
I. Growth		
1. Initiation	Extra teeth	Congenital absence of teeth
2. Proliferation	Cysts	
3. Histodifferentiation	Atypical structure	Amelogenesis imperfecta Dentinogenesis imperfecta (abnormal quality)
4. Morphodifferentiation	Atypical form and tooth size	Peg teeth Small teeth
5. Apposition	Excessive size	Hypoplasias
II. Calcification	Fluorosis (mottled teeth)	Mottled or chalky teeth
III. Eruption	Crowding and malocclusion	Late eruption Submerged teeth Impacted teeth
IV. Attrition	Excessive wear Night grinding	

anterior teeth and first molars, the jaws widen slightly. Since the space available for all the permanent teeth has been essentially determined and the jaws will widen only minimally to accommodate the larger permanent teeth, maintenance of space becomes important. The primary teeth act as natural space maintainers. If primary teeth are lost, appliances must be used to hold spaces open until the permanent teeth erupt.

Adolescence is the period when rapid facial growth occurs and the permanent canines and premolars erupt. From about 10 years to 20 years of age, 35% of facial growth occurs. The jaws grow downward, giving the adolescent a more adult appearance. Adolescence is therefore a critical time for orthodontic problems. Early intervention by a dentist can preclude orthodontic difficulties. In the child with delays, early intervention is even more critical in light of possible associated craniofacial malformation and intellectual retardation, both of which can complicate treatment.

Development of Dental Caries and Gingival Disease

Dental caries and gingival (gum) disease are both infectious diseases. In the general population, about 50% of children experience dental caries by age 2. Gingival disease tends to begin in childhood and early adolescence as gingivitis (gingival inflammation) and, if untreated, progresses later to periodontal disease with destruction of the tooth-supporting tissues and bone. The child or adolescent with a developmental delay may be more prone to infectious dental disease because of a host of physical and social factors discussed later in the chapter.

Disease occurs when three factors are present: bacteria capable of initiating disease; a diet that encourages growth of these bacteria; and an individual who is susceptible to disease. When any one factor is eliminated, disease does not occur. For example, thorough toothbrushing removes plaque from the teeth and gingiva, thus eliminating the bacteria. In addition, fluoride, when ingested during the development of teeth or applied topically after teeth have erupted, makes the teeth less susceptible to caries.

PREVENTION AND HIGH RISK FACTORS

Once a developmental delay or defect is suspected or identified in a child, the focus of intervention often assumes a problem or illness orientation specifically related to the delay or disability. Although this approach is essentially preventive in nature, it emphasizes problems and can result in severe neglect of other "nonrelated" areas. Dental health frequently is relegated to this latter status, creating a situation in which minor dental problems are ignored until they become major and require treatment.

The ultimate goal of prevention in dental health is to motivate individuals to seek and practice preventive care throughout their lifetime. For children identified as having a developmental disability, a further objective is to prevent dental disease from becoming an additional handicap.

To meet these goals, various "high risk factors" can be identified. These factors pertain to any child, but are particularly relevant for the handicapped child. Table 3 outlines these high risk factors and lists specific examples and the associated dental concerns.

GATHERING DENTAL HEALTH DATA

Outline for an Oral Screening

Procedures for conducting an oral screening are outlined below. Discussion of these screening aspects comprises the remaining sections of this chapter.

I. Identify high risk factors and treatment obstacles: psychosocial, accessibility, communication, mobility, stability, finances, medical problems.

II. Clinical Examination
   Soft tissue examination
   1. Skin
   2. Lips
   3. Mucosa
   4. Palate
   5. Tongue
   6. Throat
   7. Floor of mouth
   Hard tissue examination
   1. Dental age
   2. Tooth number, color, size, shape, position
   3. Caries

Historical Data

Due to a largely private practice system of dental care in this country and the fact that only 15% to 20% of the population seeks professional dental care on a routine basis (Young and Stiffler, 1969), dental professionals must in many instances rely on other health professionals to identify problems and initiate referrals. This referral "network" is particularly important for handicapped children. Preliminary information about a child is usually acquired through an intake interview or home visit, where it is also feasible and appropriate to gather dental health information. Table 4 illustrates questions that may be asked during an intake interview or home visit to elicit valuable preliminary information about the dental needs and high risk factors of children with developmental disabilities.

Table 3. High risk factors for dental problems

Factors and dental concerns	Important historical data
I. Prolonged Bottle Feeding ↑ risk for caries, malocclusion	1. How and when (night, naps, whenever asked for, propped)? 2. Contents (Kool-Aid, juice, milk, sugar additives, special formula)? 3. Presence of teeth (how long erupted)?
II. Inadequate Diet ↑ risk for caries, disturbed tooth and bone development	1. Nutrient intake (quality and quantity)? 2. Vitamin/mineral supplements? 3. Frequency of eating? 4. Snacking patterns (type of food and frequency)? 5. Level of feeding skills? 6. Feeding problems? 7. Stress around mealtime? (Check prenatal, infancy, and present status.)
III. Special Diets ↑ risk for general dental problems	1. Reason for (medical problem, oral dysfunction)? 2. Types of foods used and eliminated? 3. Frequency of intake? 4. Duration of diet? 5. Special feeding techniques (gavage, bottle)?
IV. Food Reinforcers ↑ risk for caries	1. Who uses (parents, educators, babysitters)? 2. When used (specific program, for certain behavior at home)? 3. Where (home, school)? 4. What used (candy, pop, cereal)?

Table 3. *Continued*

Factors and dental concerns	Important historical data
V. Perioral Sensitivity ↑ risk for poor oral hygiene and dental disease	1. When (always, certain textures, just during toothbrushing)? 2. Where elicited (intraoral, extraoral, hypersensitive gag)? 3. How manifested (pulls away, closes mouth, fights)?
VI. Oral Motor Dysfunction ↑ risk for poor oral hygiene and general dental problems ↑ risk for interference with dental/home care procedures	1. Which parts of mouth affected (tongue, lips)? 2. How severe is dysfunction—does it interfere with speech, feeding, home care procedure? 3. How is it manifested? 4. Any asymmetry in physical appearance or function? 5. Is muscle tone abnormal?
VII. Gross Motor Delays or Dysfunction ↑ risk for interference with dental/home care procedures	1. Which parts of body affected (all extremities, head, and trunk)? 2. How is body affected (range of motion, muscle tone, paralysis, motor control)? 3. With what activities does the problem interfere (walking, sitting, eating, brushing)? 4. Is any adaptive equipment used (wheelchairs, walkers, adapted spoons)?
VIII. Less than Optimal Fluoride Supplementation ↓ resistance to caries	1. When first received? 2. What type (systemic—tablets, drops, water; topical—toothpaste, rinse, gel; home, school, dental office)? 3. Frequency?

186

IX. Poor Oral Hygiene
   ↑ risk for caries and periodontal disease

1. Type (plaque, debris, calculus)?
2. Pattern (localized, generalized)?
3. Home care procedures:
   a. Who performs (self, other)?
   b. Frequency and adequacy?
   c. Degree of supervision?
   d. Materials (electric or manual toothbrush, floss)?
   e. Need for adaptations?

X. Oral Habits
   ↑ risk for malocclusion

1. What type of habit (grinding, self-abuse, thumbsucking)?
2. How often—occurs at any particular time?
3. What techniques, if any, tried to use to eliminate?
4. Any motivation to eliminate the habit?

XI. Crisis Orientation to Care
   ↑ risk for severe and chronic dental problems

   ↑ risk for behavior problem

1. What prompts seeking care?
2. How severe before deciding to seek care?
3. Who recognizes problems?
4. Is attitude reflected in total life style?
5. How consistent are home care procedures?

XII. Preoccupation with Handicap/Illness
   ↑ risk for general dental problems and
   ↑ risk for behavior problems

1. Parent's perceptions of patient's functioning level, future goals, expectations for:
   a. Self-care skills
   b. Transportation skills
   c. Social skills
   d. Acceptance of dental environment
2. Define patient's strengths.
3. Define patient's problems.
4. What activities does patient enjoy?
5. What upsets patient?

↑, Increased; ↓, decreased.

Table 4.   Dental health questionnaire

Child's Name _____ **Date of Birth** _____
Please circle the appropriate response

Yes   No

Yes	No		
Y	N	1.	Are you concerned about your child's dental status?
Y	N	2.	Has your child ever had dental cavities?
Y	N	3.	Has your child ever been seen by a dentist?
			a. Does he or she receive regular care (at least once a year)?
			b. Are you satisfied with your child's present dental care?
Y	N	4.	Do your child's gums bleed at any time?
Y	N	5.	Is your child able to brush his or her teeth without your help?
Y	N	6.	Is your child resistant to toothbrushing?
Y	N	7.	Does your child receive fluoride in any form (toothpaste, drinking water, tablets, etc.)?
Y	N	8.	Was your child bottle-fed after birth?
			a. Did you frequently use juice, Kool-Aid, or sweeteners (Karo Syrup, sugar water) in the bottle?
Y	N	9.	Has your child ever had feeding problems (poor sucking, chewing, etc.)?
Y	N	10.	Is food used regularly as a reward at home or school?
Y	N	11.	Does your child have any medical problems?
Y	N	12.	Does your child take any medications on a regular basis?
Y	N	13.	Does your child grind or clench his or her teeth at any time?
Y	N	14.	Does your child usually put objects in his or her mouth or suck or bite on his or her fingers?
Y	N	15.	Does your child fall down or bump into things frequently?
Y	N	16.	Does your child understand simple directions?
Y	N	17.	Can your child communicate his or her needs verbally?
Y	N	18.	Does your child exhibit behavior problems that would interfere with dental care?
Y	N	19.	Do you expect dental treatment to be a traumatic or unpleasant experience for your child, or has he or she had an unpleasant experience?
Y	N	20.	Are you able to afford routine dental care for your child?

Name of person completing form _____

Relationship to child _____ **Date** _____

Once the appropriate information has been gathered, a decision must be made about whether the child is at risk for dental problems. If the child is at risk and does not at present receive regular dental care, then a clinical assessment of the child's actual dental status should be made. (A screening of the oral tissues can be performed quickly, for example, with a pocket flashlight and a tongue blade or toothbrush.) If the child resists an oral screening or demonstrates severe oral motor dysfunction that interferes with access to the mouth, then the child is exhibiting a definite high risk factor and should be referred to dental professionals for a thorough assessment.

Clinical Data Gathering

A dental screening for a child with a known or suspected developmental disability should include two parts:

1.   Examination for soft tissue disease;
2.   Evaluation of dental age, developmental problems, and dental caries —the hard tissue examination.

Soft Tissue Examination   A dental screening should begin with an examination of the perioral tissues. Swelling, asymmetry, ulceration, pain, limited function, and changes in color may each indicate soft tissue pathosis.

The skin and perioral tissues often show the effects of developmental delays or abnormalities. Chapped or crusted lips and cheeks may be the result of drooling or chronic mouthbreathing. Ulceration of the lips or face may indicate self-abuse. Attention also should be given to common oral problems such as herpetic stomatitis.

Intraoral examination begins with inspection of the oral mucosa, which should be pink and free of lesions. The palate should be intact and free of debris or inflammation. A normal hard palate can be fully visualized and palpated. The tongue should be free of lesions and have a full range of motion. The gingiva should be pink and free of redness, especially in the papilla area between teeth. Rubbing the gingiva should not elicit bleeding. Gingiva should not be swollen or cover the crowns of the teeth.

Hard Tissue Examination

Evaluation of Dental Age   An assessment of dental age is made by counting and identifying the teeth in the mouth. A rough but useful technique to quickly assess dental age in the young child is to subtract 6 from the age in months: Age (months) – 6 = average number of teeth present. This formula will yield the average number of primary teeth present for that age. *Another useful general tool is that the first primary tooth usually erupts at 6 months of age and a new primary tooth can be expected every 1 month to 2 months thereafter.* The sequence of primary tooth eruption is fairly consistent, with the anterior teeth erupting first, followed by the posteriors or molars, with the exception of the canines, which erupt after the first primary molars.

Teeth usually erupt in pairs, so bilateral patterns are expected. The permanent teeth start to erupt at about 6 years of age, beginning with the eruption of the first permanent molar, which comes in behind the last primary molar. Sometimes the permanent incisors can precede the molars. One should expect that the mandibular teeth will precede the corresponding maxillary teeth by a few months.

Teething complaints may be common in infancy, but the only verified problems associated with teething are increased drooling, increased daytime restlessness, rubbing of gingiva or digit sucking, decreased appetite, and mucosal changes. Other problems of a more serious nature such as diarrhea, fever, and infection may have more to do with general health, and teething should not be considered a catchall diagnosis that might prevent medical evaluation.

The teeth also need to be examined for size, shape, color, and position. Only experience can provide a knowledge of the range of normal. A good gage of abnormal size is to relate teeth to one another. A single small tooth or a pair of small teeth when compared to the rest may be more easily detected than generalized reduction in size. Abnormal tooth size may not be clinically significant.

Shape is another variable that is important to consider. Teeth have a fairly consistent shape, and aberrations such as peg teeth or pitted teeth should be noted. Intrinsic staining can indicate an irreversible problem (such as erythroblastosis fetalis) while an extrinsic stain (iron stain) may be corrected easily. A personal history and quick attempt to remove the stain should reveal its nature. Abnormal patterns of attrition should also be noted.

Occlusion or Bite   The assessment of tooth position is often difficult. Tooth pairs should be symmetrically placed. Primary teeth often have spaces between them, but permanent teeth usually do not unless they are recently erupted. Teeth may erupt at an angle and appear rotated. They will be eased into position eventually by the action of the tongue and oral musculature. The permanent incisors often erupt behind the primary, giving the impression of two rows of teeth. This situation will correct itself when the primary teeth exfoliate. Developmentally delayed children may have abnormal or inadequate oral movement, which may prevent development of a normal occlusion.

To assess the bite or occlusion, have the child close the teeth together. The maxillary teeth should be in front of the mandibular teeth in the incisor area so that the biting edges of the mandibular teeth cannot be seen. This relationship should extend posteriorly so that the maxillary teeth are always slightly outside the mandibular. When teeth are held together, one should not be able to see the tongue when looking directly at the teeth. Nor should there be an excessive protrusion of the front teeth. Finally, the teeth should be well-aligned. Overlapping or excessive spacing, especially in the midline, require professional attention.

Dental Caries   Dental caries take many forms. Color changes are often a key to early diagnosis of caries. White chalky areas, especially under accumulated bacterial plaque, are the first signs of decalcification. These areas may be found along with brownish stains, which indicate more advanced caries. A hole in the tooth that is yellow to brown in color means serious dental decay. A broken tooth or a large cavity that is darkly stained needs immediate attention. Localized pain or the presence of a gum boil on the gingiva directly above or below the tooth signifies pulpal disease, which also requires immediate attention. The biting surfaces of teeth tend to trap food and decay first. Darkened grooves on these surfaces may not always be signs of decay, but when these grooves are surrounded by a slight darkening or are grossly cavitated, they need to be treated. Table 5 lists examples of developmental problems and changes in the appearance of teeth.

Referral Process

Locating dental care for children is sometimes difficult and frustrating. Factors such as long waiting lists, provider attitudes, financial and transportation problems, and parental resistance can prove to be barriers to referral. Knowledge of local community resources and networks and the requirements of the dental provider help to facilitate the referral process.

Financial Assistance   Dental care is expensive, particularly if a child exhibits chronic or severe dental problems. If the child is not eligible for financial aid programs, one must determine 1) if parents can afford the care either through dental insurance, employee benefits, or extended payment plans arranged by the dentist, or 2) if any community organizations will provide financial assistance.

Occasionally, fraternal groups such as Lions Clubs or associations for children with various disabilities (for example, local chapters of the National Association for Retarded Citizens) may provide assistance on an individual basis. Health department programs such as handicapped or crippled children's programs in various states also may provide limited assistance for certain types of care or for children with specific disabilities.

Many dentists have made attempts to reduce fees for children who are indigent, handicapped or in Headstart programs, but have been overwhelmed by a flood of "needy patient" referrals or badgered with statements about societal and ethical obligations. As long as dentistry is dominated by the private practice system, provision of dental services represents a business endeavor with high overhead. Attempts to overlook this fact when securing services will only provoke anger, negative attitudes, and prejudice toward community workers and the children who require treatment.

Table 5. Examples of abnormal clinical findings and etiologies

Clinical finding	Possible dental abnormality/etiology
1. Delayed eruption (eruption that is more than 6 months beyond expected time)	*Local factors* Extra teeth Tooth bud malposition Insufficient space Overgrowth of tissue from Dilantin *Systemic factors* Endocrinopathies Malformation syndromes
2. Accelerated eruption/exfoliation (eruption that is 6 months before the expected time of eruption)	*Local Factors* Trauma Sequelae of primary infection Neoplasia *Systemic factors* Endocrinopathies Reticuloendothelioses Malformation syndromes
3. Color changes (intrinsic)—primary teeth are white, while permanent teeth may be more yellow	*Systemic Factors* White to brown (fluorosis) Purple to brown (congenital porphyria)

4. Color changes (extrinsic)

Yellow brown to gray black (tetracycline)
Blue green (erythroblastosis fetalis)
Pink (internal pulp resorption)
Gray brown or black (pulp necrosis)
Red brown to gray (dentinogenesis imperfecta)
Brownish yellow (amelogenesis imperfecta)
Local factors
Chalky white (early caries or fluorosis or hypocalcification)
Yellow to light brown (active caries)
Black (chronic or arrested caries)
Green to black (chromogenic bacteria)
Black (iron staining)

5. Pitting and grooving, altered shape (tooth surfaces are smooth, flat and glossy)

Local factors
Sequelae from trauma
Local infection
Systemic factors
Maternal infection (rubella; syphilis)
Nutritional deficiencies (vitamins A, C, D)
Nephrotic syndrome
Malformation syndromes
Poisoning (lead, radiation)
Excess fluoride

Transportation   Scheduling dental appointments can be a major problem for children with mental or physical disabilities who are totally dependent on adults for transportation. Families with nonambulatory or wheelchair-bound children encounter additional problems. Resources to assist parents in transportation may be acquired through various professional associations or through volunteers (for example, the Red Cross). In some states, Medicaid will assume transportation costs, or public clinics may provide transportation. In many instances, public health or school nurses and social workers may be asked to provide transportation.

Dental Resources   A frequent complaint of parents is the inability to find a dentist who is sensitive to the needs of their handicapped child. Referral information may be obtained through the local dental society, the dental division of the state or local health department, parent groups, dental schools, children's hospitals or health clinics, and professional associations such as the Academy of Dentistry for the Handicapped and the local chapter of the National Association for Retarded Citizens.

Assessment of Treatment Obstacles

When dental disease or high risk factors require a referral, the nondental professional should be able to provide the dentist with information on possible management problems. These problem areas are identified, along with methods of assessment, in Table 6.

An adequate referral should describe any potential problems that the dentist might expect to encounter in treatment. These problems should be considered as important as the estimate of dental disease.

ROLE OF OTHER HEALTH PROFESSIONALS

The key to prevention is continuity of care, which necessitates communication, cooperation, and coordination among all those who work with children and their parents. To encourage such cooperation and coordination, nurses and other professionals are urged to assume the following roles for the promotion of dental health in children:

1. Identify high risk factors for dental disease
2. Ask appropriate questions to determine parental dental concerns and high risk factors
3. Recognize existing dental disease
4. Counsel parents and children about high risk factors and the dental implications
5. Refer children for professional dental care or counseling
6. Facilitate follow-up of referrals by:
    a. Consultation to dental professionals
    b. Assisting families to decrease barriers to dental care

Table 6. Dental management problems and assessment with high risk patients

	Problem area		Identification of potential problem		Assessment: Interview
A.	Psychosocial (factors related to the psychological and social aspects of a handicapping condition)	A.	Does the patient have a poor attitude toward dental care? Is he or she preoccupied with daily living? Does he or she have maladaptive behaviors or emotional problems?		Multiple risk factors Existing disease Observation of behavior
B.	Accessibility (a person's ability to obtain dental care in a given place at a given time)	B.	Does the patient have physical disabilities? Does the community have transportation resources? Is a dentist available and is the dentist's office accessible? Would the patient be able to be seen in any dental office during routine hours?		Physical appraisal Knowledge of community resources
C.	Communication (ability of a patient to receive information from the dental therapist and process it into appropriate action)	C.	Can the patient communicate needs and wishes to a dental therapist in a normal fashion using speech, hearing, and sight? Is fear or emotional illness a complicating factor?		General appraisal of sensory level and intelligence Knowledge of drug and emotional history
D.	Mobility/Stability (mobility is the ability to be transferred into a dental chair; stability is the ability to be immobile for a dental procedure)	D.	Can the patient be treated in a dental chair? Does he or she have tremors, reflexes, or movements that would prevent delivery of exacting dental therapy?		Oral peripheral examination History of confinement to wheelchair/bed Physical appraisal
E.	Financial (ability to pay for dental care in the private practice sector)	E.	Can the patient pay for dental treatment or qualify for third-party payment?		Social services involvement Knowledge of qualification
F.	Medical (medical problems related to disease that affect dental care)	F.	Does the patient have a medical problem that might cause an emergency in the dental office or post-operatively?		Health history interview

REFERENCE

Young, W. O., and Sriffler, D. S. 1969. The Dentist, His Practice, and His Community. 2nd Ed. W. B. Saunders Co., Philadelphia.

SUGGESTED READINGS

American Academy of Pedodontics. 1978. Pediatric Dental Care: An Update for the Dentist and the Pediatrician. Medcom, Inc., New York.

Casamassimo, P. 1977. Toothbrushing and Flossing—A Manual of Home Dental Care for Persons Who Are Handicapped. Easter Seals, Chicago.

Entwistle, B. A. 1977. Dental needs. In: M. L. Sciantz (ed.), The Nurse and the Developmentally Disabled Adolescent, pp. 119–138. University Park Press, Baltimore.

Nowak, A. J. 1979. Pediatric Dentistry: Part I—The Pre-eruption and Eruption Periods (Birth to 36 Months). J. Contin. Educ. Pediatr. 21:11–22.

Schey, L. 1976. Home Dental Care for the Handicapped Child. Boston Children's Hospital Medical Center (distributed by National Foundation of Dentistry for the Handicapped, Denver).

U. S. Department of Health, Education and Welfare. 1977. The dental implications of epilepsy. U. S. Government Printing Office, DHEW #(HSA) 78-5217, Washington, D. C.

ADDITIONAL RESOURCES

National Foundation of Dentistry for the Handicapped. 1726 Champa, Suite 422 Denver, CO 80202 (Audiovisual materials; information about developing preventive dental health programs; dental and financial resources; bibliographies.)

Academy of Dentistry for the Handicapped. 1726 Champa, Suite 422, Denver, CO 80202 (Continuing education programs and presenters.)

American Academy of Pedodontics. 211 East Chicago Ave., Chicago, IL 60611 (Same resources as above.)

American Society of Dentistry for Children. 211 E. Chicago Ave., Suite 920, Chicago, IL 60611 (Publications; continuing education programs.)

American Association of University Affiliated Programs. 2033 "M" Street, NW, Suite 406, Washington, DC 20036 (List of interdisciplinary training programs and dental staff.)

X. Effect of Nutrition on Growth and Development

Philomena Lomena, Ed. D.

THE CHILD'S NUTRITIONAL STATUS is the sum total of the mother's nutritional status before and during pregnancy, in addition to the mother's ability to meet the child's needs at all stages of his or her development.

THE FIRST YEAR

Food is a vital factor during the child's first year. The kind, amount, method of preparation, and manner of feeding are of primary importance for a healthy, happy baby. The growth rate is greatest during the first 6 months and then gradually begins to taper off toward the end of the year. Caloric and protein requirements per unit of body weight bear a direct relationship to the growth rate, being highest when the growth rate is greatest (approximately 115 kilocalories and 2.2 g protein per kilogram body weight in the first 6 months, and 105 kilocalories and 2.0 g protein per kilogram body weight in the second 6 months).

It is important to remember that babies have very small body stores of needed nutrients and therefore must rely heavily on daily food intake to supply their needs. The well-nourished infant has all of these needs met and follows the normal growth pattern, gaining about 2 pounds per month during the first 3 months and then slowing down to about 1 pound per month. The baby almost doubles his or her birth weight in 6 months and triples it in a year. Growth in length follows a similar pattern, the baby showing a total increase of about 50% of the birth length in one year.

Diet

During the first year, infants rely substantially on milk. In addition, they need the following: 1) protein for growth; 2) carbohydrates and fats for energy; 3) vitamins and minerals to protect against infections and disease entities; and 4) adequate total calories for satiety and to support normal growth and development. Although milk supplies all of these nutrients except iron, it is inappropriate for the infant to rely on milk as the sole source of nutrients and calories after 4 months. Milk is an adequate source of certain amino acids, the end products of protein; of some vitamins, such as vitamins A and D and riboflavin; and of some minerals, such as calcium and phosphorus. However, by 4 to 6 months of age, other foods should begin to be introduced into the diet, such as cereal, with a progression to strained fruits, vegetables, and meat. By 9 to 12 months of age the child should be well on the way to a varied diet, and by 1 year, the child should be established on a variety of soft table foods. By 2 years of age, with normal oral motor development and refined chewing skills, the child is able to eat more textured foods.

Introduction of Semi-Solids

One of the concerns raised about introduction of semi-solids before 6 months of age is the development of obesity. However, when solids are introduced there should be a reduction in the milk volume. Milk plus semi-solids should equal the child's total calorie and nutrient needs. If calorie needs are thus monitored, obesity is unlikely to occur on the basis of overfeeding.

Early oral motor stimulation through a variety of textures and flavors helps to facilitate good oral motor development. This in turn assists the development of good feeding abilities, especially at the age when the child begins to eat table food. Skilled oral motor development will also facilitate speech development, since the same oral mechanism involved in feeding is also involved in speech production. Culture, maturation, neuromotor status, and feeding habits are factors that affect the time when foods are introduced.

Allergies

Allergies are another concern. It has been suggested that the more allergenic foods such as whole milk, eggs, and wheat should be withheld from the diet for the first 6 to 9 months of life to prevent or lessen the likelihood of developing allergies to these or other foods. If there is a family history of allergies, there is greater risk that a child of such a family can develop allergies. While delaying the addition of the more allergenic foods to the diet may not prevent symptoms when these foods are introduced, as a preventive measure it is best to avoid these foods in the first 6–9 months, especially among infants with a family history of allergies. It has been reported that infants do not build up normal levels of antibodies to neutralize allergenic substances in the body until about 7 months of age. The first foods introduced should be rice cereal, followed by fruits, vegetables, and meats, at appropriately suggested ages (see Table 1). It is also recommended that whole milk not be introduced before 6 months of age.

Use of Supplemental Vitamins

Until the child reaches the stage at which he or she is on a sufficiently varied diet to provide all of the needed nutrients, it is advisable to give supplemental vitamins. When the diet is adequately varied and if the child's appetite is good, supplemental vitamins are usually superfluous, since it is easy to exceed the recommended vitamin allowances.

Feeding Development

Children exhibit individual differences, and their development may follow a variety of patterns within a normal spectrum. Some children may follow

Table 1.   Normal feeding development, 0–24 months

Age	Activities
0–2 Months	Feeding is mainly reflexive. The child sucks by moving the tongue in conjunction with the lower jaw up to the hard palate with a clicking sound, and has a good suck. Liquid may be lost from the mouth in feeding, but there is enough negative pressure for adequate swallowing. Lip and tongue control are poor. Head and trunk control are poor. (Head and trunk control are important for feeding development. Swallowing is better facilitated and, later, hand-to-mouth coordination.)
2–4 Months	The child begins to develop other tongue movements and now feeds with a forward and retracting tongue action. Some up and down tongue movements may also be present. Head and trunk control are improving. Lip and tongue control are improving. Liquid may still be lost in feeding. Feeding is no longer reflexive. If fed with a spoon, exhibits poor lip closure and feeds with lips open.
4–6 Months	Variety of lip and tongue movements in feeding. Very little liquid lost in feeding. Can tolerate cereal and baby food. Hands begin to be involved in feeding; reaches out to touch the bottle. Beginning to bring hand to mouth. Better head and trunk control. Better lip and tongue control and coordination and better lip closure.
6–8 Months	Good sitting balance. Mouthing of objects and finger feeding. Reaching out to grasp bottle or spoon. Can hold bottle with both hands and feed independently. Good lip control and good closure. Can begin to drink from a cup with help but with some liquids lost.
8–10 Months	Self-feeding skills continue to develop. Spilling from the spoon and cup continues to decrease as hand-to-mouth coordination improves. Is beginning to move tongue from side to side internally and can tolerate Junior Food and some soft table food—e.g., cooked cereal, applesauce, soft mashed fruit like banana, canned pears, or peaches. Biting and munching responses to food.
10–12 Months	Good finger feeding skills. Can pick up small pieces of food (e.g., a raisin) using a pincer grasp—i.e., thumb and index finger. Tries to feed self with spoon; uses overhand grasp and spills easily. Tries to drink from cup using both hands and spills easily. Good sitting balance and can eat in a high chair. Lip and tongue control continue to develop and movements become more refined. Internal tongue lateralization continues to develop.

Table 1. *Continued*

Age	Activities
	The child can now tolerate soft table food with only very tender pieces of meat—e.g., chopped meat, fish, chicken. Chewing consists of up and down movements of the jaw (a vertical chew). There is no grinding, therefore very textured foods are difficult to eat. Food is something to play with.
12–18 Months	Self-feeding skills continue to develop. Spilling from the spoon and cup continues to decrease as hand-to-mouth coordination improves. The vertical chew develops into a rotary chew or grinding of food. The child is now able to deal with a variety of textures, although still preferring the more tender meats. Good lip and tongue control.
18–24 Months	Self-feeding skills well established with little or no spilling by 24 months. Can eat all foods except tougher meats.

the norm, others may be a month earlier or a month later. Significant lags of 3 or more months should be investigated. The following questions should be asked:

1. Are the delays related to the parent/caregivers' lack of knowledge of children's feeding abilities at different ages?
2. Is there a physical problem?

Knowing what to expect at different ages and the sequence of feeding development is very helpful (see Table 1). In the case of a physical problem, the delay is usually related to abnormalities or malfunctioning of the central nervous system resulting from the problem. Often the senorimotor system is affected, causing feeding problems.

Feeding Problems

Feeding difficulties vary and may include one or more of the following:

1. Poor lip control
2. Poor tongue control
3. Poor suck
4. Retention of oral reflexes affecting progress in feeding development, for example:
   a. Lip and tongue reflexes
   b. A rooting reflex—or movement of lips followed by head when corners of the mouth are stimulated
5. Development of abnormal reflexes, for example:
   a. An abnormal gag reflex
   b. A bite reflex

6. Difficulty swallowing
7. Difficulty chewing
8. Sensitivity to textures, temperatures, or flavors and oral tactile defensiveness

THE PRESCHOOL YEARS

Between the ages of 2 years and 6 years, growth rate decreases—the caloric needs per kilogram of body weight decrease, although totals are greater. Specific needs vary among different children, and are influenced by such factors as rate of growth, activity, and status of health.

The diet of the preschool child, as for all other individuals, should be comprised of the four basic food groups in amounts that would adequately supply nutrient and caloric needs.

Food Habits of the Preschool Child

The preschool child demonstrates an increasing determination and ability to be independent. He or she begins to exhibit this, often through food, by such negative displays: "No," "I don't want to," "I don't like it." A tactful approach is needed with this kind of display. Do not force the child; it is important to remember that the table should not be turned into a battleground.

The following facts are important when trying to encourage good food habits in preschool children:

1. Food can be used as a reward to reinforce good food habits; for instance, desserts could be used to reward full participation in the main meal.
2. Food should never be used as "punishment."
3. Preschool children tend to be picky and to have erratic food habits.
4. Preschool children may reject today what they will eat tomorrow.
5. The amount of food preschool children eat may vary.
6. An item of food once rejected may be presented again with an item well liked.

Color, flavor, and shapes are useful adjuncts in trying to create a pleasant atmosphere and encouraging a better appetite at mealtime.

Some of the factors that produce appetite variations in the preschooler are:

1. Reduced growth rate: increase in weight is about 4 pounds per year during the preschool period and increase in height is about 2 inches to 3 inches per year.
2. Variation in activity level produces a variation in calorie requirements and appetite. Because of their appetite variations and small

gastric capacity, preschoolers should have their needs met in 5 meals, including snacks. Snacks are therefore an important part of a child's intake, and should be nutritious or chosen from the basic food groups.

The preschooler's appetite can be affected temporarily by emotional and physical stress, strange surroundings, or an upset in the daily routine. At this period, also, preschoolers have developed greater interest in their environment and are less interested in food. Some factors that will help to facilitate a maximal appetite are:

1. Variation in texture with more emphasis on crispy foods
2. Creamy and easy-to-chew foods
3. Consideration for preschoolers' sensitivity to temperature and their preference for the lukewarm and not the hot
4. Mildly flavored and less seasoned foods
5. Separate foods so that preschoolers are allowed to mix food themselves
6. Bright colors and fun food such as finger foods, decorated foods, and foods of different and interesting sizes and shapes.

Serving sizes should also be kept in mind: 1/4 cup mashed potato and other vegetables; 1/2 cup cereal; 1/2 slice of bread; 1/ 2 piece of fruit; 8 ounces milk; and 2 ounces meat are the average serving sizes of the preschooler.

If the child's appetite is very picky and intake is insufficient to meet his or her nutrient needs, vitamin supplements are advisable.

THE SCHOOL-AGE CHILD (6 TO 12 YEARS)

School-age children are active. At this stage, their growth rate again begins to accelerate—thus, caloric and nutrient needs per kilogram of body weight begin to increase. The erratic eating behaviors of the preschool years have usually disappeared by this time and the child has developed definite eating patterns. There are fewer dislikes and the child has a comparatively good appetite.

Food Habits

Food habits in the school-age child are better formulated than in the preschool years. Care should be taken to see that these habits are consistent with an adequate dietary intake and acceptable forms of behavior at the table. This is important, because whether good or bad, these habits are likely to persist through life. A national survey in 1963 showed that children's diets tend to lack adequate calcium, ascorbic acid, and vitamin A

(Martin, 1974). Snacks have their place in a child's diet but should be selected from the milk, vegetable, and fruit groups.

Dietary Requirements

The diet should be representative of the four basic food groups: 1) the milk group, three or more servings: 2) the meat group, two or more servings with a total of 4 ounces to 5 ounces; 3) the fruit and vegetable group, four or more servings including: one citrus or high vitamin C fruit and one high vitamin A vegetable; 4) the bread and cereal group, four or more servings.

Factors that Affect the Child's Food Intake

Some factors that affect food intake at all ages include: culture, economic status, food habits, age, and activity.

1. *Culture.* Culture determines the kinds of foods that are eaten and those that may be taboo. It is important to first become familiar with the cultural food habits of the child's family before assessing the child's diet for inadequacies. Necessary modification to meet recommended standards may then be offered. Culture runs deep and is colored with emotional attachments. Cultural food habits can rarely be changed, but with teaching and awareness, habits can be improved.

2. *Economic Status.* This affects the kind and amount of food a family can buy. For the family of limited income, education about budgeting and the kinds of food needed for a balanced diet is vital.

3. *Food Habits.* Food habits, good or bad, will affect what the child does and does not eat. Food habits are often practiced by the entire family. Therefore, the child's food habits cannot be assessed in isolation, but must be considered in reference to family food habits.

4. *Age and Activity.* The age of a child determines appetite and food needs, and activity determines the amount of calories needed. Under normal conditions, a child's appetite serves as the control mechanism in helping him or her to adjust to food needs.

NUTRITION IN ADOLESCENCE

Adolescence is a period of rapid increase in the rate of physical growth and total physiological development. The onset of this growth period is between 9 1/2 years and 13 1/2 years, with an average of 11 1/2 years for boys; for girls, the onset is 1–2 years earlier. During this time there is linear development, with muscle mass increasing more in boys and fatty tissue more in girls, increased body cell masses, and enhanced sexual and physical maturation. Naturally, dietary needs are heightened during adolescence and there is, as well, a susceptibility to dietary deficiencies, partly because this is also a time when dietary habits frequently begin to deteriorate.

Because adolescents lead busy lives, they tend to indulge in quick, high carbohydrate empty-calorie meals. Adolescents who make a habit of such meals may maintain normal body size and not become overweight simply because of their high activity level, yet at the expense of being deficient in essential nutrients. Those inactive adolescents meanwhile, who also tend to fill up on empty calories, risk becoming overweight while still being deficient in essential nutrients.

Dietary Requirements

Generally, boys 11–14 years old have a greater growth spurt than girls of the same age and therefore usually require about 400 kilocalories more daily. The calorie need for girls peaks at menarche to about 2200 kilocalories daily and is followed by a decrease to approximately 2100 kilocalories by age 15. Boys, however, are usually already consuming 2700 kilocalories daily by age 14, with an increase to about 2800 kilocalories by age 15. It is important that family meals be planned so that calorie needs reflect a correct balance of protein, carbohydrate, and fat.

An increase in caloric intake should also reflect an increase in the intake of all essential nutrients. Those that need to be emphasized are: calcium, vitamin D, and iron. With the expanded rate of skeletal growth, calcium needs increase significantly up to 1200 mg daily. (The need for milk and milk products therefore increases.) It is also essential that the vitamin D requirement for the utilization of calcium, which remains at 400 IU throughout the life cycle, be maintained.

The increase in blood volume that accompanies growth necessitates extra iron in both boys and girls, but the need is greater in girls. It has been reported that the amount of stored iron in females is about half that found in males.

NUTRITION SCREENING

The nutrition checklist below may be used by nurses and other health professionals to assess children's nutritional status. Evaluation should include the following:

1. Physical evaluation including medical, dietary history, and anthropometric measures—e.g., height, weight, head and arm circumference, and skinfold thickness.
2. Clinical assessment for signs of nutritional deficiencies.
3. Biochemical evaluation to identify specific nutrient deficiencies.

Any necessary modification of the diet should be a joint effort on the part of the adolescent and the clinician. It is important that the adolescent participate in the decision-making process.

Feeding and Nutrition Checklist

Motor Skills:

Head control	(a) Good _____
	(b) Fair _____
	(c) Poor _____
Trunk control: without support	(a) Good _____
	(b) Fair _____
	(c) Poor _____
Hand to mouth coordination	(a) Good _____
	(b) Fair _____
	(c) Poor _____

Reaching	Yes_____	No_____
Grasping	Yes_____	No_____
Grasp-release	Yes_____	No_____
Pincer grasp	Yes_____	No_____

Primitive Reflexes Present	Yes	No
ATNR (asymmetrical tonic neck reflex)	_____	_____
STR (symmetrical tonic neck reflex)	_____	_____
Moro's reflex	_____	_____
Babinski reflex	_____	_____
Rooting reflex	_____	_____
Bite reflex	_____	_____
Grasp reflex	_____	_____
Gag reflex	_____	_____

Feeding Ability:

Sucking	Poor_____	Fair_____	Good_____
Vertical chew		Yes_____	No_____
Rotary chew		Yes_____	No_____
Swallowing	Poor_____	Fair_____	Good_____

Drooling Absent_____ Present_____

If Present: Mild____ Moderate____ Excessive____

Lip closure	Poor_____	Fair_____	Good_____
Hypersensitivity to textures		Yes_____	No_____
Hypersensitivity to temperatures Hot:		Yes_____	No_____
Cold:		Yes_____	No_____
Hypersensitivity to flavors		Yes_____	No_____
Hyposensitivity to flavors		Yes_____	No_____

Self Feeding: Yes   No
Can hold bottle   _____   _____
Can use a cup: with help   _____   _____
                without help   _____   _____
Finger feeding   _____   _____
Spoon feeding   _____   _____
Using a fork   _____   _____
Hand to mouth coordination   _____   _____

Oral Peripheral Examination:
Tongue lateralization   Poor_____   Fair_____   Good_____
Vertical tongue movements Poor_____   Fair_____   Good_____
High arched palate   Yes_____   No_____
Good teeth   Yes_____   No_____
Good gums   Yes_____   No_____

Diet:
Fruits   Refuses_____ Daily Intake: Yes_____   No_____
                                Number of times per week_____
Vegetables   Refuses_____ Daily Intake: Yes_____   No_____
                                Number of times per week_____
Meat   Refuses_____ Daily Intake: Yes_____   No_____
                                Number of times per week
Dairy products Refuses_____ Daily Intake: Yes_____   No_____
                                Number of times per week_____
Bread and cereal Refuses_____ Daily Intake: Yes_____   No_____
                                Number of times per week_____
Sweets and soft Refuses_____ Daily Intake: Yes_____   No_____
  drinks   Number of times per week_____
Problems: Yes   No   Specify
Poor appetite   _____ _____ _____
Behavior problems _____ _____ _____
Special diet   _____ _____ _____
Vomiting   _____ _____ _____
Diarrhea   _____ _____ _____

Comments:
_____
_____
_____
_____

Primitive reflexes present at birth and during the first 3 months of life must disappear so that the child can proceed to higher levels of development and improve his or her feeding abilities. Retention of these reflexes and the presence of abnormal sensitive patterns to food (hyposensitivity or hypersensitivity) often indicate a poorly functioning central nervous system. Therefore, feeding can become a screening tool for detecting early signs of neurological difficulties. An oral peripheral examination gives further clues about tongue control—lateral and vertical movements, and the ability to chew and swallow.

In addition, good head and trunk control indicate the ability to sit up, swallow well, and have good hand to mouth coordination. Poor hand to mouth coordination may indicate trouble with finger feeding and other self-feeding skills. To swallow adequately, a child must be able to hold his or her head erect. A good sitting balance that results from proper trunk and head control frees the child to use his or her hands for feeding. Reaching, grasping, an automatic grasp-release, and the pincer grasp must be present before the child can develop finger feeding and other self-feeding skills.

Nutrition and Prevention

A good diet and the absence of related problems can ensure the maintenance of good health. It bears repeating that it is easier and less expensive to prevent undernutrition by following the general guidelines for good nutrition than to try to correct undernutrition.

When clinical signs of poor nutrition appear, nutritional status is at its poorest level. Maintaining nutrition standards that support good health should be the rule rather than the exception and should prevent the appearance of clinical signs.

Some clinical signs of caloric and essential nutrient deficits include:

Deficits	Clinical Signs
Total calories	Weight loss
	Tiredness
	Lassitude
Protein	Poor growth
	Weight loss
	Dead, brittle hair
	Rough, dry skin
Vitamin A	Poor growth
	Poor dim-light vision
Vitamin D	Poor bone growth and bone deformity
	Dental caries
B vitamins	Dermatitis
	Cheilosis (cracks at corner of mouth)

Deficits	Clinical Signs
Ascorbic Acid	Soft, spongy bleeding gums
	Slow wound healing
Calcium	Bone deformity and poor bone growth
	Dental caries
	Skin pallor
	Fatigue
	Edema
Zinc	Poor growth
	Poor appetite

Routine screening can eliminate potential problems and should include:

1. Observation of gross and fine motor skills related to feeding
2. The presence or absence of reflexes that can hinder development of feeding skills
3. Signs of sensorimotor difficulties or central nervous system dysfunction
4. Self-feeding abilities
5. Oral motor function
6. The diet and problems potentially related to it

Good nutrition at every stage of development is important for health maintenance, optimum functioning, and the prevention of nutrition related illnesses. Screening help to identify areas of deficiency and potential difficulties and is therefore a significant component of preventive health.

REFERENCE

Martin, E. A. 1974. Roberts' Nutrition Work with Children. University of Chicago Press, Chicago.

SUGGESTED READINGS

Fomon, S. J. 1973. Skim milk in infant feeding. U.S. Department of Health, Education and Welfare, Maternal and Child Health Services, U.S. Government Printing Office, Washington, D.C.

Mueller, H. A. 1972. Facilitating feeding and prespeech. In: P. Pearson and C. E. Williams (eds.), Physical Therapy Services in the Developmentally Disabled. Charles C Thomas, Springfield, Ill.

Palmer, S., and Ekval, S. 1976. Pediatric Nutrition in Developmental Disabilities. Charles C Thomas, Springfield, Ill.

Pennington, A. T., and Church, H. N. 1980. Food Values of Portions Commonly Used. 13th ed. Harper & Row, New York.

Recommended Daily Dietary Allowances, 9th Ed. 1980. Food and Nutrition Board, National Academy of Sciences, National Research Council, Washington, D. C.

Wait, B. et al., 1969. Energy intake of well nourished children and adolescents. Am. J. Clin. Nutr. 22(11):1283–1296.

Wilson, E. D., Fisher, K. H., and Fruqua, M. E. 1961. Principles of Nutrition. John Wiley & Sons, New York.

XI. Environmental Factors as a Predictor of Children at Risk for School Problems

Robert H. Bradley, Ph.D.

ONE OF THE MOST DRAMATIC SHIFTS to occur in the field of child development in the past generation involves our understanding of the relationship between children's environments and their development. Prior to 1960, educational practice and medical treatment gave almost exclusive attention to working with the individual child and none to working with a child's family or the broader social network. Evidence pointing to the importance of the environment has accumulated rapidly in the intervening period. It is now clear that developmental delays often result from deficits and stresses in the child's environment and, furthermore, that risks emanating from biological conditions tend to be exacerbated or ameliorated as a consequence of a child's environmental surroundings.

RATIONALE FOR ENVIRONMENTAL ASSESSMENT

Research over the past two generations makes clear that children's mental performance and social adjustment are strongly related to their family environments (Bloom, 1964; Caldwell, 1968; Deutsch, 1973). This relationship has been observed across a wide variety of cultural, racial, and social class groups.

While environmental data seem generally useful in programs involving all children, the use of environmental measures may be especially significant when assessing children at biological risk. A good example of how environmental quality influences development in biologically at-risk children can be found in the Drillien's (1964) classic study of premature infants. When children in this study reached the age of 4 years, the developmental quotient (DQ) was found to differ within each birthweight group for each social class. The greatest difference—33 DQ points—occurred between the smallest infants from the lowest social class and the smallest from the highest social class. In a more recent study, Parmalee and colleagues (1974) described a follow-up of 126 premature infants. The infants' DQs at age 2 showed no relation to obstetrical complications or postnatal complications. By contrast, when mother/infant observations were included in the cumulative risk score, significant differences were observed. Moreover, in situations where there is an established, organically based risk to development (i.e., Down syndrome), the actual course of development is clearly dependent on the quality of the child-rearing environment.

USING ENVIRONMENTAL MEASURES

As evidence of the environment's effect on health and development has accumulated, greater numbers of child development professionals have begun to use environmental measures. The most commonly employed environmental measures are socioeconomic status (SES) indices. However, Bradley and Caldwell (1978) present evidence arguing against total dependence on SES indices when working with families. Their arguments may be summarized as follows: First, empirical studies show that homes at every SES level vary widely in the types and amounts of stimulation available to children (Bloom, 1964; Littman, Moore, and Pierce-Jones, 1957). Second, Walberg and Marjoribanks (1976), in their review of family environment and cognitive development, contends that there is little if any direct effect of social status variables on cognitive performance unmediated by environmental process variables. Third, a number of empirical investigations show that environmental process measures are more strongly related to measures of development than are SES indices (Bradley, Caldwell, and Elardo, 1977; Marjoribanks, 1972; Moore, 1968). Fourth, socioeconomic indices tend to be static and too gross as measures of the environment to be useful in program planning.

While studies published 15 years ago regarding children's development and specific environmental processes were replete with inconsistencies and research gaps, more recent findings are both more complete and more reliable. Bradley and Tedesco (1982), in a recent review of the observational literature, categorized findings under three major headings: 1) cognitive home environment; 2) socio-emotional home environment; and 3) physical home environment. Following is a summary of these findings.

Cognitive Home Environment

A child's cognitive home environment includes those transactions and events within the family environment that facilitate cognitive capability. It includes such factors as the quality and quantity of language used, the emphasis placed on intellectuality, the variety of sensory and social experiences available, and the extent to which parents encourage achievement.

The studies reviewed indicated that the amount and quality of language used by parents is related significantly to children's mental and language competence (Elardo, Bradley, and Caldwell, 1977; Marjoribanks, 1972; Wachs, Uzgiris, and Hunt, 1971; Wulbert et al., 1976). By contrast, parents' emphasis on intellectual pursuits and intellectuality only appears important once children enter school.

A third cognitive environmental variable frequently studied is the variety of social and sensory stimulation available to children. In general, the findings show that such stimulation is related to children's cognitive development from infancy to adolescence (Dave, 1963; Elardo, Bradley, and Caldwell, 1975; Henderson, Bergan, and Hurt, 1972; Moore, 1968; Wachs et al., 1971; Yarrow et at., 1973).

A fourth feature of the child's cognitive home environment is parents' encouragement of achievement. Research by White and Watts (1973) makes the importance of such parental encouragement during infancy clear. McCall, Appelbaum, and Hogarty (1973) found that parental encouragement of achievement in the first 3 years of life was associated with increases in IQ through age 17.

Socio-Emotional Home Environment

A second major component of a child's developmental environment is the social home environment (SES). It entails such environmental features as: degree of parental responsiveness; amount of warmth and nurturance made available; level of encouragement provided for independence and maturity; extent that parents restrict the child's behavior; and types of discipline practices used.

Perhaps no other aspect of a child's environment is more frequently cited as critical for development as is the degree of parental responsivity to a child's needs and interests. The studies reviewed revealed substantial empirical support for the centrality of parental responsiveness, especially during the early years (Clarke-Stewart, 1973; Elardo et al., 1977; Henderson et al., 1972; Tulkin and Covitz, 1972; Yarrow et al., 1973).

A social environment variable of continuing interest is parental warmth and nurturance. In contrast to research findings that show that parental nurturance has a generally positive import on children's development, research typically shows that restrictiveness has a mildly negative impact (Bradley and Caldwell, 1976a; Engel and Keane, 1975; Kagan and Freeman, 1963). Closely related to the issue of restrictiveness is that of discipline. Results on this subject are mixed, with discipline practices such as punishment, use of fear to control, and strictness all showing a modest negative correlation with children's development (Baumrind and Black, 1967; Bayley and Schaefer, 1964; Bradley and Caldwell, 1976b,1978; Kagan and Freeman, 1963). In summarizing the research reviewed, however, it should be mentioned that few instances of prolonged or severe physical punishment were recorded.

The final component of the social environment that was reviewed was the parents' encouragement of independence and responsibility. The studies examined showed little evidence that early encouragement of independence facilitates cognitive development (Gordon, 1970; Hanson, 1975; McCall et al., 1973). By contrast, there is some evidence that an emphasis on acting independently during the school years does have a modest relation to cognitive gains (Hanson, 1975; Marjoribanks, 1972).

Physical Home Environment

The third major category of environmental inputs is the physical home environment, which comprises aspects such as: toys and learning materials; the level of sensory input; and the extent to which the environment is organized.

A number of investigations conducted during the past decade have shown a pronounced relation between the amount, variety, and appropriateness of the toys and materials children have and children's cognitive performance during the preschool period (Clarke-Stewart, 1973; Moore, 1968; Wachs, 1976; Wulbert et al., 1976).

Distinct from specific objects and events that a child encounters is the envelope of auditory and visual stimulation that constantly surrounds a child in the home. One of the background environmental variables that has been investigated in the last 10 years is nonspecific background noise. Findings generally show that high noise levels are associated with poorer cognitive scores and decreased school performance (Michelson, 1968; Wachs, 1976; 1978). On the other hand, there is evidence that too little sensory stimulation can lead to retardation just as too much can (Dennis, 1973).

Parents provide indirect support for development by organizing the environment so that the child can receive maximum benefit. As Parke (1978) has noted, "This secondary role may be even more important than the role of stimulator, since the amount of time that infants spend interacting with the inanimate environment far exceeds their social interaction time." There is also a growing body of evidence that frequent, drastic changes in the environment are a threat to mental health (Dean and Linn, 1977; Holmes and Rahe, 1967).

THE HOME INVENTORY

Accompanying the dramatic increase in studies of specific environmental processes has been the development of techniques to assess those processes to determine potential risks for development. One of the most widely used environmental process measures is the Home Observation for Measurement of the Environment (HOME) Inventory, developed by Caldwell and colleagues (Caldwell and Bradley, 1980). (Forms and manuals to administer can be ordered from: Center for Child Development and Education, University of Arkansas at Little Rock, 33rd & University Avenue, Little Rock, Arkansas 72204.)

Currently, there are two versions of the HOME Inventory; one for use with infants (birth to 3) (Table 1) and one for use with preschoolers (ages 3 to 6) (Table 2).

Information needed to score items on the inventory is obtained through a combination of observation and interview. The inventory, which takes about 1 hour, is administered in the child's home with information

Table 1.   Samples from HOME Inventory (birth to 3)

	YES	NO
I. Emotional and Verbal Responsivity of Mother		
1. Mother spontaneously vocalizes to child at least twice during visit (excluding scolding).		
2. Mother responds to child's vocalizations with a verbal response.		
II. Avoidance of Restriction and Punishment		
12. Mother does not shout at child during visit.		
13. Mother does not express overt annoyance with or hostility toward child.		
III. Organization of Physical and Temporal Environment		
20. When mother is away, care is provided by one of three regular substitutes.		
21. Someone takes child into grocery store at least once a week.		
IV. Provision of Appropriate Play Materials		
26. Child has some muscle activity toys or equipment.		
27. Child has push or pull toy.		
V. Maternal Involvement with Child		
35. Mother tends to keep child within visual range and to look at him often.		
36. Mother "talks" to child while doing her work.		
VI. Opportunities for Variety in Daily Stimulation		
41. Father provides some caretaking each day.		
42. Mother reads stories at least three times weekly.		

Table 2.   Samples from HOME Inventory (preschool—ages 3-6 years)

	YES	NO
I. Stimulation through Toys, Games, and Reading Materials		
1. Toys to learn colors and sizes and shapes—pressouts, play school, pegboards, etc.		
2. Three or more puzzles		
II. Language Stimulation		
12. Toys to learn animals—books about animals, circus, games, animal puzzles, etc.		
13. Child is encouraged to learn the alphabet.		
III. Physical Environment: Safe, Clean, and Conducive to Development		

19. Building has no potentially dangerous structural or health hazards (e.g., plaster coming down from ceiling, stairway with boards missing, rodents, etc.)
20. Child's outside play environment appears safe and free of hazards. (No outside play area requires an automatic "No.")

IV. Pride, Affection, and Warmth

26. Parent holds child close ten to fifteen minutes per day—e.g., during TV, story-time, visiting.
27. Mother converses with child at least twice during visit (scolding and suspicious comments not counted).

V. Stimulation of Academic Behavior

33. Child is encouraged to learn colors.
34. Child is encouraged to learn patterned speech (nursery rhymes, prayers, songs, TV commercials, etc.).

VI. Modeling and Encouragement of Social Maturity

38. Some delay of food gratification is demanded of the child—e.g., not to whine or demand food unless within one-half hour of mealtime.
39. Family has TV, and it is used judiciously, not left on continuously. (No TV requires an automatic "no"—any scheduling scores "Yes.")

VII. Variety of Stimulation

43. Real or toy musical instrument (piano, drum, toy xylophone or guitar, etc.).
44. Family members have taken child on one outing (picnic, shopping excursion) at least every other week.

VIII. Physical Punishment

52. Mother does not scold (yell?) or derogate child more than once during visit.
53. Mother does not use physical restraint, shake, grab, or hit child

supplied by the child's primary caregiver. The child must be present and awake during the time of the home visit. Each item is scored using a "yes/no" format.

Infant HOME

The HOME scale was intended for use in assessing home environments to identify those that pose a risk to a child's development. The efficiency of the HOME scale as a screening instrument has been explored in a variety of studies (Bradley and Caldwell, 1978), focusing on such factors as under-nutrition, malnutrition, cognitive development, language delays, and IQ levels. The studies have also examined use of the HOME with children from minority populations. One of the studies emphasizing health-related outcomes using the HOME Inventory was a prospective longitudinal study by Cravioto and DeLicardie (1972) of a group of 229 Mexican infants. Extensive environmental, health, and developmental data were gathered on all children, including HOME assessments twice yearly up to age 3 and once yearly thereafter. Of the 229 infants, 19 were identified as having experienced severe clinical malnutrition some time prior to age 30 months (with most of the cases occurring between the ages of 1 and 3 years). After the 19 index cases of malnutrition had been identified, Cravioto and DeLicardie selected from the remaining 210 children a matched sample of 19 children for a comparison group, and then examined the 6 month HOME scores of the two groups. The results indicated that the children who developed malnutrition were living at age 6 months in homes much lower in stimulation than were the comparison children. When the homes were assessed again at 48 months, the picture was essentially the same.

One particularly interesting long-term study (VanDoorninck et al., 1975) examined the screening efficiency of the HOME. It found that 43% of the children from lower class families has school problems, including low scores in achievement tests, low grades, and poor performance in reading and math. Only 7% of the higher social class had children with such school problems. These low-SES, high-achievement families would have been needlessly identified and "assisted" with supplemental programs. These investigators noted that the overinclusion of the low-SES children in the high-risk group could have been avoided to a large extent if HOME scores would have been employed to classify children at risk. When 12-month HOME scores were used, prediction was much more accurate (VanDoorninck, 1977). Of 24 children whose families received low HOME scores, 16 (67%) developed significant school problems. By comparison, 81% of the children whose families received high HOME scores had no apparent school problems.

Preschool HOME

Relatively fewer studies have been published using the preschool version of the HOME Inventory. The most extensive data available on the pre-school version are reported in Bradley and Caldwell (1979). The study involves 117 preschool-age children and their families. Sixty-two percent of the sample were black. Families represented diverse socioeconomic backgrounds with a disproportionate number from lower to lower-middle class. Assessments of the home environment at age 3 showed moderate correlations with IQ at age 3, with the highest correlation being for Toys,

Games, and Reading Materials and Variety of Stimulation. Essentially, the same level of relation was observed between 3-year HOME scores and IQ assessed at age 4½ years. The total HOME score was correlated 0.54 with IQ. Home assessments at 4½ years also showed moderate correlations with IQ. The strongest correlations were for Stimulation of Academic Behavior, Toys, Games, and Reading Materials, and Variety of Stimulation.

HOME INTERVENTION

Identification of children at risk for developmental problems due to inadequate home environments is but a single step in the overall process leading to effective treatment (Meier, 1976). The information obtained from environmental process measures would seem potentially useful in helping to plan appropriate interventions, since the measures index the quality, quantity, and patterning of specific transactions, events, and objects in the child's environment. Despite this, most home-based intervention models prescribe the same general pattern of experiences for all families involved and deal with only a narrow range of environmental processes. So far, an environmental measure as broadly focused as the HOME scale has not been used for the purposes of intervention. Nonetheless, home-based activities such as those found in some widely used early childhood programs would seem natural follow-ups to deficits found in an infant's home environment.

For example, homes that score low on such HOME factors as provision of appropriate play materials and maternal involvement with the child would likely benefit from experiences like those found in the Mother/Child Home Program (Levenstein, 1970; Levenstein et al., 1973). The program centers around the relationship between the mother/child dyad and a home visitor. The home visitor functions as a "toy demonstrator" during the biweekly home visits, showing the mother how to use toys or other educational aids. No direct teaching of the mother occurs; the emphasis is on how to use toys and materials. Follow-up evaluation of this program has indicated its effectiveness with a wide range of mothers. One component of such a program, a toy lending library, is easy and inexpensive to duplicate.

As a second example, caregivers who score low on the responsivity factor might benefit from an approach to home programming such as that in the UCLA project (Bromwich, 1976), whose aim is to develop awareness and sensitivity in parents so that they might be more responsive to their infant's needs. Parents are shown techniques for physical and social caregiving designed to promote social bonding and involvement.

Third, families scoring low on language stimulation and variety of stimulation may be good candidates for programs such as those described by Gordon (1970a). The curriculum is not fixed but emphasizes activities between parent and child that are well-planned and enjoyable. Activities for children under 3, such as those found in *Baby Learning Through Baby Play* (Gordon, 1970b), are demonstrated by the home visitor. Not only is there emphasis on fun but also on extensive verbal interchange.

Low scores on the organization of the environment subscale of the HOME Inventory are particularly likely to occur with young, inexperienced mothers. Modeling is a major thrust in programs, in which teenage mothers are paired with adult volunteers to help them with the difficult transition to motherhood. The volunteers make regular visits to the home, assist the teenage mother in developing good plans; help them obtain needed social services; demonstrate caregiving techniques; and act as a person-to-person counselor; they also make themselves available for emergencies. Modeling, accompanied by some direct instruction tailored to the individual client, can be an effective technique for helping mothers organize the environment.

CONCLUSION

Our present understanding of the relationship between environment and individual development is far from complete (Bronfenbrenner, 1979). Given the complex nature of the human organism and the complexities of the society we live in, few simple direct linkages between specific environmental features and children's development are likely to emerge (Sameroff, 1978). Nonetheless, our present abilities in environmental measurement should allow us to move into another area of human service activity: prevention.

Nurses should thus consider incorporating specific environmental assessment as part of the nursing process. Detailed systematic information about the home environments of their client/patients would provide nurses with a basis for preventive activities. Such prevention activities might be especially significant for those families where risk would ordinarily be higher (low income, single parent, teenage parent, parent of handicapped child, and so forth). Thus, the greatest value of systematic environmental assessment may be not so much in predicting school failures as in planning prevention activities, thereby promoting cognitive growth, social adjustment, and general mental health.

REFERENCES

Baumrind, D., and Black, A. 1967. Socialization practices associated with dimensions of competence in preschool boys and girls. Child Dev. 38:291–327.
Bayley, N., and Schaefer E. 1964. Correlations of maternal and child behaviors with the development of mental abilities: Data from the Berkeley Growth Study. Monographs of the Society for Research in Child Development, Vol. 22, no. 6.

Bloom, B. 1964. Stability and change in human characteristics. John Wiley & Sons, New York.

Bradley, R., and Caldwell, B. 1976a. Early home environment and changes in mental test performance from 6 to 36 months. Dev. Psychol. 12:93–97.

Bradley, R., and Caldwell, B. 1976b. The relation of infants' home environments to mental test performance at fifty-four months: A follow-up study. Child Dev. 47:1172–1174.

Bradley, R. and Caldwell, B. 1978. Home Observation for Measurement of the Environment: A validation study of screening efficiency. Am. J. Ment. Defic. 81:417–420.

Bradley, R., and Caldwell, B. 1979. Home Observation for Measurement of the Environment: A revision of the preschool scale. Am. J. Ment. Defic. 84:235–244.

Bradley, R., and Caldwell, B. 1980. The relation of home environment, cognitive competence, and IQ among males and females. Child Dev. 51:1140–1148.

Bradley, R., and Caldwell, B. 1981. The HOME Inventory: A validation of the preschool scale for black children. Child Dev. 52:708–710.

Bradley, R., Caldwell, B., and Elardo, R. 1977. Home environment, social status, and mental test performance. J. Educ. Psychol. 69:697–701.

Bradley, R., and Tedesco, L. (1982) Environmental correlates of mental retardation. In: J. Lachenmeyer and M. Gibbs (eds.), The Psychology of the Abnormal Child. Gardner, New York.

Bromwich, R. 1976. Focus on maternal behavior in infant intervention. Am. J. Orthopsych. 46:439–446.

Bronfenbrenner, U. 1979. The Ecology of Human Development: Experiments by Nature and Design. Harvard University Press, Cambridge, Mass.

Caldwell, B. 1968. On designing supplementary environments for early child development. BAEYC Rep. 10:1–11.

Clarke-Stewart, K. A. 1973. Interactions between mothers and their young children: Characteristics and consequences. Monographs of the Society for Research in Child Development, Vol. 38, nos. 6, 7.

Cravioto, J. and DeLicardie, E. 1972. Environmental correlates of severe clinical malnutrition and language development in survivors from Kwashiorkor or Marasmus. In: Nutrition: the Nervous System and Behavior. Scientific Publication No. 251. Pan American Health Organization, Washington, D.C.

Dave, R. 1963. The identification and measurement of environmental process variables that are related to educational achievement. Unpublished doctoral dissertation. University of Chicago, Chicago.

Dean, A., and Linn, N. 1977. The stress-buffering role of social support. J. Nerv. Ment. Dis. 165:403–417.

Deutsch, C. 1973. Social class and child development. In: B. M. Caldwell and H. N. Riccuiti (eds.), Review of Child Development Research, Vol. 3. University of Chicago Press, Chicago.

Drillien, C. 1964. Growth and Development of the Premature Infant. Ed Livingston, Inc., Edinburgh.

Elardo, R., Bradley, R., and Caldwell, B. 1977. A longitudinal study of the relation of infants' home environments to language development at age three. Child Dev. 48:595–603.

Elardo, R., Bradley, R., and Caldwell, B. 1975. The relation of infant's home environments to mental test performance from six to thirty-six months: A longitudinal analysis. Child Dev. 46:71–76.

Engel, M., and Keane, W. 1975. Black mothers and their infant sons: Antecedents, correlates, and predictors of cognitive development in the second and sixth year of life. Paper presented at the annual meeting of the Society for Research in Child Development, Denver.

Gordon, I. 1970a. Reaching the young child through parent education. Child Educ. 46:247–249.

Gordon, I. 1970b. Baby Learning through Baby Play. St. Martin's Press, New York.

Hanson, R. 1975. Consistency and stability of home environmental measures related to IQ. Child Dev. 46:470–480.

Henderson, R., Bergan, J., and Hurt, M. 1972. Development and validation of the Henderson Environmental Learning Process Scale. J. Soc. Psychol. 88:185–196.

Holmes, T., and Rahe, R. 1967. The social readjustment rating scale. J. Psychosom. Res. 11:213–218.

Kagan, J., and Freeman, M. 1963. Relation of childhood intelligence, maternal behaviors, and social class to behavior during adolescence. Child Dev. 34:899–911.

Levenstein, P. 1970. Cognitive growth in preschoolers through verbal interaction with mothers. Am. J. Orthopsychiatry 40:425–432.

Levenstein, P. Kochman, A., and Roth, H. 1973. From laboratory to real world: Service delivery of the mother-child program. Am. J. Orthopsych. 43:72–78.

Littman, R., Moore, R., and Pierce-Jones, J. 1957. Social class differences in child-rearing: A third community for comparison with Chicago and Newton, Massachusetts. Am. Sociol. Rev. 22:694–704.

McCall, R., Appelbaum, M., and Hogarty, P. 1973. Developmental changes in mental performance. Monographs of the Society for Research in Child Development, Vol. 38, no. 3.

Marjoribanks, K. 1972. Environment, social class, and mental abilities. J. Educ. Psychol. 43:103–109.

Meier, J. 1976. Developmental and Learning Disabilities. University Park Press, Baltimore.

Michelson, W. 1968. The physical environment as a mediating factor in school achievement. Paper presented at the annual meeting of the Canadian Sociology and Anthropology Association, Calgary, Alberta.

Moore, T. 1968. Language and intelligence: A longitudinal study of the first eight years, Part II: Environmental correlates of mental growth. Hum. Dev. 11:1–24.

Parke, R. 1978. Children's home environments: Social and cognitive effects. In: I. Altman and J. Wohlwill (eds.), Children and the Environment. Plenum Publishing Corp., New York.

Parmalee, A., Sigmund, M., Kopp, C., and Haber, A. 1974. The concept of a cumulative risk score for infants. Paper presented at the Symposia on Aberrant Development in Infancy, Gatlinburg, Tenn.

Tulkin, S., and Covitz, F. 1972. Mother-infant interaction and intellectual functioning at age six. Paper presented at the biennial meeting of the Society for Research in Child Development, Denver.

VanDoorninck, W. 1977. Families with children at risk for school problems. In: M. Krajicek and A. Tearney (eds.), Detection of Developmental Problems in Children. University Park Press, Baltimore.

VanDoorninck, W., Caldwell, B., Wright, C., and Frankenburg, W. 1975. The relationship between the 12-month inventory of home stimulation and school competence. Paper presented at the biennial meeting of the Society for Research in Child Development, Denver.

Wachs, T. 1976. Utilization of a Piagetian approach in the investigation of early experience effects: A research strategy and some illustrative data. Merrill-Palmer Q. 22:11–29.

Wachs, T. 1978. The relationship of infants' physical environment to their Binet performance at 2½ years. Int. J. Behav. Dev., 1:51-65.

Wachs, R., Uzgiris, I., and Hunt, J. 1971. Cognitive development in infants from different age levels and different environmental backgrounds: An exploratory investigation. Merrill-Palmer Q. 17:283-317.

Walberg, H., and Marjoribanks, K. 1976. Families and cognitive development. Twelve analytic models. Rev. Educ. Res. 45:527-552.

White, B., and Watts, J. 1973. Experience and Environment. Prentice-Hall, Englewood Cliffs, N. J.

Wulbert, M., Inglis, S., Kriegsmann, E., and Mills, B. 1976. Language delay and associated mother-child interactions. Dev. Psychol. 2:61-70.

Yarrow, L., Rubenstein, J., Pedersen, F., and Jankowski, J. 1973. Dimensions of early stimulation and their differential effects on infant development. Merrill-Palmer Q. 19:275.

SUGGESTED READINGS

Caldwell, B. and Bradley, R. Home Observation for Measurement of the Environment. The Dorsey Press, New York. In press.

Chase, H., and Martin, H. 1970. Undernutrition and child development. N. Engl. J. Med. 282:933-993.

Dennis, W. 1973. Children of the Creche. Appleton-Century-Crofts, New York.

Hartup, W. 1979. The social worlds of childhood. Am. Psychol. 34:944-950.

Keeves, J. 1972. Educational Environment and Student Achievement. Almquist & Wiksell, Stockholm.

Kessen, W. 1979. The American child and other cultural inventions. Am. Psychol. 34:815-820.

Larson, C. 1980. Efficacy of prenatal and postpartum home visits on child health and development. Pediatrics 66:191-197.

Levenstein, P. 1969. Individual variation among preschoolers in a cognitive intervention program in low income families. Proceedings of Conference on Council for Exceptional Children or Early Childhood Education, New Orleans.

Sameroff, A. 1978. Infant risk factors in developmental deviancy. In:E. Anthony, C. Koupernik, and C. Chiland (eds.), The Child in His Family. John Wiley & Sons, New York.

Saxon, S. A., and Witriol, E. 1979. Down's syndrome and intellectual development. Pediatr. Psychol. 1:45-47.

Siegel, L. 1981. Infant tests as predictors of cognitive and language development at two years. Child Dev. 52:545-557.

Trotman, F. 1977. Race, IQ, and the middle class. J. Educ. Psychol. 69:266-273.

Wolf, R. 1964. The identification and measurement of environmental process variables related to intelligence. Unpublished doctoral dissertation. University of Chicago, Chicago.

XII. The Nurse and Abused Children
Implications for Developmental Disabilities

Harold P. Martin, M.D.

CHILD ABUSE IS DEFINED AS the physical or mental injury, sexual abuse, negligent treatment or maltreatment of a child under the age of 18 by a person who is responsible for the child's welfare under circumstances which indicate that the child's health or welfare is harmed or threatened thereby. This includes, then, not only intentionally inflicted physical trauma, but neglect, abandonment, and passive mistreatment. When the adult caregiver is not providing an adequate environment, and the child's physical or mental status is thereby harmed or *threatened*, the child is being mistreated.

Since 1962, when Kempe et al. (1962) coined the term, "battered child," and reported a nation-wide survey of child abuse, all 50 U. S. states have passed laws defining child abuse and have made it mandatory to report suspected abuse and neglect. The definitions and reporting laws vary from state to state; thus, it is imperative for nurses to obtain information regarding their community's views and laws about child abuse.

As a conservative estimate, at least 1 of every 100 children in the U. S. is significantly mistreated through physical abuse and neglect. Some estimates of maltreatment go as high as 10%–15% of all children in this country. In any case, given the high incidences of both the morbidity and mortality of abused children in the U. S., abuse and neglect represent a major health and developmental problem in our society.

DYNAMICS OF CHILD ABUSE

At least three factors should be considered in understanding why and how children come to be mistreated. The first factor involves the type of adult who abuses or neglects children. This factor is complex, inasmuch as there is no one single personality profile of abusive adults. Indeed, it is thought that any one of us has some potential to mistreat children; yet, certain characteristics are found frequently enough to suggest that they are important dynamics in the abuse situation. One aspect of the background of many abusive adults is well-documented: the majority of adults who mistreat children were themselves abused or neglected as children (Steele and Pollock, 1968). And almost all abusive adults give histories of poor parental treatment in some form during their childhoods. This factor alone may well be the basis for the following characteristics of abusive adults, as suggested by Steele (1975):

1.   Immature and dependent. Abusive adults may be dependent on the child or on other adults or agencies.
2.   Socially and emotionally isolated. Abusive adults have few social friends, and rarely have special people in their lives to whom they can turn for help, nurturance, or friendship.

3. Poor self-esteem. Abusive adults have poor images of themselves, probably from growing up with the reinforcement that they are bad, inadequate, and incompetent. Such adults have often played out this inadequacy through repeated failures in school, jobs, and love relationships.

4. Difficulty seeking or obtaining pleasure. Abusive adults are generally unhappy people who have little joy in their lives and engage in few fun activities.

5. Distorted perceptions of the child. This may take the form of role-reversal, wherein the parent turns to the child for comfort and emotional sustenance, rather than the reverse. There is frequently a distorted idea of what children should be able to do and accomplish at various ages.

6. Fear of spoiling the child.

7. A belief in the value of punishment, especially physical punishment.

8. Impaired ability to empathize with the child's needs and to respond adequately. Abusive adults have little capacity to empathize with other people (children or adults), especially those to whom they are emotionally close.

The second factor that leads to abuse is stress, often taking the form of socioeconomic stress. It is unclear whether it is the personalities of abusive adults that lead to the socioeconomic stress or the reverse, but this author feels that both can be true. Clearly the stresses of unemployment, poor housing, poverty, large families, and marital instability increase the chances of abusive behavior, and are factors that need to be addressed in the treatment process.

Finally, the third factor to consider is the type of child that might increase the chances of abuse or neglect. Six characteristics have been noted:

1. Any attributes of the child that make him or her more difficult to care for and nurture, or that make the child less capable of responding to and reinforcing parenting. Perhaps this is a major reason why small birth weight babies are over-represented in almost all cohorts of mistreated children.

2. Medical problems during the pregnancy, labor, or delivery, or during the early months of life, have been indicated in Lynch's (1976) work as putting a child at higher risk for abuse.

3. When a child does not meet the parent's expectations, or is a "special" child, the potential for mistreatment rises. This mismatch may come from unrealistic expectations of an adult that no child could meet, or it may be a situation in which the child, for whatever reason, cannot and does not meet normal expectations.

4. Disruptions in attachment and bonding may play a role in increasing the propensity for mistreatment.
5. The developmental level of the child. Some children, for example, may be well parented as dependent infants, but when they start to display the more independent characteristics of the preschooler or early adolescent, abusive behavior by a parent may result.
6. It is said that some children invite or provoke abuse or neglect. In this author's experience and opinion, this occurs almost exclusively in children who have been previously abused. Indeed, foster parents often comment on the provocations of abused children in their homes.

DEVELOPMENTAL IMPLICATIONS

The most serious consequence of child abuse and neglect is the mortality, estimated to be between 3,000 to 6,000 children per year in the U. S. Less attention has been paid to the morbidity of the survivors, a brief summary of which follows.

Health Risks

1. The immediate harm from inflicted injuries or neglect is obvious— i.e., fractures, burns, hemorrhage, and so on.
2. Long-term medical effects of the abusive environment, as well as health problems that are of higher incidence in mistreated children than in control groups, include:
    a. Brain damage and the subsequent disabilities (discussed below under neurodevelopmental risks).
    b. Abused children have, as a group, less adequate health care than other children.
    c. Anemia is more common in abused children, probably due to inadequate supply of iron-containing foods.
    d. There is reason to believe that mistreated children have increased risk of hearing deficits, probably due to inadequately treated otitis media.
    e. Undernutrition may be found in up to 35% of abused children, and is the usual hallmark of neglected children.
    f. Microcephaly may accompany brain damage or undernutrition in the mistreated child.
    g. Some workers are impressed that abused and neglected children have more infections than other children, probably related to inadequate nutritional and health care in the past.
    h. Up to 50% of abused children suffer trauma about the face and mouth. In addition to trauma, neglect feeds into a high incidence of dental problems in the abused or neglected child.

i. There is disagreement as to whether abused children have more congenital anomalies than the population at large.

j. As noted previously, children are at increased risk of abuse when there have been medical complications of the pregnancy, labor, or delivery (Lynch, 1976). Further, disruptions in attachment often are secondary to medical problems in the newborn. Hence, the nurse should be aware that the mistreated child may have had a history of health-related high risk events prior to abuse or neglect.

Neurodevelopmental Risks

Various studies place the percentage of mistreated children with developmental problems from 15% to 88%, using criteria of mental retardation, physical defect, language deficit, and emotional disturbances (Martin, 1976). Retarded intellectual function is certainly one of the most common consequences of brain damage from injury and, in abused children, may also be a consequence of growing up in a neglectful and usually disturbed family environment.

In the course of this author's experience and research, the majority of the intellectual and developmental disabilities in mistreated children are *not* due to biological damage from trauma, but to the pathological family milieu in which the child has lived. This suggests a greater chance for reversibility of impaired function than if the disabilities or delays were secondary to structural damage to the central nervous system. It also emphasizes the need for identification and treatment.

Psychological Risks

There is not one stereotypic personality profile of mistreated children. However, one can assume that, with few exceptions, abused and neglected children have psychological scars.

1. The behavior of most abused children will tend to be either at one end of the spectrum or the other, with few treading the middle road of expected behavior. For example, the child is apt to be excessively shy and inhibited, or excessively aggressive and provocative. Some will tend to be compulsive and neat, while an equal number will be disorganized in thought and behavior.

2. Most mistreated children are noticeably unhappy children, sharing their parents' difficulty in enjoying and taking pleasure from life.

3. Mistreated children usually have deficits in interpersonal relationships. Here, again, both ends of the spectrum are represented. It is notorious for many abused children to be indiscriminately friendly with strangers and mere acquaintances. Other abused children will react with unusual stranger anxiety and fearfulness, with little capacity to trust.

4. It must be emphasized that the treatment regimes often prescribed for abused children add to the psychological stress the children undergo, even if the therapeutic regimes are necessary. The children must often deal with separation from parents, hospitalization, foster care, rare visits with parents, and, typically, repeated changes in foster home placements. These stresses should be minimized and anticipated.

Long-term Consequences

The long-term effects of maltreatment cannot be known with scientific accuracy. However, what is known emphasizes the need for identification and treatment of the abused child. The most obvious logic stresses the risk that the mistreated child will grow up to be much like his or her parent(s). As noted above, it is known that there is a generational transmission of child abuse. It is also known that populations of learning-disabled children, juvenile delinquents, and aggressive criminals have a shockingly high incidence of histories of abuse and neglect as children (Martin, 1981).

IDENTIFICATION REPORTING AND INITIAL MANAGEMENT

In the majority of instances, abuse or neglect are obvious to the nurse clinician. The following are common signs and symptoms that should alert one to the possibility of abuse:

1. Multiple injuries or fractures.
2. History or evidence of recurrent injury. This may be suspected when radiographs show fractures (often unsuspected) in different stages of healing.
3. The injury(ies) is not adequately explained by the history. For example, bruises rarely occur in the axillae, or on several surfaces of the body from a fall.
4. The history the parent(s) gives keeps changing, or the parents give different explanations for the injury.
5. The parents delay in seeking medical care for the child's injuries.
6. There may be pathognomonic lesions, such as cigarette burns, cord or belt-buckle marks, bites, strap marks, trauma in the front of the mouth due to forced feeding, and so forth.
7. Unusual parent behavior—e.g., parents disappear during hospital admission, show anger at the child for the injuries, do not visit the child in the hospital, or show unusual indifference.
8. Signs of problems or pathology in the parent-child interaction.
9. There are signs of physical, medical, or emotional neglect. Neglect is not as clearcut a syndrome as abuse. In addition to the signs of abuse

noted above (since abuse and neglect often coincide), signs of neglect include:

a. Poor physical growth with no organic reason for the failure to thrive.
b. Neglected hygiene and physical care.
c. Insufficient medical attention for past and present illnesses.
d. History of inadequate diet.
e. Parents who do not demonstrate usual caring behaviors.
f. Leaving the child unattended when the age of the child does not warrant.
g. Inappropriate dress for the weather.

The first task of the clinician is to be aware of abuse and neglect when seeing the child, since the professional is legally required to report suspected abuse and neglect in all states, and is ethically required to report suspected abuse and neglect in *all* communities. It is essential to consider the reporting of abuse and neglect as taking action to help a patient, not as breaking confidentiality or as accusing an adult of criminal or bad behavior. The hope of the nurse is that the family can obtain help so that the child's environment becomes a safe and healthy one. If the suspicion of abuse or neglect is confirmed by legal or social agents, the thrust of action is to improve the situation, not to punish the adults. In fact, most abuse and neglect cases are heard in civil, not criminal, court. This is indicative of the intent to remediate a situation, rather than taking punitive approach.

It is also essential to note that state laws require people to report *suspicions* of abuse or neglect. The nurse is not required to make a clear-cut diagnosis or to undertake an investigation to "prove" abuse or neglect. What is required is a reasonable concern or belief that a child's injuries or condition is likely, or probably, the result of abuse or neglect.

Each state has official forms for use in reporting suspected abuse and neglect. Usually these are to be filled out and submitted within 24–48 hours after seeing the child. Often, the nurse should also make immediate phone contact with the local child welfare agency or the police (depending on local laws). The nurse should inform the parents that he or she is making the report. It is advisable for the nurse to indicate to the family that a report is required so as to minimize any parental feelings of malice toward the nurse.

When there is a suspicious injury, the following should be done:

1. Immediate attention to the injuries and wounds is required.
2. Perform a thorough physical examination—or see that it is done—and record all injuries, describing size, color, location, etc. Look for hidden injuries such as in the mouth, around the genital and anal areas, in the fundus of the eye, and under the hair.

3. If the child is under 5 years of age, or comatose, a skeletal X-ray survey should be done to look for unsuspected fractures from past injuries.
4. If there is any bruising, a laboratory screening for bleeding disorder should be done, so that if court action occurs, one can state definitively that the bruising was not due to some bleeding diathesis.
5. Talk with the older child (who has language) and inquire from the child as to the etiology of the injuries.
6. Talk with the parents, and in addition to getting a history of the child's injuries and condition, take a social history—e.g., how do parents discipline the child, what stresses are the family under, and what social resources do they have.
7. The child must be provided an immediate place of safety. This may be in a hospital, a foster home, or a receiving home, or it may be felt that it is safe to let the child return home. This decision must be made jointly with the appropriate local agency—i.e., police, welfare, or child protection agency, judge, etc.

One cannot ignore the upsurge of emotion that abuse and neglect elicits in the health professional. Since health professionals are taught to be nonjudgmental, reporting the suspicion of abuse and neglect is often equated in a professional's mind with accusing adults of "bad" behavior. Discovery of a significantly injured child, especially an infant, can engender anger, shock, or disgust in the health professional; it may seem impossible, or appalling, that any adult could be so malevolent to a defenseless child. In addition, professionals are often afraid to confront the parent with their suspicions. It is essential for the nurse to recognize and deal with these feelings. This is especially true when sexual abuse occurs. The nurse, as a health professional, may need some other person to assist him or her; many hospitals, for example, have a CAN (Child Abuse Neglect) team who can help with such an emotionally draining situation.

LONG TERM MANAGEMENT OF THE CHILD AND FAMILY

Developmental Concerns

Conservatively estimated, at least 50% of abused and neglected children have developmental problems. This highly at-risk group should *all* be formally screened for developmental status. Further, the siblings of the abused child should be seen and examined; while only one child in a particular family may be mistreated, it is just as common for several children in the same family to be victimized. Certainly, home visits should be part of the management plan, and school testing results and teacher comments should also be sought.

There is frequently a need for more in-depth evaluation of children who indicate, by screening, the likelihood of developmental delays. Treatment services for these problems are often required, perhaps under the aegis of a therapeutic day care center or preschool.

Psychological Concerns

Since most mistreated children bear psychological wounds, some screening of the child's psychological status is indicated. The nurse can assess this parameter of development in the following ways:

1. Children display psychological and social milestones, just as they show language and motor skill achievement. With development, for example, children smile, recognize strangers, have stranger anxiety, and so forth. The nurse can use his or her knowledge of personality growth stages to determine if the child is developing at a normal rate.
2. A time-honored method of psychological screening is used to identify symptoms. A child may display behaviors that seem abnormal, unusual, or even bizarre. Health professionals tend to note especially those symptoms that are disturbing to adults—i.e., aggression, hyperactivity, and misbehavior. The nurse should be just as concerned, however, about a child's undue shyness, fearfulness, inhibition, or fear of failure, for example. Affect should be assessed, as should the child's ability to relate to other adults and children. When the nurse suspects or feels that the child is emotionally suffering, a consultation from a mental health professional may be in order to ascertain whether the child needs psychological treatment.
3. The nurse may also assume a therapeutic role with the child. When a child is identified, he or she is frequently afraid, in pain, and must often deal with the stress of separation from parents, hospitalization, and even placement in a strange family environment. The child needs someone to be there, to explain what is happening, and to help by listening to and eliciting emotional responses. Of primary importance is that the child have someone to allay his or her irrational fears and fantasies about what happened and what will happen. When the child is in foster placement particularly, there is a great need for an individual who will maintain contact with the child. With the tremendous turnover in child protection workers and the frequent foster home changes, the involved nurse may be the only person who can give this continuity.

Help for the Family

At least 75% of abused and neglected children can remain with their biological parents or return to them very quickly. Abusive parents need a great deal of professional help, which will require more than one person. The needs of the parents, any component of which the nurse can supply, will include:

1.   Parent education. Abusive adults typically are deficient in child crafting skills, as well as in knowledge of child development, ways to stimulate development, discipline methods, and medical care of children. Abusive parents can best benefit from modeling, in-home demonstrating and reinforcement, and the more subtle and gentle teaching that can be given in one-to-one personal contact in the home. Child-crafting skills (e.g., formula preparation, how to bathe the baby), while important, are not nearly as essential as teaching how to empathize with the child's needs and affect, how to use behavioral management, and how to supply love and nurturance to the child. These latter abilities are acquired slowly, but are essential for a lasting change in the abusive and neglectful home environment (Martin, 1980).

2.   A therapeutic relationship. This is the most important need of most abusive parents. The emotional deficits of abusive adults are amazing, and are taxing on the professional's own emotions. The nurse, in this role, functions partly as a "friend," partly as a parent surrogate, and partly as an expert professional with knowledge and skills to offer. The friendship, stability, nonjudgmental acceptance, and offer of emotional, professional, and *personal* support that the nurse supplies may play a key role in reversing an abusive situation.

Advocacy and Coordination

The nurse can assume the essential role of advocate for the child and his or her needs. Commonly, in abuse cases, a team addresses the case by providing the child with a safe placement, and then proposes a treatment package for the parents. In addition, however, someone must guarantee that the child's health, developmental and emotional status are evaluated, and that a treatment program for the child is instituted. Furthermore, the ongoing progress of the child must be monitored and efforts made to insure that the child's views and interests are taken into account. There is also a need for an individual to coordinate the ongoing management of the child and the family. The many professionals and agencies typically involved in the abuse situation need to pool their information periodically and assure that coordination of efforts is maintained. It is often the nurse who must assume the above roles.

The Child in School

While the health, developmental, and psychological consequences of mistreatment are largely the same in older as in younger children, special problems posed by children who are identified by school personnel as abused require some emphasis:

1. The school-age child is more apt to verbalize his or her history of mistreatment.
2. Learning disorders, discussed above, and behavioral problems are more obvious consequences of years in a suboptimal home.
3. Since schools are not health facilities, the child in school is not regularly examined, and mistreatment is more likely to be noted by physical neglect—e.g., the child inadequately dressed for the weather.
4. Schools sometimes resist identifying and reporting abuse or neglect. The school nurse *can* help change this attitude by: a) providing inservice education to teachers and school administrators regarding the laws pertaining to reporting suspected mistreatment; b) establishing in the schools a system for reporting suspected abuse. Teachers as individuals should not be expected to carry out the reporting per se; the school nurse in collaboration with the school social worker, or another school staff member, can more comfortably play this role. School nurses are especially helpful in this role because: a) They can adequately examine the child and confirm suspected abuse and neglect; b) They are part of the health profession; and c) They do not usually need to have regular daily contact with the child and/or family, as does the teacher—therefore, they can be objective staff members.

   The frequency of abuse cases reported has greatly increased in schools where: a) inservice education to school staff has occurred; b) systems of dealing with abuse and neglect were developed that removed the teacher from being in the position of personally contacting social services; and c) the school administration, especially the principal, was satisfied with the developed system of handling suspected abuse.
5. Among girls approaching 10–12 years of age, more cases of sexual abuse will be identified by school personnel. Sexual abuse is a more emotionally-charged issue than physical abuse, and handling it requires greater skill on the part of the school nurse.
6. Physical abuse of adolescent children has only recently been recognized with any frequency; yet, it is reported in a large majority of adolescents with school problems, truancy, delinquent, and antisocial behavior. While it is not clear that the mistreatment by parents is the *cause* of these behaviors, identification of physical injuries, with appropriate help to the adolescent and the family, may decrease the chances of such maladaptive reactions to unhappy family life.

In summary, the school nurse works in an educational agency, rather than in a health care facility. He or she may be instrumental in bringing an abusive situation to the attention of school administrators, with suggestions as to how schools can properly assume their legal and ethical responsibilities in identifying abusive families.

PREVENTION OF ABUSE AND NEGLECT

There are two aspects of preventing abuse or neglect in which the nurse can play a critically important role. At this point, enough is known about the dynamics of abuse and neglect to enable identification of many parents who are "at risk" for mistreating their children. Any method used to screen for at-risk adults will identify not only parents who are likely to abuse their children, but also a much larger group of people who are at increased risk of having serious problems in interacting with their children. It is important then, to use screening tools to identify these latter adults, a small percentage of whom will actually abuse or neglect their children. If adults at-risk are offered regular health care from a professional, and are contacted frequently by that professional (through home visits and by telephone) this can positively influence the parenting such persons provide. The goals of preventive contacts by the nurse include:

1. Providing the message that the nurse is someone who cares about and is interested in the adult.
2. Providing information and education about parenting, discipline, and child-crafting skills.
3. Helping the parent develop social networks to turn to for pleasure, as well as in times of crisis.
4. Helping the parent learn to develop alternatives when the child is especially stressful—i.e., using a neighbor to watch the child when stress is high.
5. Increasing the parent's self-concept.
6. Helping the parent learn ways to problem solve, and prevent and resolve crises.
7. Helping the parent with specific problems, as well as directing the parent to resources such as marital therapy, parents' groups, job training, etc.

It should be emphasized that although abuse and neglect may occur more frequently in the lowest socioeconomic classes, they occur also in middle- and upper-class families. In fact, the vulnerability and increased risk of well-to-do families is often ignored, since the professional assumes that economic and social or educational advantage preclude poor impulse control, psychic stress, and unhappiness. Nothing is farther from the truth. Another group of parents who may be overlooked are those who adopt children; the dynamics of abuse or neglect can exist in adoptive parents as easily as in biological parents.

Primary Prevention

Another method of decreasing future abuse and neglect is to provide needed treatment services to abused and neglected children. Inasmuch as most abusive parents were abused or neglected themselves as children, it should be clear that mistreated children are at risk of growing up to imitate their parent(s). This author offers the view that providing intervention, especially for the psychological and developmental problems of mistreated children, holds the opportunity for decreasing abuse and neglect in the next generation.

CONCLUSION

Abuse or neglect are signs of a troubled parent-child interaction. Over 50% of surviving mistreated children will have health problems, neurodevelopmental delays, and/or significant psychological problems. Nurses are legally (in most states) and always ethically bound to identify and report suspected cases of abuse or neglect so that the pathological parent-child relationship can be improved.

REFERENCES

Kempe, C. H., Silverman, F., Steele, B., Droegmeuller, W., and Silver, H. 1962. The battered child syndrome. JAMA 181:17-24.

Lynch, M. 1976. Risk factors in the child: A study of abused children and their siblings. In: H. Martin (ed.), The Abused Child: An Interdisciplinary Approach to Developmental Issues and Treatment, pp. 43-56. Ballinger, Cambridge, Mass.

Martin, H. P. (ed.). 1976. The Abused Child: A Multidisciplinary Approach to Developmental Issues and Treatment. Ballinger, Cambridge, Mass.

Martin, H. P. 1980. Working with parents of abused and neglected children. In: R. Abidin (ed.), Parent Education and Intervention Handbook, pp. 252-271. Charles C Thomas, Springfield, Ill.

Martin, H. P. 1980. The consequences of being abused and neglected: How the child does fare. In: R. Helfer and C. H. Kempe (eds.), The Battered Child. 3rd Ed. pp. 347-365. University of Chicago Press, Chicago.

Martin, H. P. 1981. The neuro-psycho-developmental aspects of child abuse and neglect. In: N. Ellerstein (ed.), Child Abuse and Neglect: A Medical Reference, pp. 95-120. John Wiley & Sons, New York.

Steele, B. 1975. Working with abusive parents: From a psychiatric point of view. U. S. Department of Health, Education and Welfare, Office of Child Development, #H 75-70, Washington, D. C.

Steele, B. F., and Pollock, C. B. 1968. A psychiatric study of parents who abuse infants and small children. In: R. Helfer and C. H. Kempe (eds.), The Battered Child, 1st Ed. pp. 103-148. University of Chicago Press, Chicago.

SUGGESTED READINGS

Heindl, C., Krall, C. A., Salus, M. K., and Broadhurst, D. D. 1979. The nurse's role in the prevention and treatment of child abuse and neglect. U. S. Department of

Health, Education and Welfare, National Center on Child Abuse and Neglect, U. S. Government Printing Office, #OHDS 79-30202, Washington, D. C.

Helfer, R. E., and Kempe, C. H. (eds.). 1976. Child Abuse and Neglect: The Family and the Community. Ballinger, Cambridge, Mass.

Helfer, R. E., and Kempe, C. H. (eds.). 1981. The Battered Child. 3rd Ed. University of Chicago Press, Chicago.

Korbin, J. E. (Ed.). 1982. Child Abuse and Neglect: A Cross-Cultural Perspective. University of California Press, Los Angeles.

Martin, H. P. 1979. Treatment for abused and neglected children. U. S. Dept. of Health, Education and Welfare, National Center on Child Abuse and Neglect, U. S. Government Printing Office #OHDS 79-30199, Washington, D. C.

XIII. Behavior Modification
Changing Children's Behavior

Marilyn J. Krajicek, R.N., Ed.D.
Nancy Weaver, M.S.

BEHAVIOR MODIFICATION IS A USEFUL TOOL for nurses and other health care professionals who work with children with problems. It is also helpful for parents and teachers who wish to relate more effectively to children and to assist them to grow in the most healthy way, both physically and mentally. Once health care professionals are familiar with behavior modification procedures, they can guide parents and teachers in learning about this method of relating to children.

DEFINITIONS OF TERMS

Reinforcement

Reinforcement is a consequence following a behavior that is designed to increase the behavior's occurrence in the future. A child will pick up his toys if each time he does so his mother lets him know how much she appreciates his efforts.

Punishment

Punishment is a consequence following a behavior that is designed to decrease the behavior's future occurrence. Example: If a child is told to sit in a chair each time he hits his sister, the child will stop hitting his sister.

Extinction

Extinction is not responding to a behavior in order to decrease that behavior. Example: A child engaging in temper tantrums who is not given attention by his mother (ignored) will stop having a tantrum.

Shaping

Shaping is the reinforcement of closer and closer approximations to the desired behavior. Example: In helping a mother to toilet train her 2-year-old child, the procedure must be broken down step by step and each step rewarded. Suggested sequence:

1. The child should be taken to the bathroom approximately every 2 hours. Mother should reinforce the child for going with her to the bathroom and sitting on the potty.
2. Mother should continue taking the child every 2 hours, but reinforce the child only when he or she uses the toilet.
3. When mother takes the child to the bathroom, she should reinforce the child only when he or she is dry and then uses the toilet.
4. When child indicates by gesturing or vocalization a need to go to the bathroom, mother should take the child to the bathroom and then reinforce the child for indicating his or her need. The child should be

taken to the bathroom on a regular schedule and then reinforced for being dry and going to the toilet.

5. Mother should reinforce the child for the child's assistance in pulling pants down, for using the toilet, and for the child's assistance in pulling pants up.

6. Mother should reinforce the child for pulling pants down, using the toilet, and pulling pants up on his or her own.

7. Mother should reinforce the child for completing the entire toileting process on his or her own.

Each of the above steps takes time, depending on the child's readiness, so patience is important. As the child progresses from step to step, the reinforcer for the previous step should be eliminated.

Consistency

Consistency is following through with a selected approach. Example: *Each time* a child gets out of bed after being put to bed, the parent needs to immediately return the child to bed.

Observation

Observation is watching behavior for a specific period of time in order to determine the frequency of the behavior's occurrence. Example: A child has frequent temper tantrums in preschool; the teacher records the number of times she observes the child having a temper tantrum.

Recording

Recording is the systematic record keeping of the number of times a behavior occurs (Figure 1).

Consequence

Consequence is the event that follows the occurrence of a behavior. Example: A child finishes his or her dinner and receives dessert as a reward (consequence).

Baseline

Baseline is the frequency of occurrence of a behavior prior to intervention. Example: An observer records the frequency of whining behavior before attempts are made to change that behavior.

Manipulation

Manipulation is the intervention technique introduced in order to change a behavior. Example: A child throws his toys. In order to decrease the throwing behavior the child is placed in a chair each time he throws a toy.

Child's Name_____

Date _____

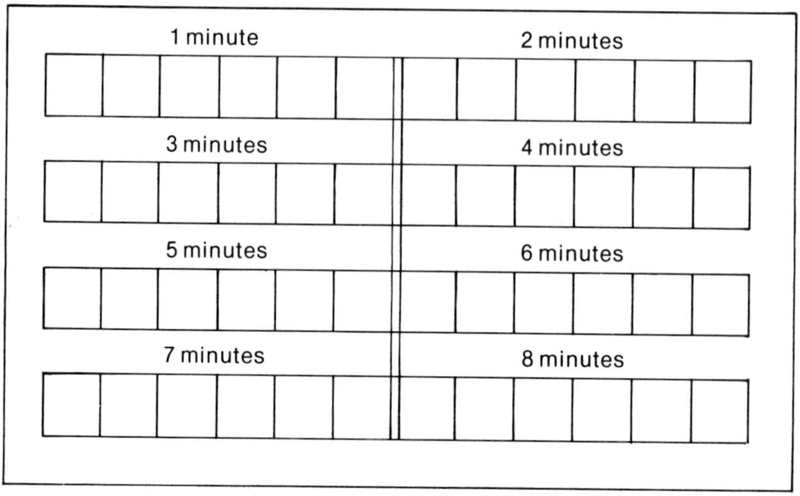

Figure 1.   Sample of chart for systematic record keeping of times a behavior occurs.

OBSERVATION

Accurate observations must occur before any procedures are undertaken to modify a behavior. One must communicate to the parent or teacher that the observation is being done to select an appropriate intervention technique. It is necessary to know, through observation, what behaviors the subject is demonstrating, rather than assuming or accepting that a behavior occurs. When observing, it is important to remain silent and not interact with the child or any other person in the environment. An observation is performed in two steps: The first step is the running record; the second is the objective observation.

Running Record

The running record observation is used to identify what behaviors are occurring and what behaviors need to be modified. It is done by observing the child two different times for 30 minutes each, in his or her natural environment (home or school), and writing down as much as possible about what is observed. Behaviors should be recorded that seem inappropriate, as well as the events that occur before (stimulus) and after those behaviors (consequences). It is important also to observe the parent or teacher's behavior in interacting with the child. A particular behavior can thus be identified for use in making a more objective observation.

Example:

Name: Janet Brown ("S" stands for subject)
Date: 6/4/81
Time: 10:04 A.M.
Place: Home
S is going to get a cookie from the cookie jar—pulls chair over—climbs
up on counter—mother says, "no, no"—mother gets S down—S cries
and throws herself on floor—mother gives cookie.

Objective Observation

An objective observation is made to count accurately the number of times
a certain behavior occurs. In this observation, the observer need not use
his or her subjective judgment, but should define what he or she is observing and record only what has been defined.

Example:

If the behavior being observed is a tantrum or getting out of bed after
being put to bed, the observer should define those behaviors as follows:
1.   Tantrum—the subject cries, screams, throws himself on the floor
     or holds his breath.
2.   Getting out of bed—any point at which no part of the body touches
     the bed.

After defining what behavior is being observed, prepare a recording
sheet (Figure 2) on which to record the behavior. In Figure 2, each square

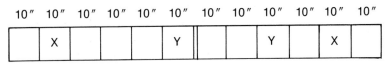

X = crying behavior   Y = screaming

Figure 2.   Recording sheet (see text for explanation).

represents 10 seconds; each group of six squares represents 1 minute. A
symbol, such as "X," should be designated to represent the behavior. The
observer starts at the first square, moving the pencil from square to square
as each 10-second interval passes (Figure 3). (The observer will need to

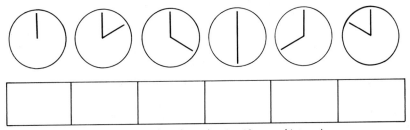

Figure 3.   Recording sheet showing 10-second intervals.

have a watch with a second hand, or a stopwatch.) Place an X in the 10-second square in which the behavior occurs each time it occurs.

After 30 minutes of observation, count the number of times the behavior occurred during the observation. Mark the number of times the behavior occurred on the graph (Figure 4). The observer will need to do three of these observations.

Using the baseline data (see previous definition) begin to work with a teacher or a parent around a behavior. This technique of observing and recording will help professionals train themselves to be better observers.

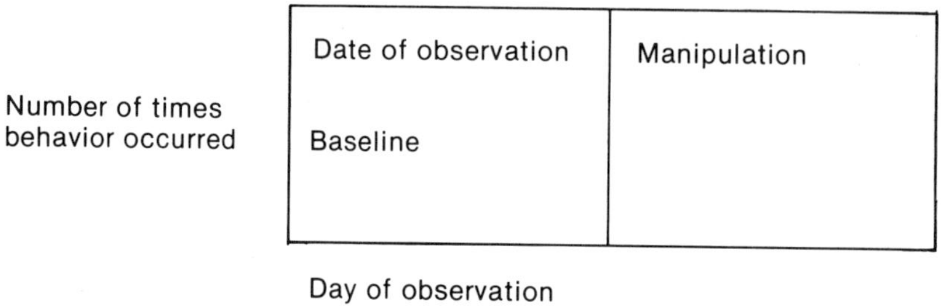

	Date of observation	Manipulation
Number of times behavior occurred	Baseline	

Day of observation

Figure 4.   Graph of number of times behavior has occurred.

Parent or Teacher Observation

Once a nurse or other health care professional knows what behaviors need to be modified, it is important to talk to the parent or teacher about what behaviors they see as inappropriate. The nurse and parent and/or teacher should then agree on *one* behavior that needs to be changed. *Caution*: It is a great temptation to want to change many behaviors at one time. It is important not to give in to this temptation. Parents and teachers need to be aware of how often the inappropriate behavior occurs. Frequently, it is difficult for them to be consistent when charting or responding to a child's behavior, but consistency is essential if behavior change is to occur. Make a chart for the parent or teacher and ask them to place it in an accessible area. A good idea is to tape it to the wall. Have them record each time the behavior occurs.

Figure 5 is an example of a chart that can be used by a parent or teacher. The chart should be kept for at least 4 days. At the end of the 4 days review the chart with the parent or teacher and determine the behavior pattern and an intervention technique. Once the intervention has begun, the parent or teacher should continue to chart the behavior so that they will see it decrease. *Warning*: Often after manipulation occurs there is a testing period between the child and adult, during which time the behavior occurrence will increase. This is normal and it is important to help the parent or teacher cope with this time and see a change.

Inappropriate Behavior

Baseline		Intervention	
Mon. Oct. 1	/𝑋𝑋/ /𝑋𝑋/ /	Fri. Oct. 5	/𝑋𝑋/ /𝑋𝑋/ /𝑋𝑋/
Tues. Oct. 2	/𝑋𝑋/ /𝑋𝑋/	Sat. Oct. 6	/𝑋𝑋/ /
Wed. Oct. 3	/𝑋𝑋/ /𝑋𝑋/	Sun. Oct. 7	/𝑋𝑋/
Thurs. Oct. 4	/𝑋𝑋/ /𝑋𝑋/		

Figure 5.   Chart to be used by parent or teacher to record inappropriate behavior.

Child Observation

When working with a school-age child the child can learn to keep records of his or her own behavior. Awareness of one's own behavior is a critical component for changing one's behavior. The child can keep a chart on the wall of his or her room and mark when a behavior occurs. Some examples of these behaviors may include bed wetting, fighting with a sibling, or not getting up to get ready for school. At school the child could keep the chart on his or her desk and record such behaviors as talking without permission, getting out of the seat, or failing to turn in assignments on time.

Follow-up Observation

After the manipulation has been in progress for 2 weeks, two more objective observations should be conducted. Put the data on the original graph (Figure 4) on the manipulation side. After the third week of manipulation, do a third observation, and chart the results (Figure 6).

INTERVENTION SUGGESTIONS

The same intervention techniques can often be applied to the same problem behaviors in different children. Whatever interventions are used, be consistent with the child. The following are suggestions for intervention:

1. Temper tantrums may occur when a child does not get what he or she wants or must do something he or she does not want to do.
    a. Ignore the child as long as the temper tantrum is in progress.
    b. Reinforce the child when the tantrum has stopped. One can actually reward the child by getting the child involved in another activity.
    c. If the tantrum occurs in a public place where it cannot be ignored, remove the child from the situation.

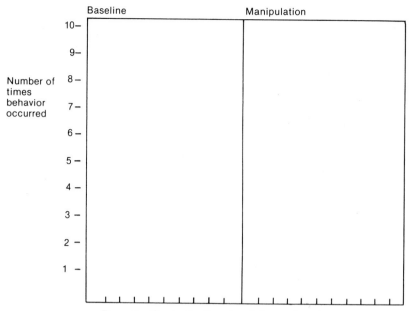

Figure 6.   Graph after 3 weeks of observation.

2.   Other discipline problems that parents often must handle include: engaging in over-aggressive behavior toward siblings, getting into the refrigerator, throwing toys and other items, or refusing to perform a task when told to do so.
   a.   Put the child in the same chair in the same place and require him or her to sit there for 3 minutes.
   b.   If the child tries to get out of the chair, return him or her to the chair and firmly tell the child to sit there.
   c.   Put the child in the chair *every* time the behavior occurs.
3.   The parent may experience a problem of the child not remaining at the table during a meal. Expecting a child to sit at the table and eat a child's portion of food that is liked by the child is not an unreasonable request to make of a normal 4-year-old. However, the child needs to be encouraged to taste foods that are unfamiliar or disliked.
   a.   Parents should communicate their expectations to the child: "Johnny, you need to stay at the table until you have finished what is on your plate." (Remember to give small portions.)
   b.   If the child gets down from the table, the parent should place the child back in his chair at the table and give one warning: "Johnny, if you get down from the table again, you will not get any more to eat."

    c. If the child will not stay at the table, the parent should ignore the child when he is away from the table, and not give the child any solid food until the next scheduled eating time.

4. The child may have a "picky" appetite. He or she may refuse to eat what the parent has prepared for a meal, and eat only selected foods. In order to change this behavior, consider the following:

    a. Introduce 2 teaspoons of a food the child has previously refused.

    b. Tell the child that he or she will get a dessert when the plate is cleaned. (Remember to give small portions of all foods.)

    c. Reinforce the child for eating new food and cleaning his or her plate. Do not get discouraged if the child will not clean his or her plate. Continue to introduce new foods by using the above method. It is important for the adult to remain calm and not to demonstrate disappointment if the child does not eat the new food. Be consistent in the approach used. Do not give the child dessert if his or her plate is not clean.

5. The child may refuse to stay in bed.

    a. Parents should put a night light in the child's room if the child is afraid of the dark. Another idea is to give the child a flashlight in bed to enable him or her to shine the light on "scary" objects in the room.

    b. Parents should establish a routine to perform each night, which may consist of bathing time, putting pajamas on, getting a drink, telling family members "good night," going to the bathroom, and/or reading a story to the child.

    c. After this routine the child needs to know it is time to go to sleep and remain in bed.

    d. Parents should ignore a child's request, whining, or crying if they are certain nothing is wrong.

    e. If the child gets out of bed and makes a request, the parents should not fulfill the request, but put the child back to bed immediately, and tell him firmly, "You must stay in bed." Getting up and being put back to bed may occur several times for several nights until the child stays in bed.

6. Toilet training: See previous discussion in this chapter under definition of *Shaping*.

7. The school-age child may not return home at the time agreed upon by the child and parent.

    a. Discuss with the child the agreed upon time for arriving home.

    b. If the child is unable to be home at this time, the child is to call.

    c. If the child does not return home on time, or fails to notify the parent, then the parent needs to institute an appropriate consequence(s).

   d. Grounding the child for the following day is an appropriate
       consequence.
8. Siblings over 5 years of age may engage in fighting behavior.
   a. Place a chart in each child's room.
   b. When fighting occurs, each child should record the incident on
       his chart.
   c. The child should remain in his or her room for a 15-minute
       period.
   d. Initially, if the child goes without fighting for 1 day, he or she
       should receive a small reward. Let the child work toward in-
       creasing the time span for no fighting, giving the reward for
       longer periods of not fighting.

FADING OUT THE MANIPULATION

When and how does the parent or teacher eliminate the manipulation and
still maintain the desired behavior? This is a difficult question. The answer
depends both upon the individual child and the situation. Once the desired
behavior is achieved, the manipulation procedure is no longer necessary.
However, if the behavior appears again, the manipulation procedure
should be reintroduced.

Maintaining Desired Behavior

In order to maintain any desired behavior such as picking up toys and
putting them away, self-dressing, carrying out requests of others, or self-
entertaining when mother is busy, it is important to consistently reinforce
these behaviors. Attention is often given to the child only when he or she is
misbehaving. This pattern needs to be reversed and emphasis given to
positive behavior.
   Example:

   Frequently, when a child is quietly looking at a book, the child is ignored
   by the adult. However, when the child begins to tear the pages, he or she
   is given attention by being reprimanded. Although this may be considered punishment, if it is the only attention the child gets, he or she will
   learn to misbehave in order to get attention.

CONCLUSION

Behavior modification, if appropriately used, will change undesirable behaviors and increase desirable ones. If the behaviors identified as needing
to be altered appear complex, it is advisable to consult with a person who
has expertise in the concepts of behavior modification. The key to a suc-
cessful program for changing behavior is consistency.

SUGGESTED READING

Azrin, N., and Besalel, V. 1980. How to Use Overcorrection. H&H Enterprises, Lawrence, Kans.

Dreikurs, R., and Grey, L. 1970. A Parent's Guide to Child Discipline. Hawthorn Books, New York.

Hall, R. V., 1971a. Behavior Modification: The Measurement of Behavior, #1. H&H Enterprises, Lawrence, Kans.

Hall, R. V., 1971b. Behavior Modification: Basic Principles, #2. H&H Enterprises, Lawrence, Kans.

Hall, R. V., 1971c. Behavior Modification: Application in School, and Home, #3. H&H Enterprises, Lawrence, Kans.

Hall, R. V., and Hall, M. 1980a. How to Use Planned Ignoring (Extinction). H&H Enterprises, Lawrence, Kans.

Hall, R. V., and Hall, M. 1980b. How to Use Systematic Attention and Approval (Social Reinforcement). H&H Enterprises, Lawrence, Kans.

Hall, R. V., and Hall, M. 1980c. How to Use Time Out. H&H Enterprises, Lawrence, Kans.

Kinshourne, M. 1973. Diagnosis and treatment—School problem. Pediatrics 52:699–700.

Macht, J. 1975. Teaching Our Children. John Wiley & Sons, New York.

O'Neil, S., McLaughlin, B., and Knapp, M. 1977. Behavioral Approaches to Children with Developmental Delays. C.V. Mosby Co., St. Louis, Mo.

Panyan, M. 1972. Behavior Modification: New Ways to Teach New Skills, #4. H&H Enterprises, Lawrence, Kans.

Patterson, G. 1979. Families. Research Press, Champaign, Ill.

Patterson, G., and Gullion, M. E. 1979. Living with Children: New Methods for Parents and Teachers. Research Press, Chicago.

Ullman, L. P., Krasner, L. (eds.). 1965. Case Studies in Behavior Modification. Holt, Rinehart & Winston, New York.

Watson, L. 1972. How to Use Behavior Modification with Mentally Retarded and Autistic Children: Programs for Administrators, Teachers, Parents and Nurses. Behavior Modification Technology, Libertyville, Ill.

Wright, L. 1978. Parent Power: A Guide to Responsible Child-rearing. Psychological Dimensions, Oklahoma City, Okla.

Index